ICONS OF THE
FANTASTIC

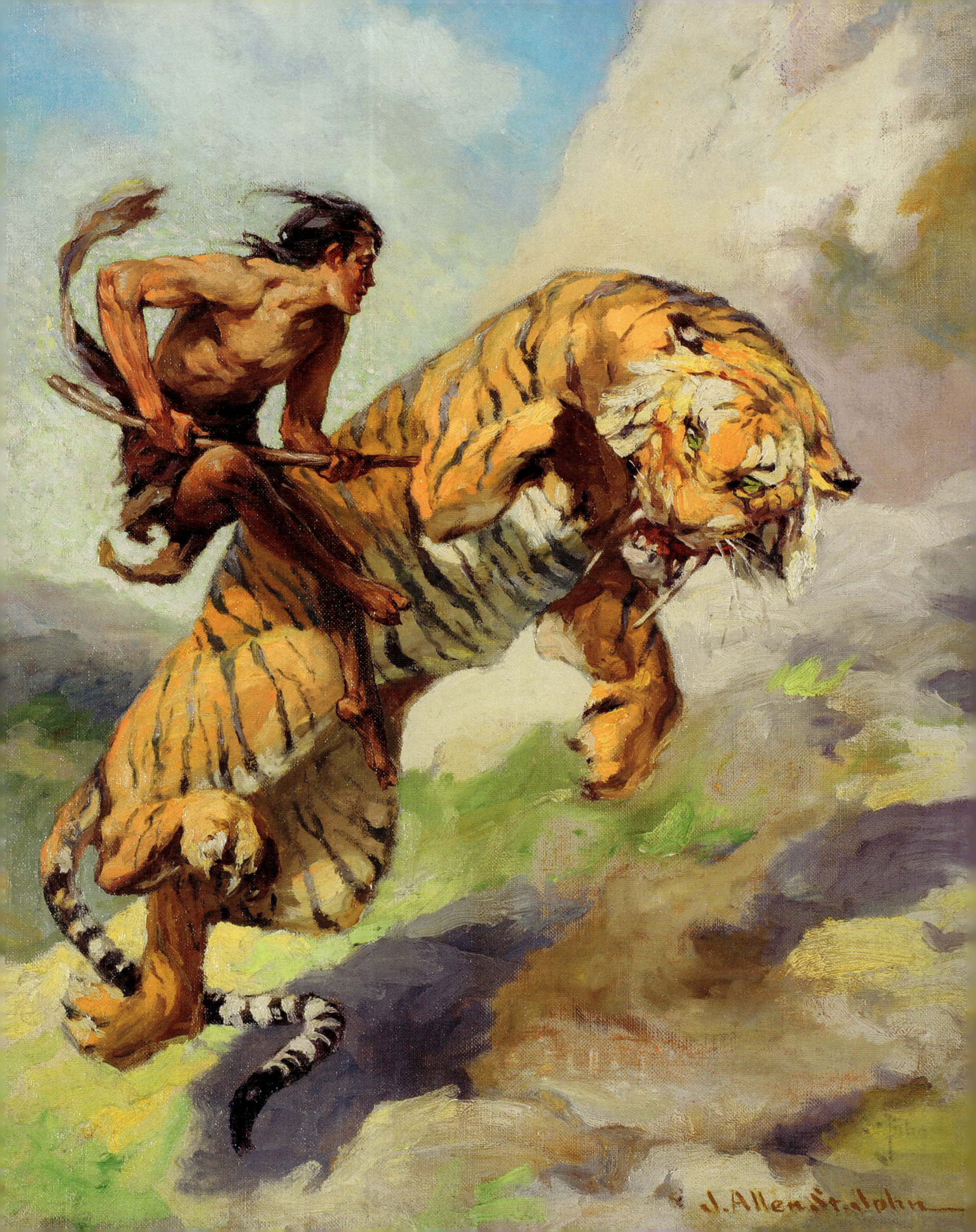

J. Allen St. John

ICONS OF THE FANTASTIC

ILLUSTRATIONS OF IMAGINATIVE LITERATURE FROM THE KORSHAK COLLECTION

Edited by Amanda T. Zehnder and David M. Brinley

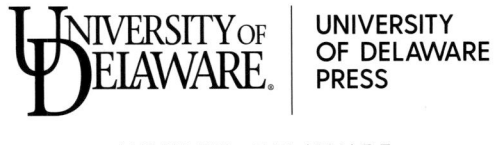

UNIVERSITY OF DELAWARE PRESS

NEWARK, DELAWARE

ISBN 978-1-64453-405-2 (cloth)
ISBN 978-1-64453-406-9 (ebook)
ISBN 978-1-64453-418-2 (special edition cloth)

Library of Congress Cataloging-in-Publication Data
Names: Zehnder, Amanda T., editor | Brinley, David M., 1971–, editor
Title: Icons of the fantastic : illustrations of imaginative literature from the Korshak collection / edited by David M. Brinley and Amanda T. Zehnder.
Description: Newark : University of Delaware Press, [2025] | Includes bibliographical references and index.
Identifiers: LCCN 2025016920 | ISBN 9781644534052 cloth | ISBN 9781644534069 epub
Subjects: LCSH: Fantasy in art | Illustrated books—Private collections—United States | Korshak, Stephen D.—Art collections
Classification: LCC NC961.7.F36 I29 2025 | DDC 771.6/47—dc23/eng/20250519
LC record available at https://lccn.loc.gov/2025016920

A British Cataloging-in-Publication record is available from the British Library.

References to internet websites (URLs) were accurate at the time of writing.

Neither the authors nor University of Delaware Press are responsible for URLs that may have expired or changed since the manuscripts were prepared.

♾ The paper used in this publication meets the requirements of the American National Standard for Information Sciences—Permanence of Paper for Printed Library Materials, ANSI z39.48-1992.

Composed in Zapf Renaissance Antiqua and Optima (Hermann Zapf); and Aboreto (Dominik Jáger)

Book design by Robert L. Wiser, Silver Spring, MD

udpress.udel.edu

Distributed worldwide by Rutgers University Press

Manufactured in the United States of America

Every reasonable effort has been made to acquire accurate rights information for the images in this book. If there are errors or omissions in the credits included herein, please contact the University of Delaware Press, so that corrections may be addressed in any subsequent editions.

FRONTISPIECE. J. Allen St. John (American, 1872–1957), *The Eternal Lover*, 1925, oil on canvas board, 25 × 18 inches.

CONTENTS

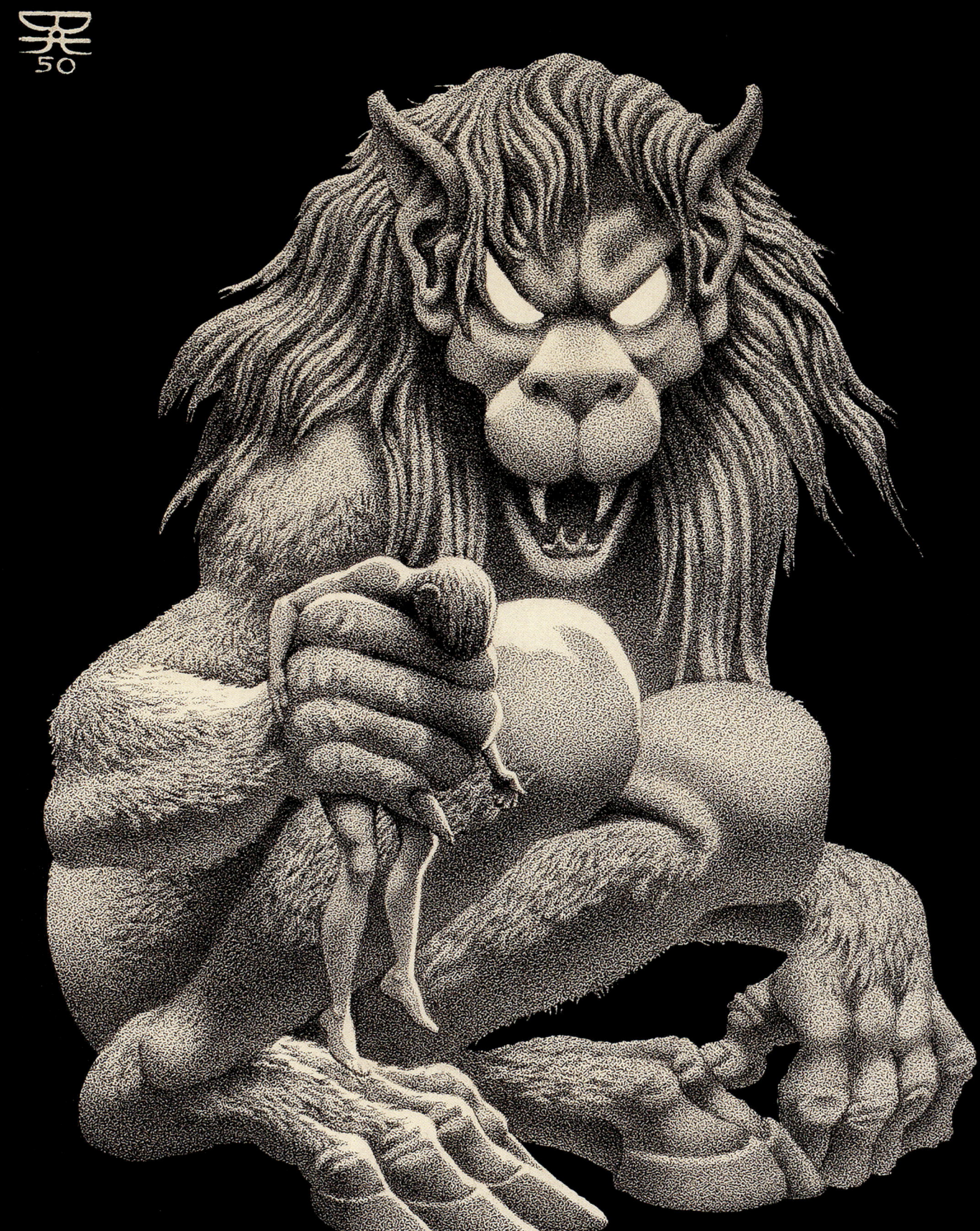

FOREWORD:
A Cabinet that Holds the World

We, as collectors, serve as guardians of a language or a past in order to secure a future. No piece of art in a collection belongs to those that paghold it. It belongs to the world and its life will invariably outlast our own.

That said, our curation often becomes self-portraiture. As custodians of images, we define our own view of the world. Thus, the Korshak Collection is not only one of the most important fantastic art collections in the world, but also a window into Stephen Korshak's soul, and the souls of his family before him, and their longing for the sublime, the bizarre, and the extraordinary.

The essays in this book tackle the artists and inventory featured in the collection with sufficient attention that I need not repeat the details here, but I would like to expand on the advantages of holding a collection, a cabinet of curiosities of sorts: collecting became an art in and of itself as the world inched its way toward enlightenment. Travel was difficult and the world was full of mystery, so few brave explorers—or warriors—ventured beyond and carried home intriguing traces of creatures and places. One could imagine what laid beyond the mists—faraway lands where cyclopes roamed the land in search of human flesh and roc birds nested in islands full of precious stones....

It is said that the first organization of the great museums was simply done to organize the spoils of war. Art was parceled and divided according to the time and place of acquisition and creation: Egyptian Art, Renaissance Art, Flemish Art, etc. Soon, the spoils of war revealed an unexpected, hitherto unknown, aesthetic and sense of self amongst collectors that revealed chronology and national identity and influenced artists across the globe. And in these explorers' collections, fantasy and reality collided—narwal horns and elephant heads became avatars for a zoology of invention, and coral and nautilus shells laid side by side with pygmy skulls or Hands of Glory. The collection of Japanese and Egyptian art helped many European artists to reformulate their own aesthetic and philosophical approach to image-making and to reenvisioning the world through the eyes of others.

Fantastic art, then, carries the breeze from an impossible ocean shore—it liberates us not only of geography and chronology but of the mundane and

PLATE 1. Hannes Bok (American, 1914–1964), *Pickman's Model*, 1950, mixed media, pen and ink on illustration board, 8¾ × 6¾ inches.

7

the rational. The marriage of new forms, new architecture, and newly discovered biology gives us hope in the fact that, perhaps, we are not limited by the vulgarity of our lives. We can represent larger realities and concepts, tackle the cosmology of fairy tales about the very foundational myths and concepts that constitute the language of *what* we are, not only *who* we are. The divine and eternal, the numinous and uncanny lie side by side in the images on these pages, and we have the privilege of walking the corridors of their artists' minds while holding the hand of an expert guide, a man that knows that the first act of love is to hold, and the second one is to share.

Indeed, I collect and study many of the very same subjects the Korshak Collection has enshrined and preserved, so I am grateful to have the collection as a resource. The most beautiful thing is to encounter a collection that almost perfectly mirrors your own or, simply put, is a mirror that becomes a window to a landscape, known and new at the same time.

The Korshak Collection is a portrait and biography of a man and his family, who once looked upon the dark skies and saw Immortals, gods hunting in the storm clouds. Stephen Korshak decided to dedicate his life to tell us all how the thunder sounded and preserve the outlines of the cosmos for the awe of us all.

Enjoy, believe—be amazed.

Guillermo del Toro
Los Angeles, California
2025

PREFACE

Some artwork can evoke emotions or cause a shift in your way of thinking. Other artwork can inspire entire universes.

The varied, startling, and amazing pieces in the Korshak Collection comprise a vast library and toy store of imaginative scenes and places. Take a journey across the galaxy, or into wondrous fantasy lands, or deep into the twisted depths of hell.

———

These images were created by some of the greatest artists in the history of science fiction, fantasy, and horror. They graced the covers or interiors of classic pulp magazines from the 1930s through the 1960s, and of hardcover or paperback books written by masters of the genre such as Edgar Rice Burroughs, Robert E. Howard, H.P. Lovecraft, and L. Ron Hubbard. Working for the earliest pulp fiction magazines, many imaginative artists had a challenging job that went beyond simply illustrating a featured work of fiction. They had to make their point with a shout amidst the chaos of competing titles on newsstands filled with *Amazing Stories, Weird Tales, Fantastic Adventures, Wonder Stories,* and other tantalizing and eye-popping titles. Their vibrant images had to capture the imaginations of potential customers and conjure tantalizing hints of the marvelous adventures that awaited the reader.

The practice of illustrating a science fiction or fantasy story is less common in modern publishing, but the works of the pulp-era masters featured in the Korshak Collection are the pinnacle of interior art. No issue of *Weird Tales* or *Amazing Stories* would have been complete without elaborate line drawings that were just as captivating or thought-provoking as the dazzling covers. Due to the limitations of black-and-white printing, this art is darker and moodier, but just as effective as a striking cover, even when printed on coarse, yellowing paper.

In the golden age of the pulp magazines, writers were workhorses, penning novelettes to order, often for the minuscule pay of one-quarter cent per word. They wrote fast and with furious energy, and they told compelling, bombastic stories. The genre artists did the same, producing dazzling works of bug-eyed alien monsters and scantily clad damsels in distress. They depicted alien worlds, liberating dreamscapes, or nightmarish dimensions. The audiences were entertained, amazed, and inspired. And that creative process went both ways. Pulp magazine editors might commission paintings, pastels, watercolors, or drawings based on a story to lead off the issue, or the artist might deliver a brilliant cover image, and the publisher would tap their stable of authors for someone to write a new story inspired by the art.

Later, cover art styles evolved for a less transient book-buying market, as science fiction publishing grew from specialty fan presses in the 1950s to major publishers of commercial paperback and hardcover releases. The Korshak Collection includes lavish illustrations that graced the covers of landmark works of the genre. Such work, both the fiction and the paintings, did not often receive respect or attention in literary and artistic circles—and yet these works are powerful and enduring. The images created popular conceptions of cultural icons including Tarzan of the Apes, John Carter of Mars, King Kull, Conan the Barbarian, and more.

These artists knew their audience. Their illustrations were not designed for admiration by those who would spend an afternoon in a leisurely stroll through an art gallery. They had a different purpose, functioning like a power source connected directly to the imaginations of generations of readers.

KEVIN J. ANDERSON

A picture is worth a thousand words, and these images have triggered hundreds of thousands of words of my own fiction, as well the stories of countless other authors. As a young aspiring writer who lived in a small Midwestern town, I pored over the books and magazines these pictures illustrated, absorbed by the breathtaking sense of wonder that the art evoked. I remember standing at the paperback spinner rack in my high school library, enthralled by the kaleidoscope of alien worlds and heroes. I wanted to read *all* the stories like that. I wanted to *write* stories like that!

The covers of paperbacks, comics, and magazines transported me to amazing lands unknown, just as the spirit of John Carter was swept away to Barsoom in *A Princess of Mars*, or as Lovecraft's narrator was terrified when he gazed upon the bone-chilling ancient temple of Dagon. These epic images ignited my sense of wonder like a nuclear detonation.

————

Science fiction and fantasy artwork is commercial, yes, created to entice readers to buy a book or a magazine, but it also tells a story. It fires your imagination. When the artist helps to bring an author's imaginative story to life in a reader's mind, there is no greater accomplishment. Even if you aren't familiar with the associated stories, these illustrations will inspire stories of your own.

The myriad pieces in the Korshak Collection show the triumphant range of illustration in fantastic genres, from space landscapes to dreamworlds and painstakingly detailed depictions of the most horrific monsters. Just page through this book and you'll see for yourself.

Note the intense and exotic colors of Hannes Bok, the bright classic covers of Ed Emshwiller, the haunting details of Virgil Finlay, the energetic drama of Frank R. Paul, the lyrical grace of Arthur Rackham. The collection also includes classic book covers from masters such as Frank Frazetta, Kelly Freas, and Paul Lehr, and modern landmarks ranging from the evocative to the amazing to the terrifying—from Brian Froud, Jim Burns, J.K. Potter, and Michael Whelan.

Let yourself experience these works of art—you will certainly feel them at the core of your imagination. You can be an armchair explorer of all the planets in the galaxy, or all the lands of myth and legend.

Reawaken your sense of wonder.

Kevin J. Anderson
Monument, Colorado
2025

Michael Dirda

INTRODUCTION TO
THE KORSHAK COLLECTION

In a famous line from the opening page of *Alice's Adventures in Wonderland*, Alice thinks, "'What is the use of a book without pictures or conversations?'" While Lewis Carroll's heroine sounds distinctly exasperated, even a bit cross, her remark certainly wouldn't apply to the volume you now hold in your hands. It's chock-a-block with pictures that will surprise and delight you, as well as essays that, all together, call to mind a lively, many-sided conversation about the myriad connections between words and art. There's even one actual conversation, an interview with Michael Whelan, whose covers for science fiction novels won him multiple honors, including an astonishing fifteen Hugo Awards. As all these scholars and creators make clear, the best illustrations don't replicate a text, they augment it.

This catalogue also makes clear one other important aesthetic point: though originally designed to enhance pulp magazines and specialty press books, these paintings and drawings from the Korshak Collection can stand on their own as works of art. They aren't just eye candy meant to capture your attention or set your pulse racing. They do that, of course, but then what art worth that name doesn't aim to please, shock, propagandize, elicit religious awe, or offer aesthetic bliss? The one thing it never does is leave the viewer indifferent. Moreover, representational art, like that in the Korshak Collection, exhibits one additional quality, what one might call narrativity. In the words of an old catchphrase, every picture tells a story. The moment captured in paint or pencil functions like a highly dramatic movie still, a single frame from a motion picture we've never seen: we react to what the artist shows us, but also formulate a context for the image. What does it mean? What actions preceded it? What will happen next?

For a long time, many people naively dismissed these spectacular visions of space, fairyland, and the future as simply throwaway commissions produced by harried freelancers working with scratchboards and other cheap materials. Yet, commercial origins don't preclude the creation of things of beauty. All artists, even Old Masters, must work within the constraints imposed by their medium, their patrons, and their audience. A bishop requires a particular saint for a church fresco; a Renaissance grandee wants his bedroom ceiling decorated with sportive nymphs and satyrs; a Gilded Age mogul desires a portrait of his daughters for the Newport summer retreat. In all these cases, the end product can be forgettable, merely adequate, or an immortal masterpiece by Tiepolo, Titian, or John Singer Sargent. What matters isn't the material used, the time spent, or the amount paid, but the quality of the finished picture.

To be industrious and prolific, as many of these artists had to be, doesn't mean that quantity has inevitably replaced quality. Would you want Mozart to have composed less music or Dickens to have scribbled just two or three novels? In many cases, time pressure actually liberates the imagination, forcing one to tap deep into the wellsprings of the unconscious. Is there, for example, a more frightening, more archetypal demon from the id than that pictured in Hannes Bok's *Pickman's Model* (Plate 1)! Once seen, it is never forgotten.

For the most part, fantasy illustrations, whether whimsical or dark, never strike us as period pieces. The works of N.C. Wyeth and Howard Pyle (Plates 2 and 3), to mention two American masters represented here, are joys forever, though created well over a hundred years ago. However, like science fiction itself, science fictional art tends to reveal more about the time in which it was made than it does about the future. Many of the treasures in the Korshak Collection reflect a particular moment of twentieth-century idealism and wishful thinking about technology and the space age. Here are sleek rocket ships captained by the prototypes of Flash Gordon and Buck Rogers, buxom heroines in metallic sports bras, tentacled aliens and comical BEMs (bug-eyed monsters), flying saucers, and cosmic visions of life on other planets—all of them aspects of that vision of a gleaming future that reached its zenith at the 1939 New York World's Fair. Since then, such hopeful visions of the twenty-first century and beyond now elicit nostalgic wistfulness. Captured in them is the World of Tomorrow before it became today; the original, untarnished dream of a new frontier among the stars.

Looking at these pictures induces a small pang: we cannot help but impute to them a certain endearing but definitely lost innocence. These days, we dread a future out of a Philip K. Dick novel—an overcrowded Earth devastated by climate change, strewn with debris, and racked by never-ending wars. In this regard, the Korshak Collection celebrates two overlapping Golden Ages: one of magazine and book illustration, the other of the American dream when know-how, drive, and hard work might accomplish anything, together creating an age of wonder and of wonders.

MICHAEL DIRDA

All the works in this catalogue convey a sense of awe and enchantment. As Stephen D. Korshak writes in his essay here, "Key to building a great collection is a guiding principle that organizes individual items into a set." His own "set," he emphasizes, "focuses on fantastic illustrations of imaginative literature that exhibit a sense of wonder." While pulp fantastika started him on his collecting career, Korshak soon recognized that masterpieces by J. Allen St. John, Frank R. Paul, Virgil Finlay, Hannes Bok, and others transcended the purely parochial uses for which they were initially made. They could rightly take their place in the wider history of fantasy illustration. Refusing to ghettoize the paintings and drawings he'd loved since childhood, Korshak instead contextualized them. By integrating showpieces from Aubrey Beardsley, Arthur Rackham, Edmund Dulac, and other European book artists into his collection, he has demonstrated that quality recognizes no boundaries. Not even Dulac could produce a more haunting, *Thief of Bagdad*-like vision than Margaret Brundage's pastel *The Altar of Melek Taos* (Plate 4).

This catalogue, consequently, highlights the sheer ecumenical variety of the Korshak Collection. Consider the range of its scholarly, fact-filled essays. In her close parsing of Aubrey Beardsley's *Le Morte d'Arthur* or *Woman Playing the Violin and Satyr Playing the Pipes for Le Morte d'Arthur* (Plate 40), Margaret D. Stetz reminds us that this consummate (and perverse) master of pen-and-ink drawing insisted that he always created "autonomous images" independent of any text they were reproduced in. Partway through Ashley Rye-Kopec's analysis of Arthur Rackham's depiction of the sleeping Rip Van Winkle surrounded by fairy folk (Plate 41), she points out that Washington Irving's five-thousand-word story inspired the artist to produce "fifty-one color illustrations, plus three line drawings and one decorative initial." This means "that, on average, there is an illustration by Rackham for every hundred words of Irving's text." She notes, again, the stand-alone character of his pictures, quoting a newspaper review that Rackham took "from his author's text nothing more than a hint and an opportunity."

In her own genial essay, Amanda T. Zehnder, a coeditor of this catalogue, probes Edmund Dulac's scene from Shakespeare's *The Tempest* (Plate 42) and his use of blue in *The Snow Queen* (Plate 43), while also touching on the evolution of color printing and the history of lavish Christmas gift books. To aid our understanding of the skeletal figures in Władysław Benda's *The Army of the Dead* (Plate 44), Rachael Kane relates the actual history of Poland's Winged Hussars, then uses Benda's piece to reflect on the fraught relationship between art and nationalist propaganda.

Not least, Lauren Stump offers what is, in effect, a concise biography of the still too-little-known José Segrelles. His quietly ominous painting of jellyfish-like Martian warships sending tentacles down toward an isolated cottage in *War of the Worlds* (Plate 46) might well be my favorite picture in the Korshak Collection—unless it's one of a dozen others, among them *Pickman's Model*, Paul's *Seeds from Space* (Plate 5), Brian Froud's *Voice of the River* (What a wonderful scaly creature!) (Plate 6), Rackham's *The Mock Turtle* (Plate 7) from *Alice's Adventures in Wonderland*, or Robert Lawson's *The House of Usher* (Plate 8). That last one was a surprise. Who would have thought that Lawson, best known for his drawings of the flower-loving bull of Munro Leaf's *The Story of Ferdinand*, could capture Poe's sinister melancholy almost as well as Harry Clarke (Plate 9)?

As the pulps developed, certain artists gradually became associated with particular authors and magazines. St. John excelled at drawing the youthful male body and worked closely with Edgar Rice Burroughs in depicting Tarzan and John Carter of Mars. The exceptionally prolific Paul produced many of the most famous images of early American science fiction, starting in 1927 with his iconic *War of the Worlds* cover for *Amazing Stories* and—to mention only examples from the Korshak Collection—quickly going on to picture, sometimes in psychedelic color, the futuristic architecture of *The Glass City of Europa*, Earth's watery devastation in *Moon Doom*, the eerie vegetal aliens of *Seeds from Space*, and the strange wonderland of *Life on Neptune*. Finlay, the Seurat of pulp fantasy, used tiny pen-and-ink dots—stippling is the technical term—to conjure up the elegant and mysterious women of A. Merritt's fiction, often surrounding these goddess-like beings with bubbles and swirling mists. One might argue that Finlay's women are the stuff of dreams, actually more alluring than Margaret Brundage's more blatant nudes. See, for instance, his 1956 cover painting for *Other Worlds Science Stories* (Plate 10).

That said, many of Brundage's originals have been lost, partly because her pastels are so fragile that if you breathe heavily on them half the image will fly away as chalky dust. Still, the two examples in the Korshak Collection, especially *The Witch's Mark* (Plate 11), hint at why her work has long been viewed as kinky and sado-masochistic. As the science fiction writer L. Sprague de Camp once wrote: "Mrs. Brundage earned the title 'Queen of the Pulps' with her pictures of naked heroines being tortured, raped, and disemboweled."[1] That's something of an overstatement, but most of Brundage's covers, notably for *Black Colossus* and *A Witch Shall Be Born* (neither in the Korshak Collection), certainly seem to be catering to "the male gaze." Is her work, then, just extra-spicy pinup art? In her compelling essay, Lisa Yaszek neatly overturns this reflexive interpretation.

Brundage's *Weird Tales* covers, she contends, spotlight empowered women taking center stage but also taking command. The long-tressed redhead in *The Witch's Mark*, for instance, stares back at the viewer with her own enigmatic female gaze. Yaszek also interprets Brundage as part of a cadre of neglected women artists of the 1930s, as well as a prominent feminist and civil rights activist. One could add an additional factoid that sets the mind speculating or even reeling: Brundage and Walt Disney were high school classmates.

In the catalogue's final essay, David Brinley considers the metaphysical, highly stylized art of Bok, eight of whose works are represented in the Korshak Collection. Perhaps the best known of these is his phantasmagorical, crisply painted dust jacket for the Arkham House compilation of Robert E. Howard stories, *Skull-Face and Others* (Plate 12). Disdaining the quotidian, Bok opts for grotesquerie: in the left background, a sailing ship lies anchored near a pink minaret, from which an eerie swirling length of pink cloth gradually morphs into the wispy dress on a bright-eyed, dark-haired young woman. Her disheveled drapery, however, looks oddly angular and one section of it resembles an extra appendage, almost a third breast. Even more unsettling, the woman appears to be fending off a somewhat humanoid and vaguely feminine creature with a single gigantic eye who floats in the air and carries a translucent green globe. From this creature's torso unravels an immensely long spiral of red scarf that has, python-like, encircled the woman's ankle. Off in the right-hand corner of this bizarre tableau squats a gigantic toad-like creature, coolly watching the action. Not all of Bok's so-called "kodachromes of the fantastic" are quite this *outré*. But looking at the cover's juxtaposition of enigmatic and disparate elements, it's hard not to think of a Dali painting or the prose-poet Comte de Lautréamont's haunting phrase, a surrealist touchstone, about the beauty of "the chance encounter of a sewing machine and an umbrella on an operating table."[2]

As it happens, at least one major artist in the Korshak Collection fully and overtly embraced the surrealist aesthetic in his signature works. Influenced by Yves Tanguy, Richard Powers repeatedly assembled squiggles and blobs, lines and splotches, along with the occasional humanoid shape, into hypnotically fascinating book covers, such as that for Frederik Pohl's story collection *The Abominable Earthman* (Plate 13). Rivaling Powers in popularity during the 1950s and early '60s, Edmund Emshwiller often set a human face or figure against an abstract expressionist background, as in the lovely example from *Spaceman* (Plate 14). By contrast, J.K. Potter's surreal but deeply unnerving *Alive and Screaming* (Plate 15) could serve as the splatter-shock finale of a modern horror film.

MICHAEL DIRDA

Artists, of course, learn from their predecessors and each other. As one surveys the pictures in this catalogue, one can detect lines of affiliation and influence. Frank E. Schoonover, for instance, was taught by Howard Pyle, whose example suffuses his pupil's cover for Burroughs's *A Princess of Mars* (Plate 16), a double portrait of the resolutely heroic John Carter and the beautiful Dejah Thoris. Brundage is a soulmate of Beardsley and Clarke (as well as of Eugène Delacroix and Jean-Léon Gérôme in their Orientalist vein). St. John's action-packed paintings established the templates for the later heroic fantasy art of Roy Krenkel (Plate 17), Frazetta, and Whelan. The two works here by Kelly Freas (Plate 18) recall Paul, Earle K. Bergey (whose heroines popularized the steel bra), and other Golden Age illustrators. While Freas's most affecting painting—the October 1953 cover for *Astounding Stories,* illustrating Tom Godwin's *The Gulf Between*—may not be part of the Korshak Collection, it clearly pays homage to two works that are. Without Finlay's *The Face in the Abyss* from 1940 (Plate 19) and Bok's *Pickman's Model* from 1951, each a close-up of a huge and terrifying creature clutching a human being, would Freas have given us a gigantic robot, with a soulful face conveying deep, almost uncomprehending pity, as it holds out a dead man in its metal palm?

Let me stop here. Inevitably, any introduction, no matter how long, can only draw attention to a few of the many artists represented in the Korshak Collection. I certainly don't mean to overlook, or in any way undervalue, Kay Nielsen (Plates 20 and 21), Sidney Sime, Dorothy Lathrop, and Joseph Clement Coll (Plate 22), or such European masters as Heinrich Lefler (Plate 24) and Heinrich Kley (Plate 25), or John Schoenherr (Plate 30), Stanley Meltzoff (Plate 34), Alex Schomburg, Jim Burns, The Brothers Hildebrandt (Plate 36), and so many others. Let me just say: their depictions of fairies and sea nymphs, of space captains and aliens, are all here, waiting to be enjoyed, studied, and learned from.

"One of the joys of collecting," as Stephen Korshak writes here, "is sharing your vision with others." Education, preservation, and stewardship matter. Above all, though, these exhilarating works of art, bursting with action, enchantment, and every sort of marvel, demonstrate the truth of William Blake's words: "Energy is eternal delight."[3] With that, let me urge you to explore over 160 years of imaginative illustration and discover for yourself the world of wonder that is the Korshak Collection.

1. L. Sprague de Camp, *Lovecraft: A Biography* (New York: Doubleday, 1975).

2. Comte de Lautréamont, *Les Chants de Maldoror* (Paris: Gustave Balitout, Questroy et Cie., 1868). The translation is mine.

3. William Blake, *The Marriage of Heaven and Hell* (London, ca. 1790), 4.

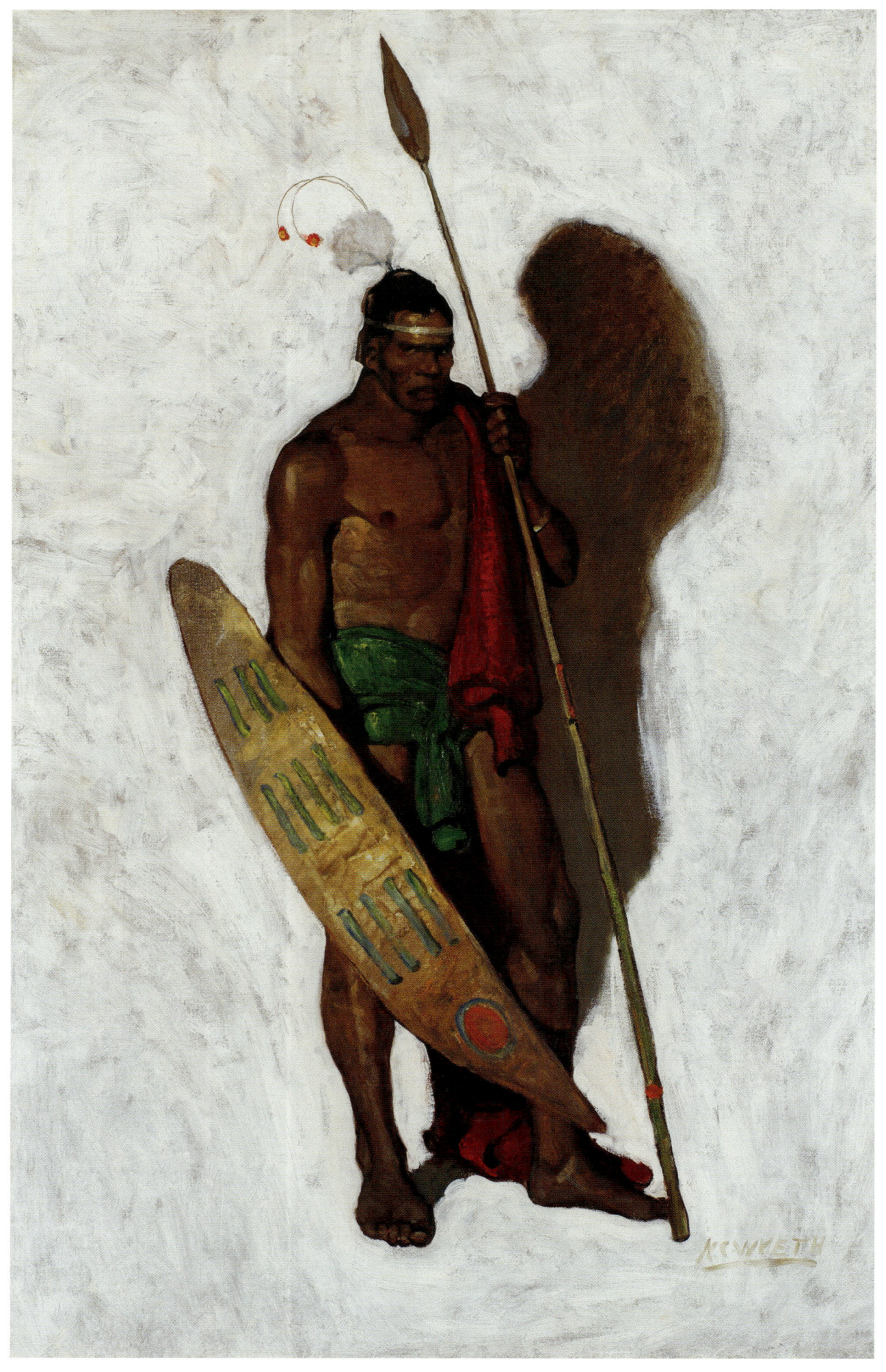

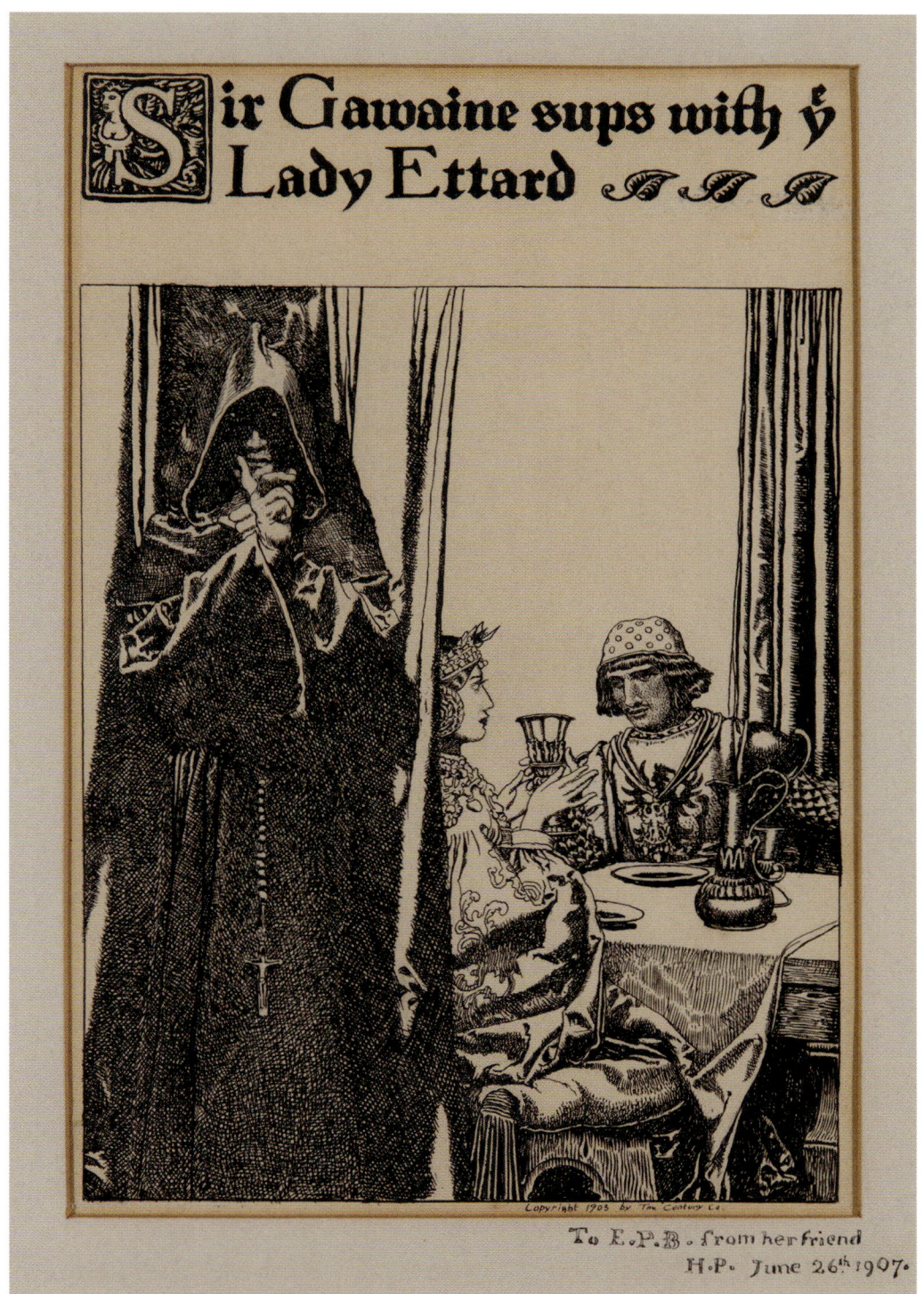

PLATE 2 (opposite). N.C. (Newell Convers) Wyeth, (American, 1882–1945), *Story of Allan Quartermain*, 1914, oil on canvas, 40 × 30 inches.

PLATE 3. Howard Pyle (American, 1853–1982), *Sir Gawaine Sups with Ye Lady Ettard*, 1903, pen and ink, 9¼ × 6½ inches.

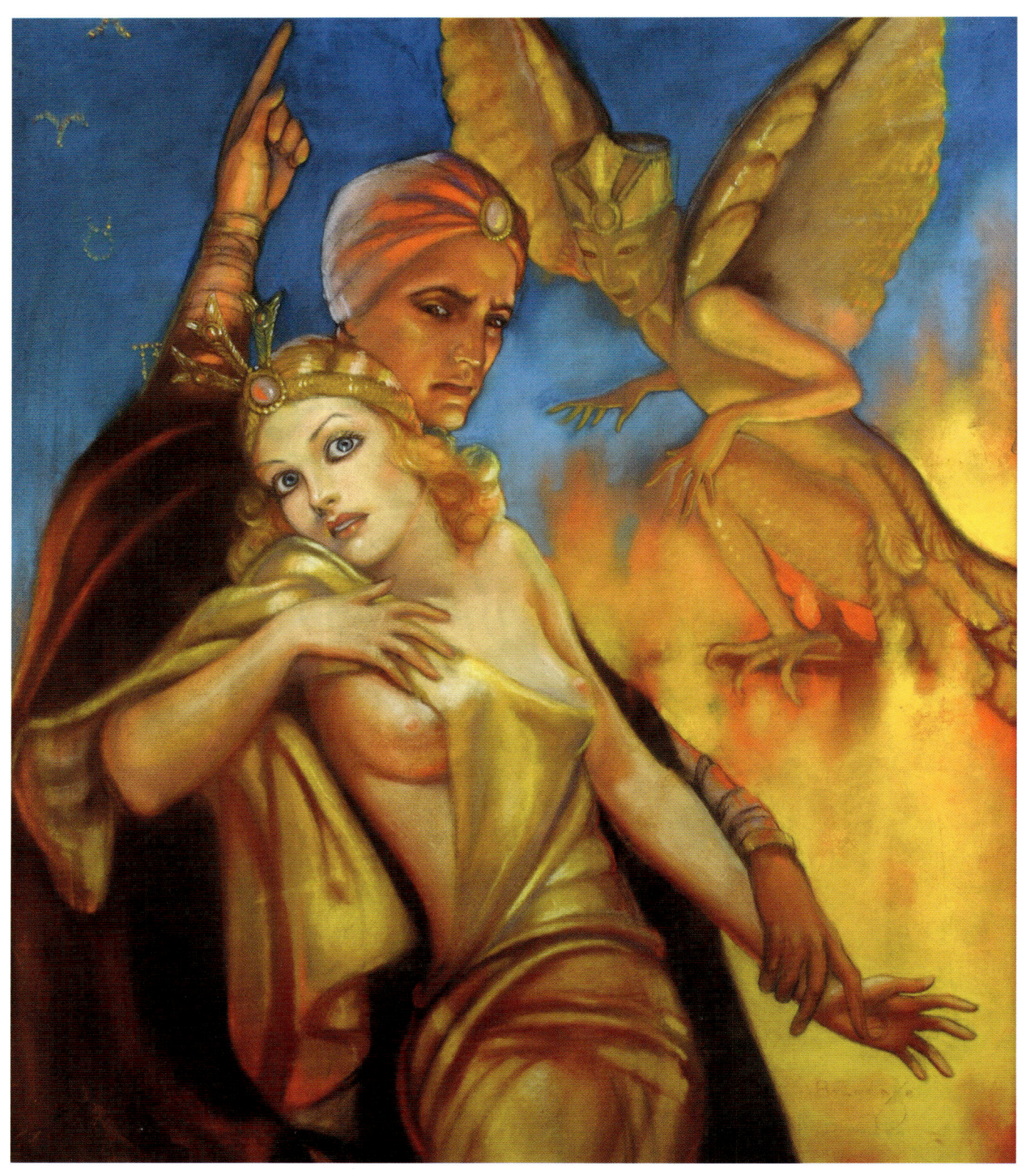

PLATE 4. Margaret Brundage (American, 1900–1976), *The Altar of Melek Taos*, 1932, pastel on paper, 23 × 16 inches.

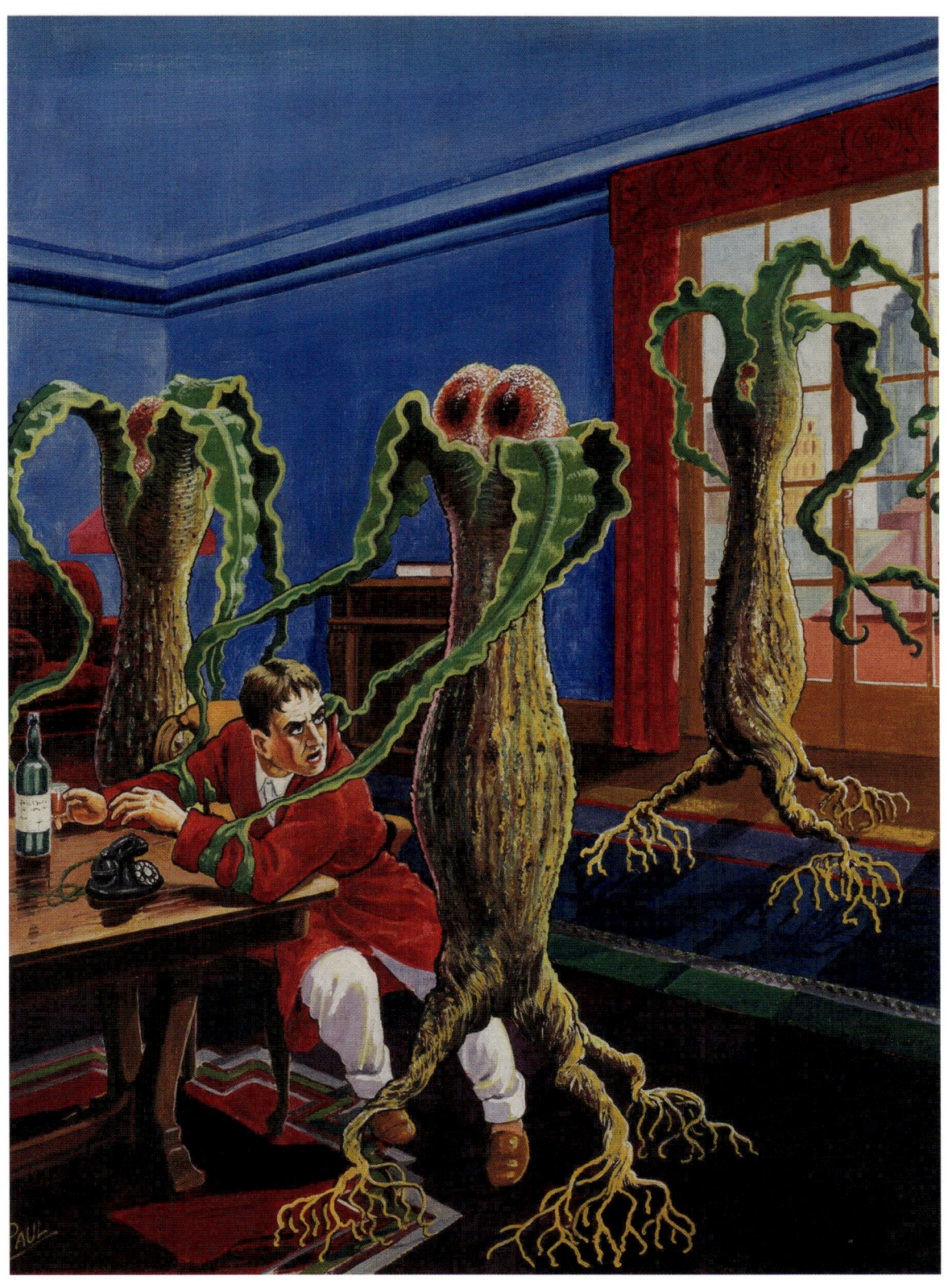

PLATE 5. Frank R. Paul (American,
1884–1963), *Seeds from Space*, 1935,
oil on canvas board, 24 × 16 inches.

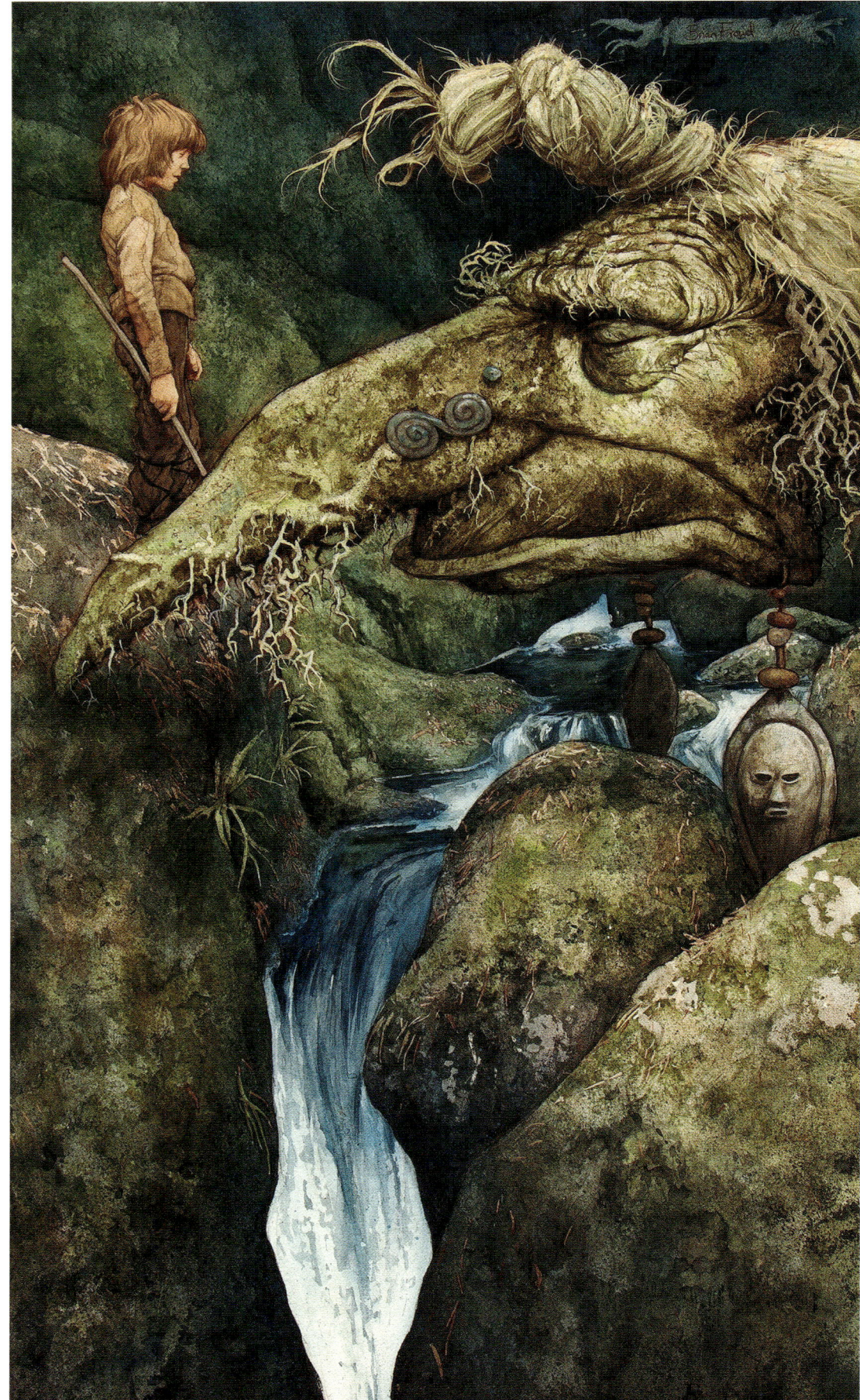

PLATE 6. Brian Froud (British, b. 1947), *Voice of the River*, 1976, watercolor, gouache on paper, 22¾ × 13½ inches, permission granted by Robert Gould.

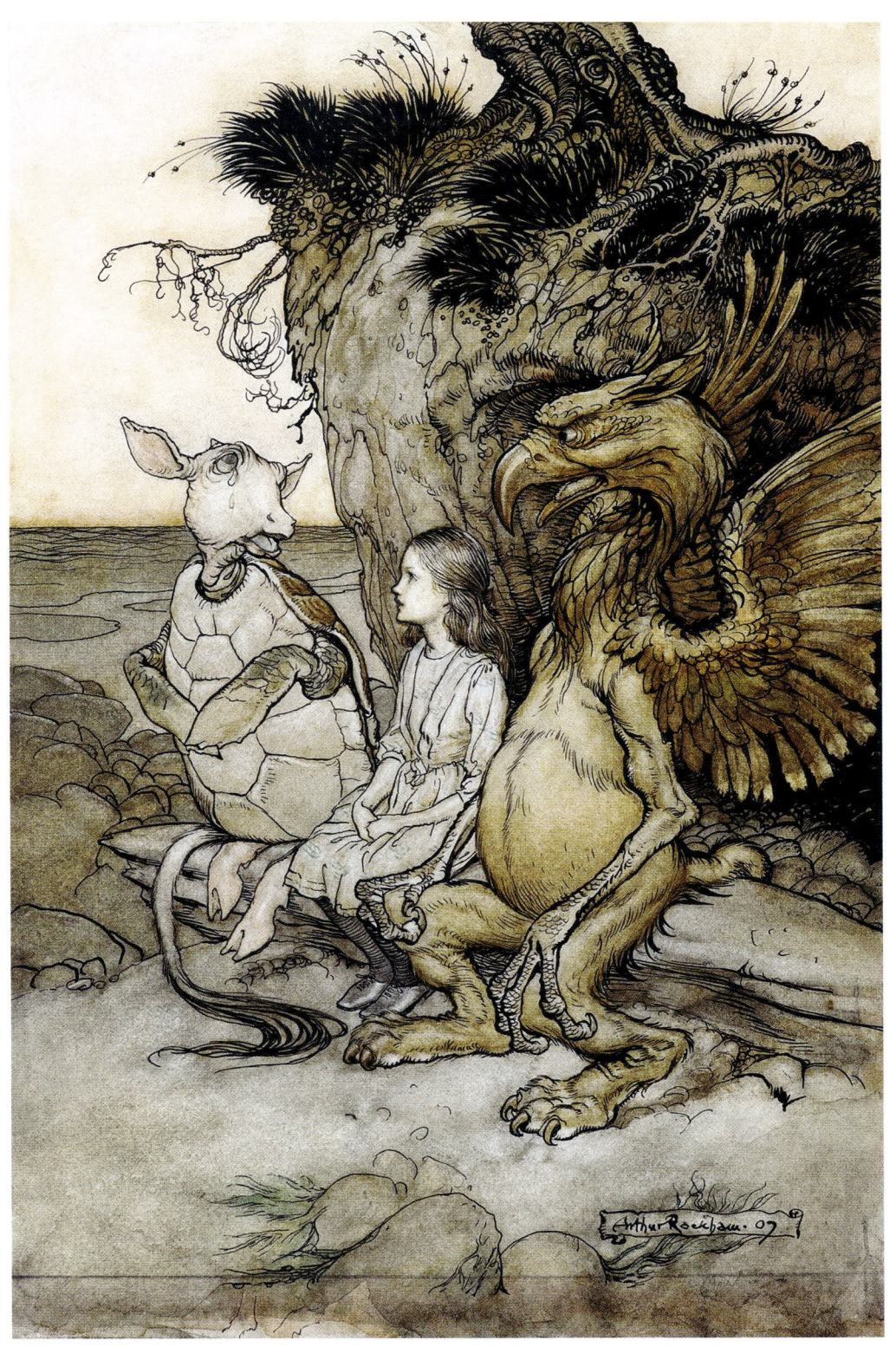

PLATE 7. Arthur Rackham (British, 1867–
1939), *The Mock Turtle* (*Alice's Adventures
in Wonderland*), 1907, watercolor, pen and
ink on paper, 10½ × 7 inches.

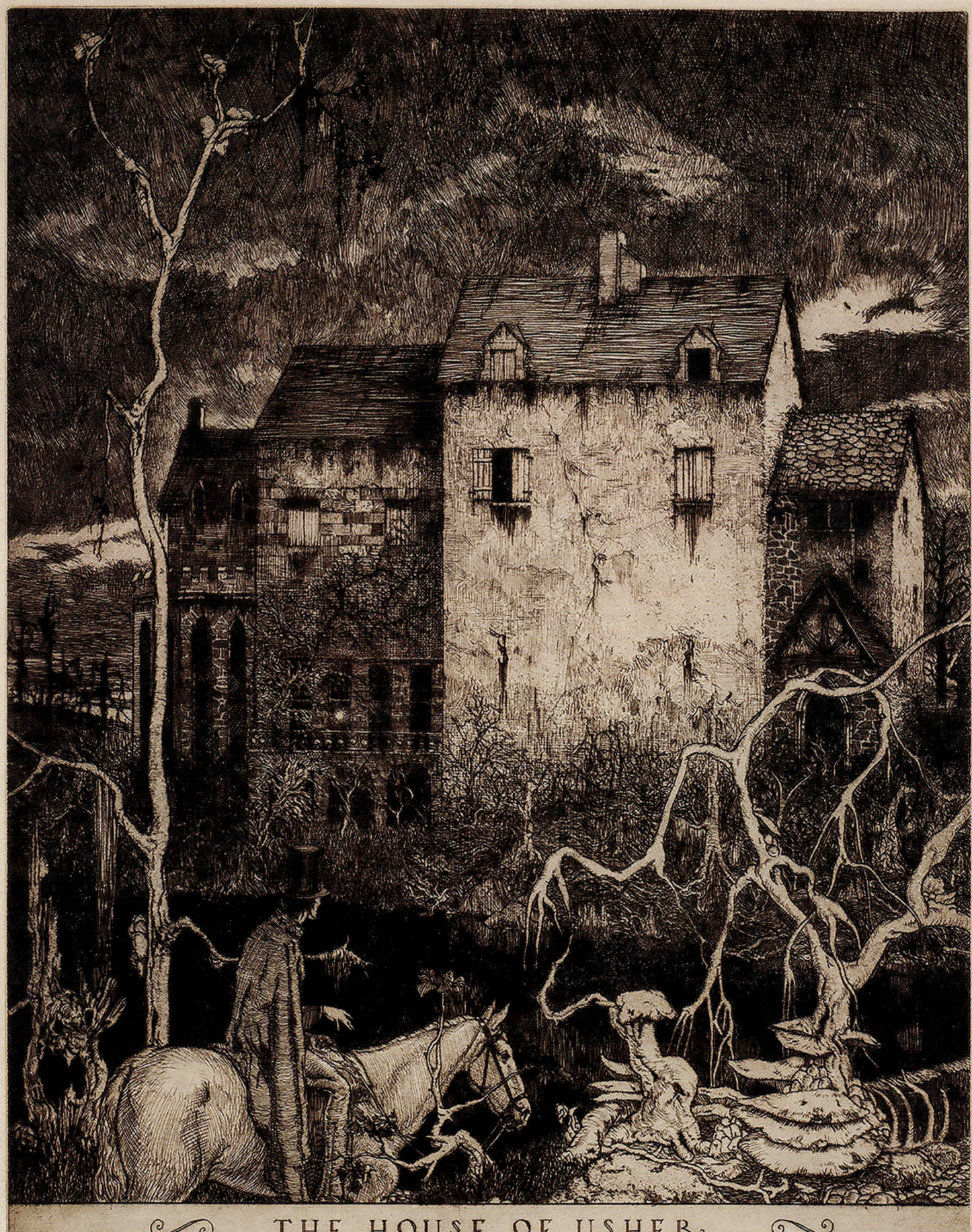

THE HOUSE OF USHER

"I know not how it was—but, with the first glimpse of the building a sense of insufferable gloom pervaded my spirit"

The Fall of The House of Usher. By Edgar Allan Poe.   This is Nº 18 of an Edition of 100 proofs.

Robert Hanson

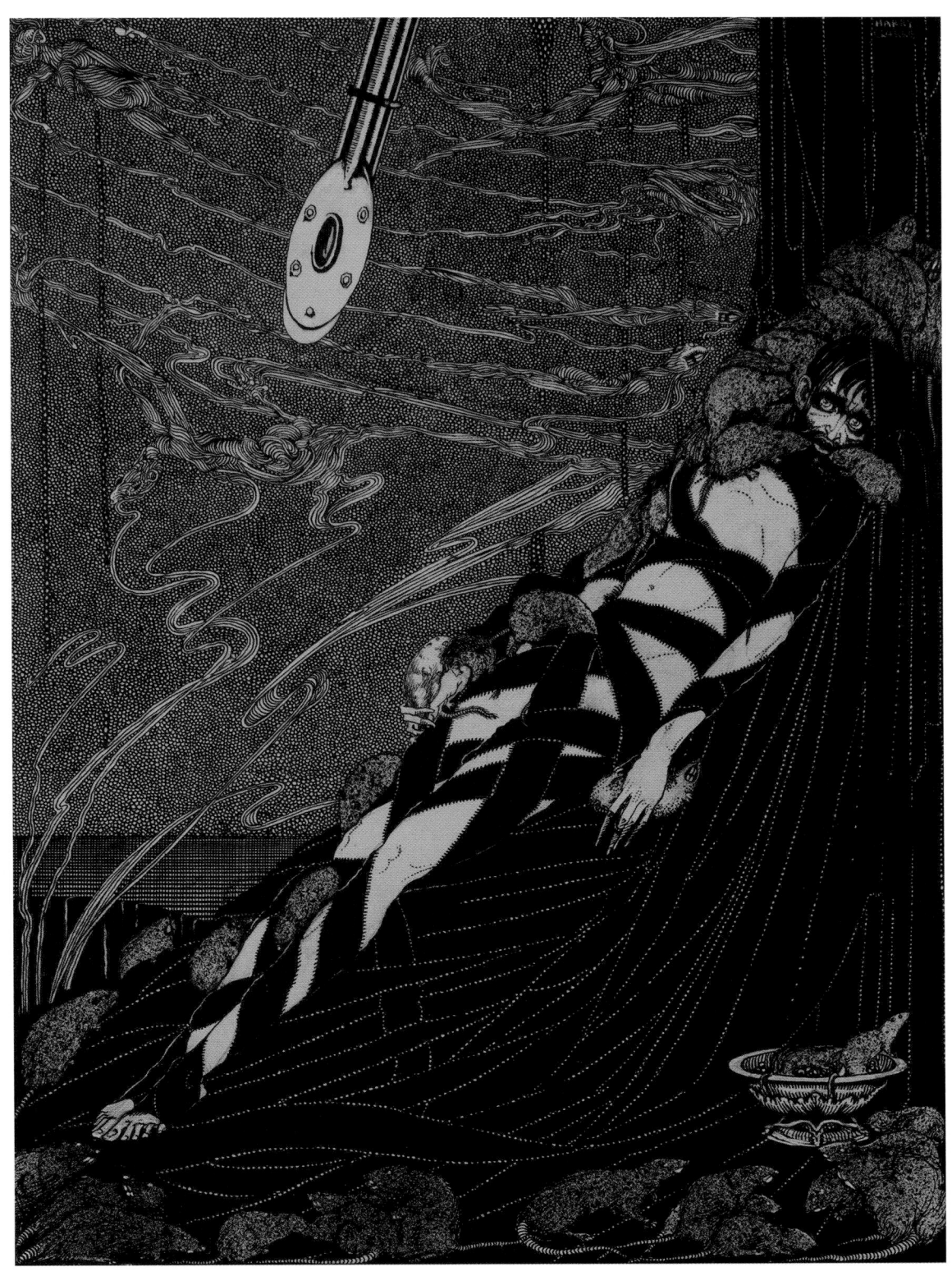

PLATE 8 (opposite). Robert Lawson (American, 1892–1957), *The House of Usher*, c. 1925, etching on paper, 12 × 9 inches.

PLATE 9. Harry Clarke (Irish, 1889–1931), *The Pit and the Pendulum*, 1919, pen and ink, 9 × 7 inches.

PLATE 10. Virgil Finlay (American, 1914–1971), *Other Worlds Science Stories cover*, 1956, gouache on illustration board, 10 × 8 inches.

PLATE 11 (opposite). Margaret Brundage (American, 1900–1976), *Witch's Mark*, 1938, pastel on paper, 26 × 20 inches.

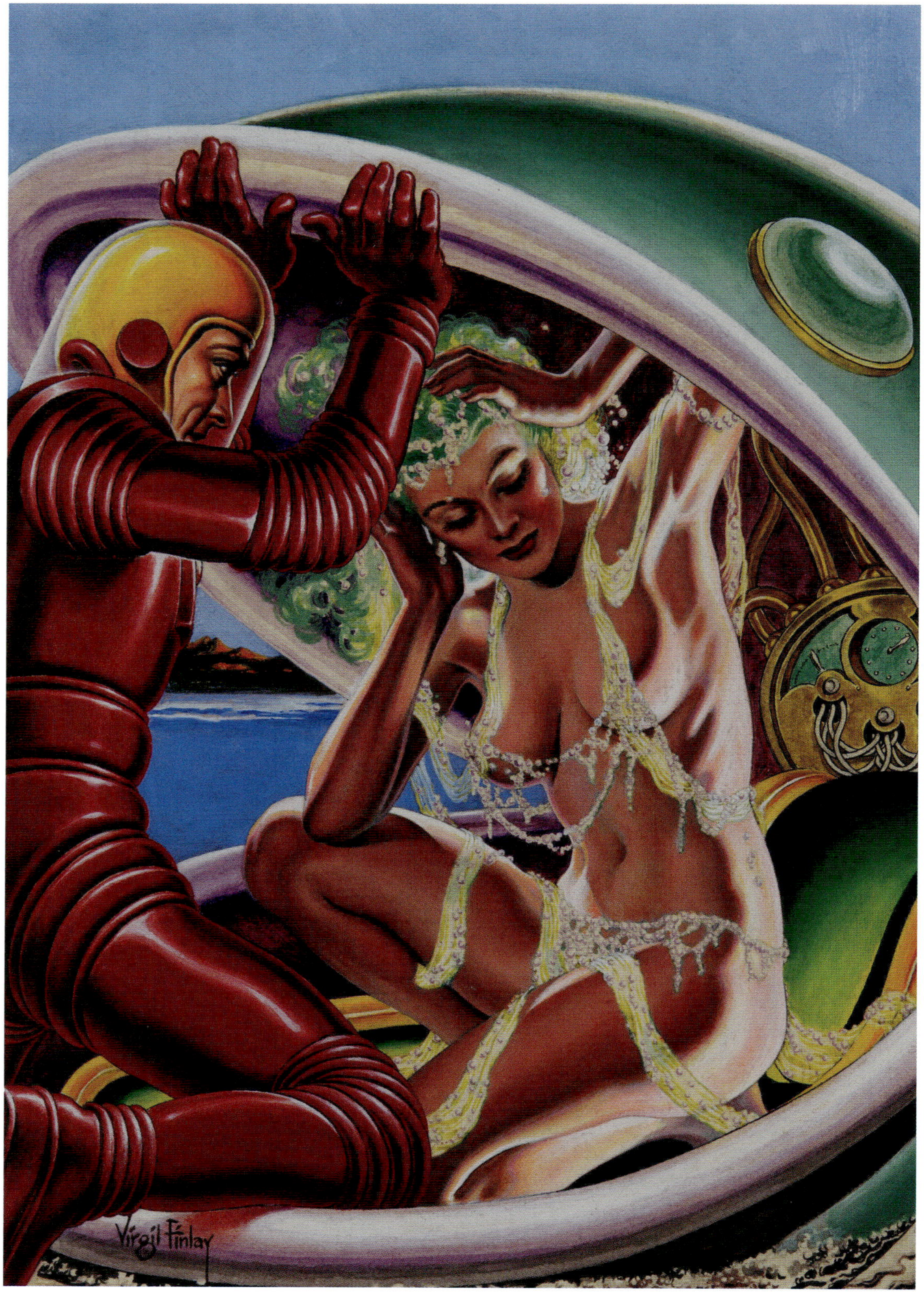

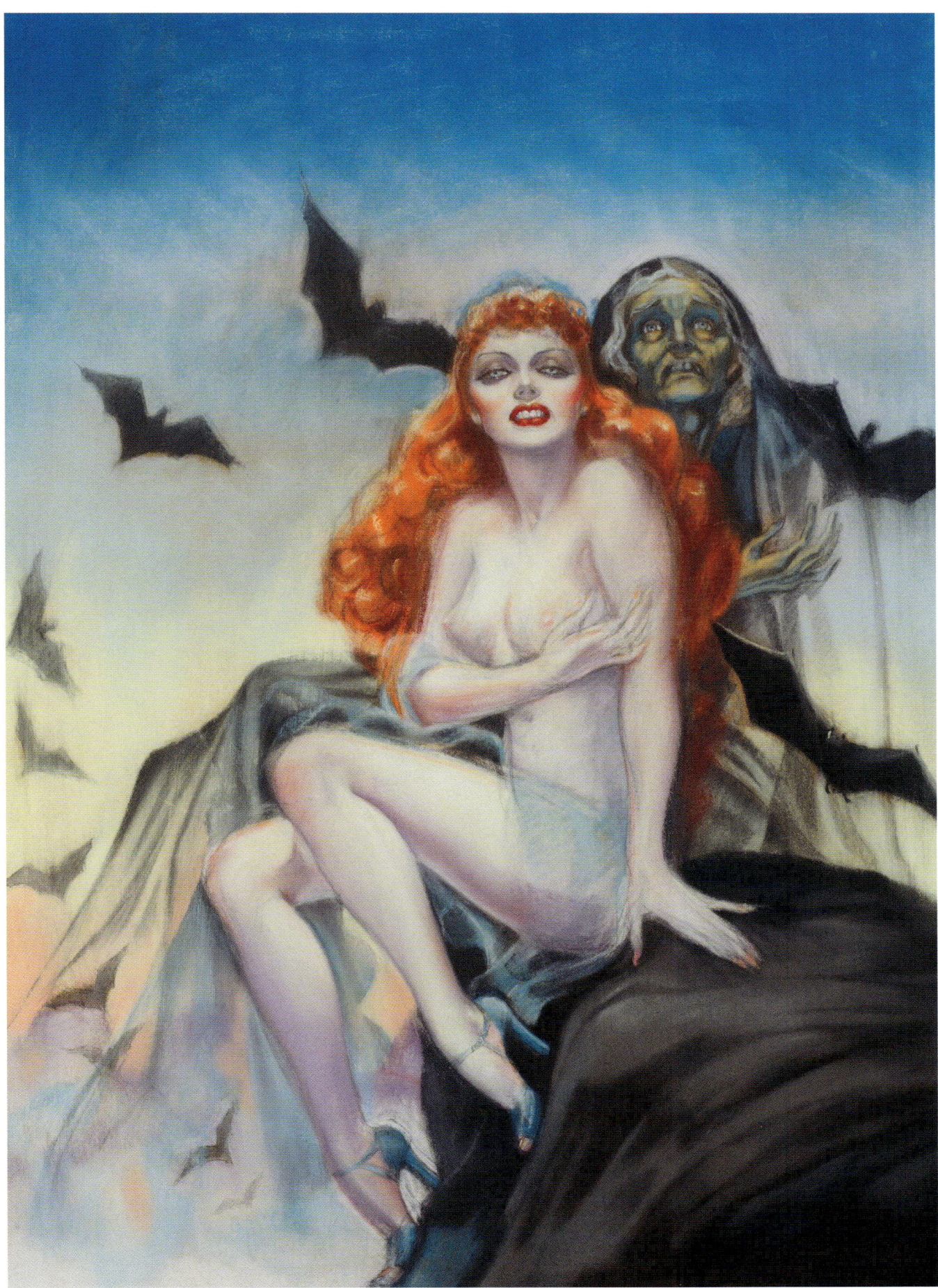

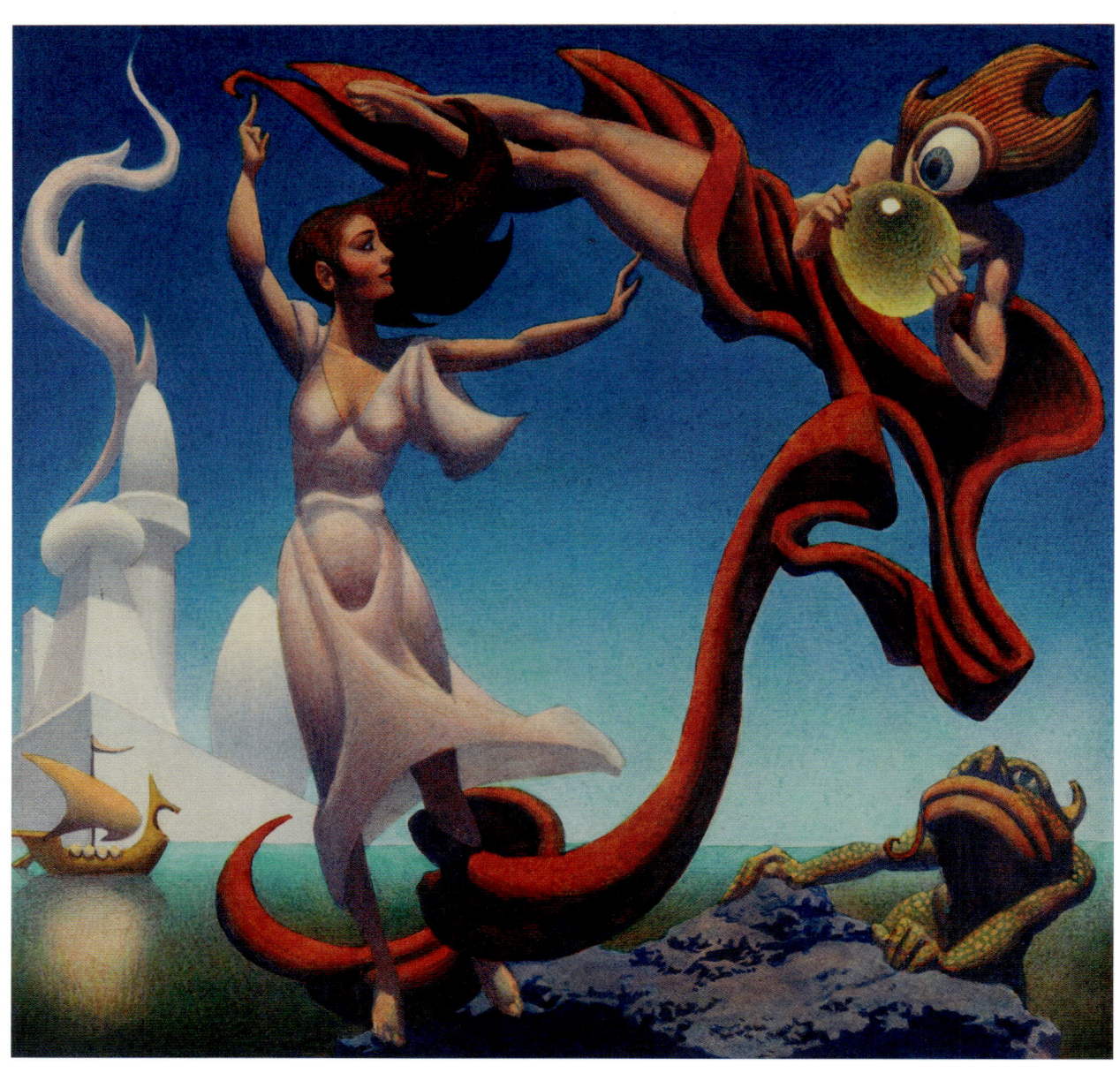

PLATE 12. Hannes Bok (American, 1914–1964), *Skull-Face and Others*, 1946, gouache on illustration board, 6 × 8 inches.

PLATE 13 (opposite). Richard Powers (American, 1921–1996), *The Abominable Earthman*, 1963, acrylic on illustration board, 17 × 11½ inches, © Richard Powers.

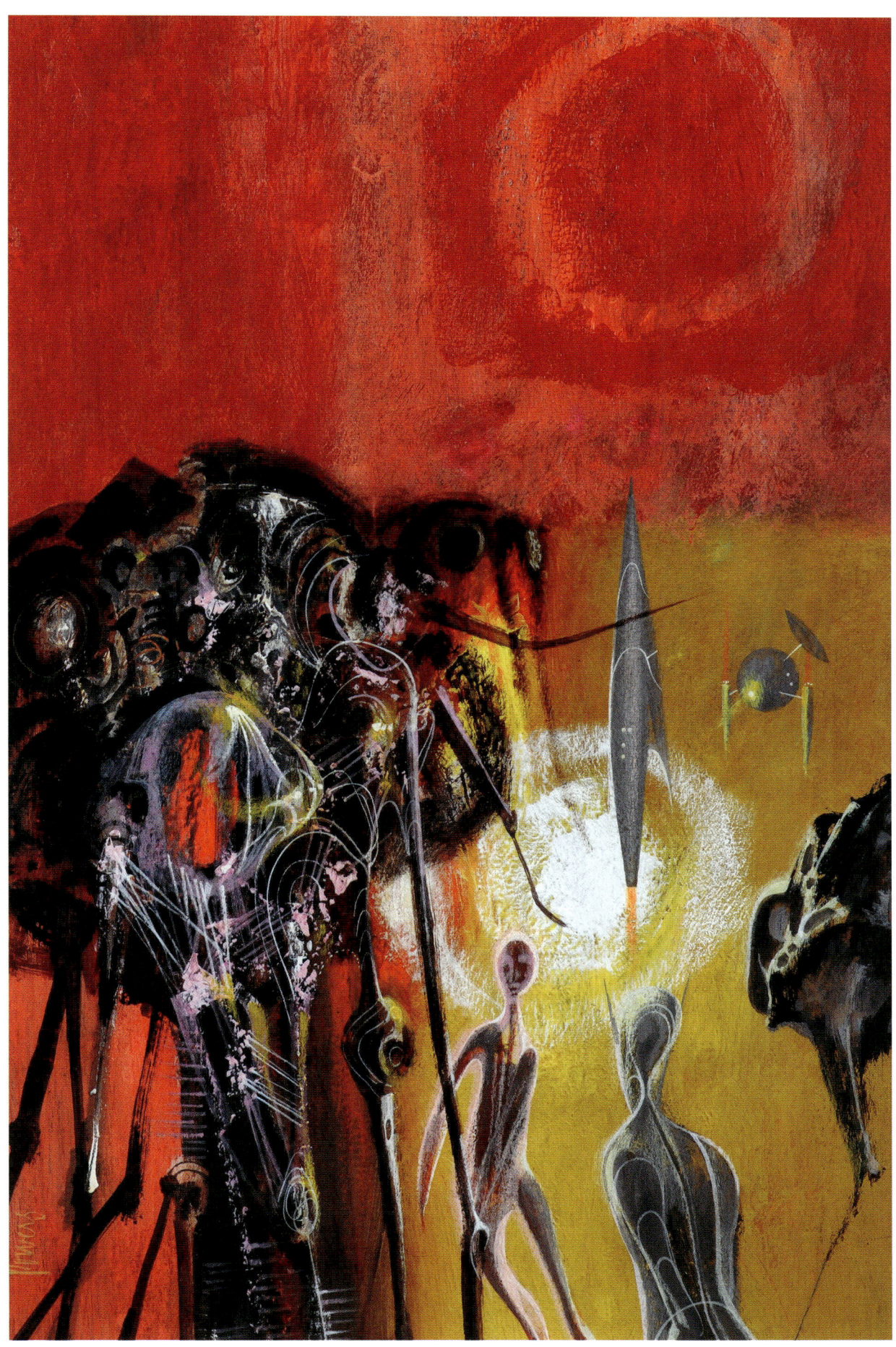

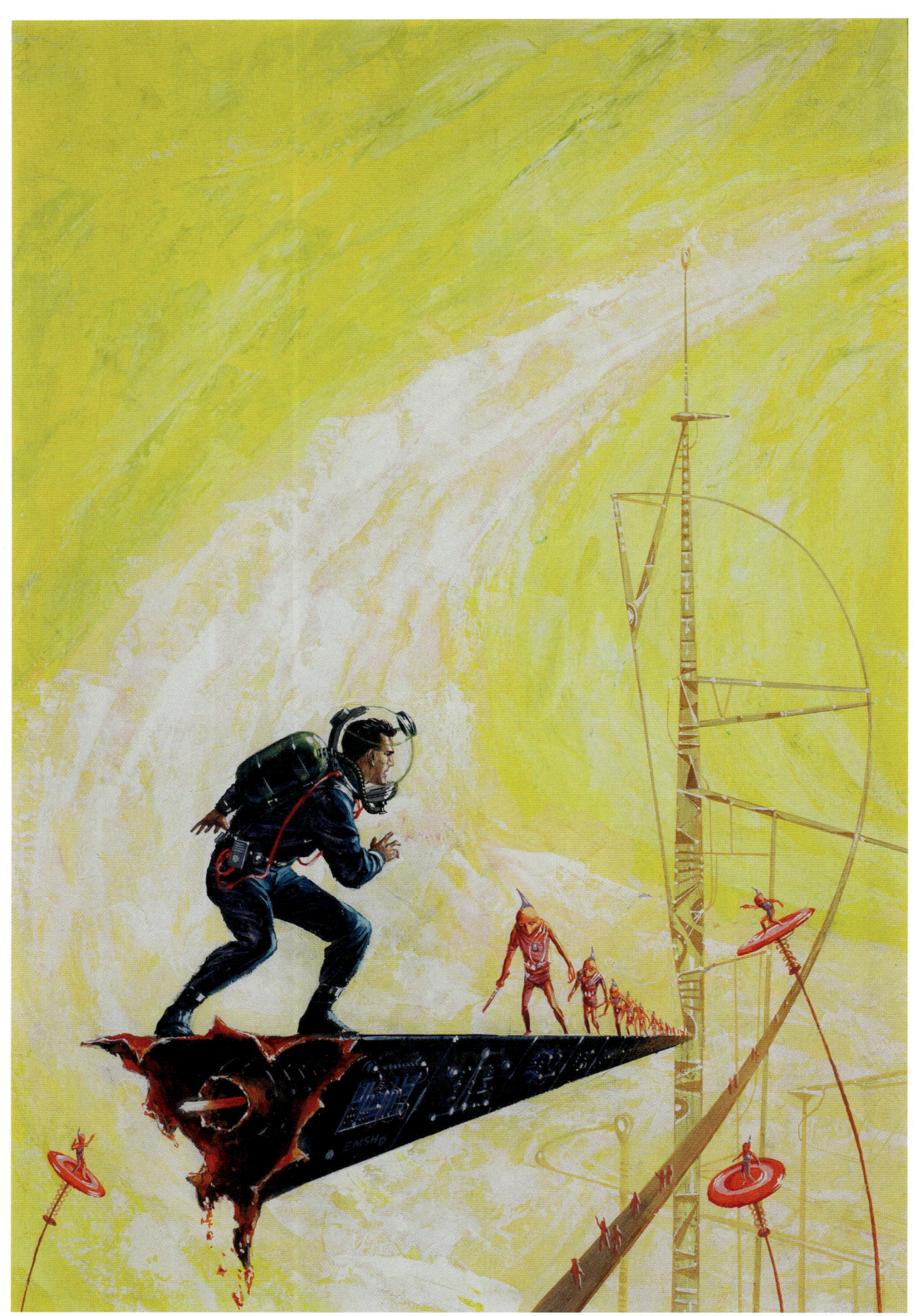

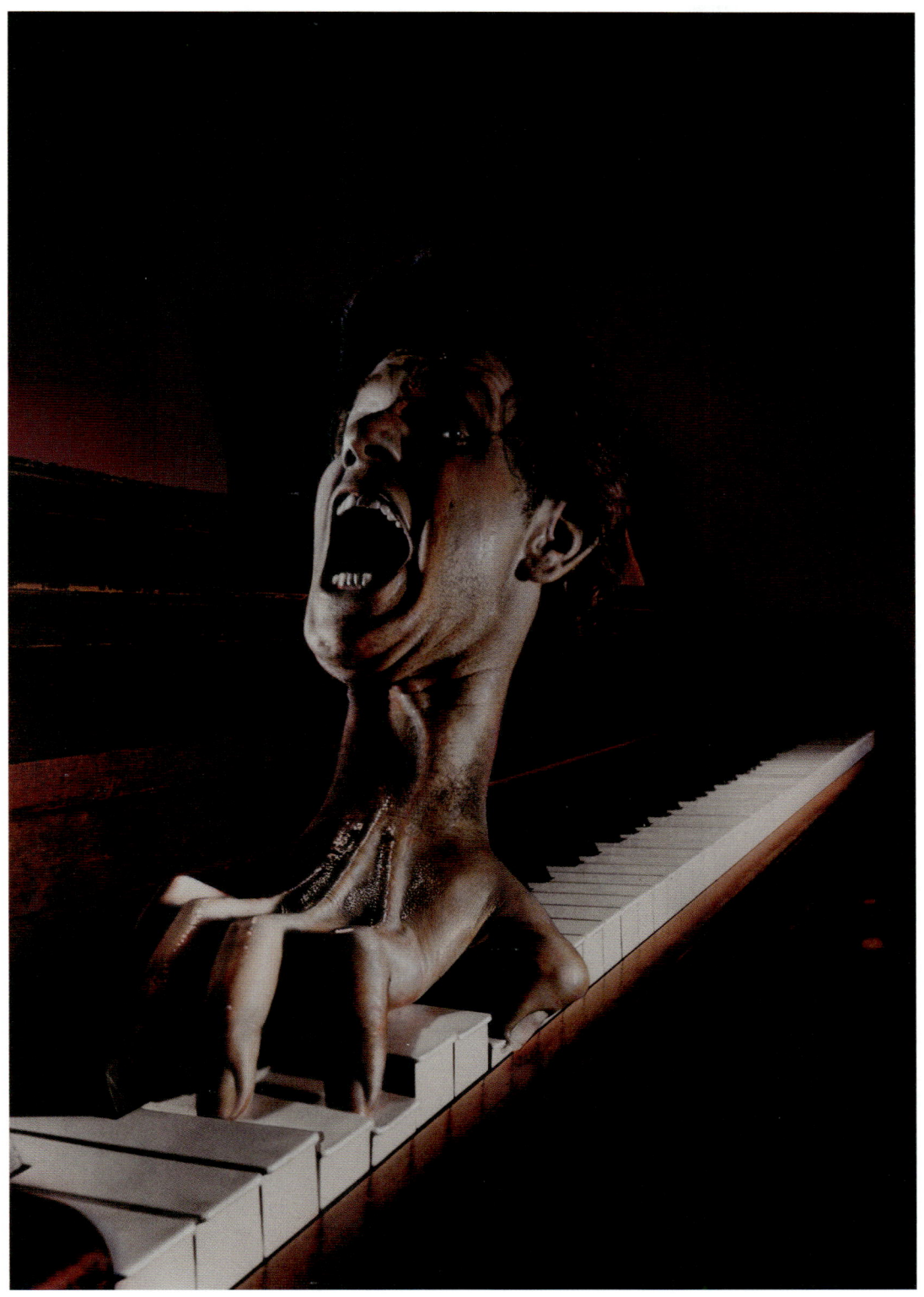

PLATE 14 (opposite). Edmund Emshwiller
(American, 1925–1990), *Spaceman*, c. 1965,
gouache on illustration board, 19 × 13
inches, courtesy of the Ed Emshwiller Estate.

PLATE 15. J.K. Potter (American,
b. 1956), *Alive and Screaming*
(*Piano Man*), 1985, photography and
digital illustration, 14 × 10 inches.

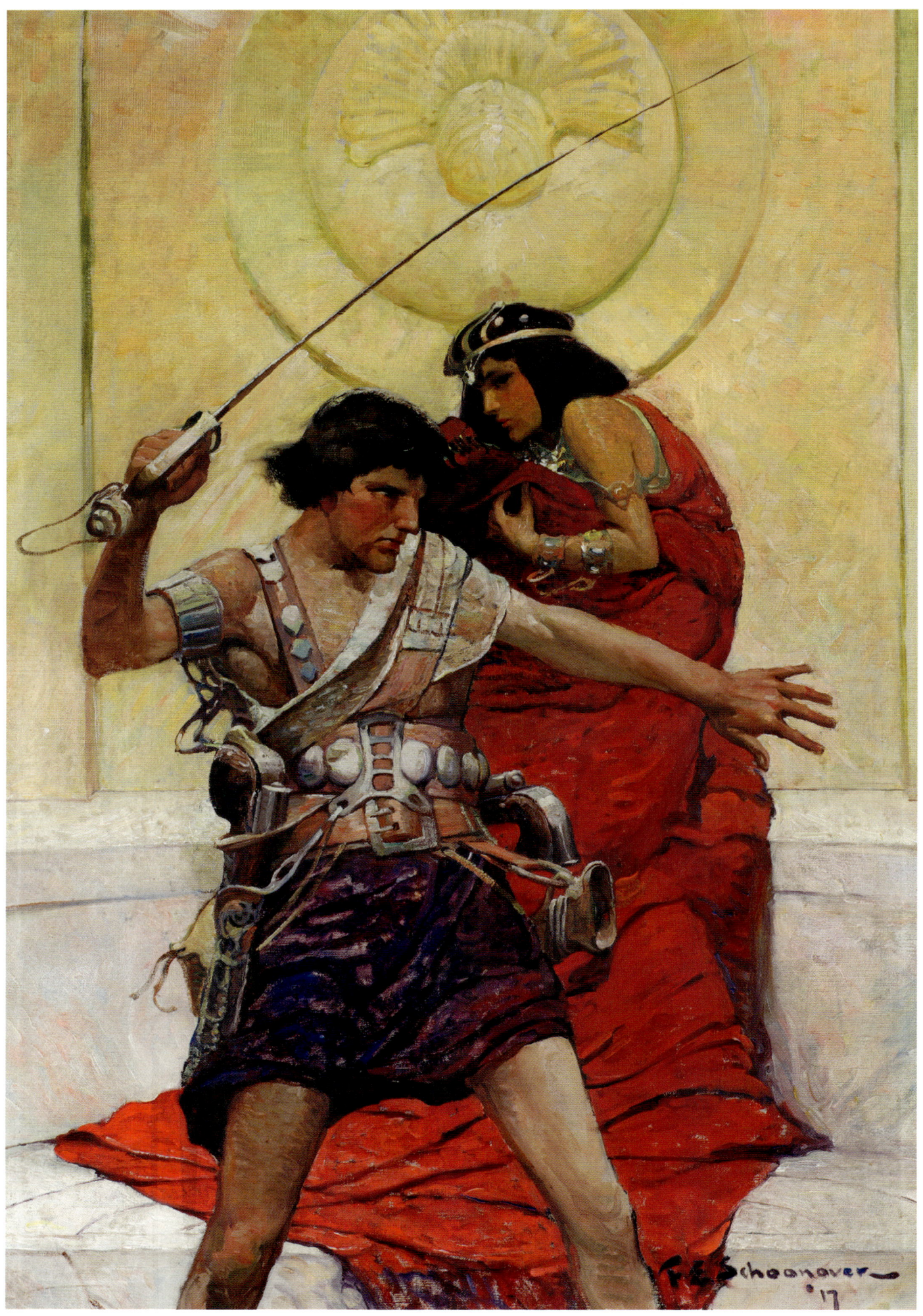

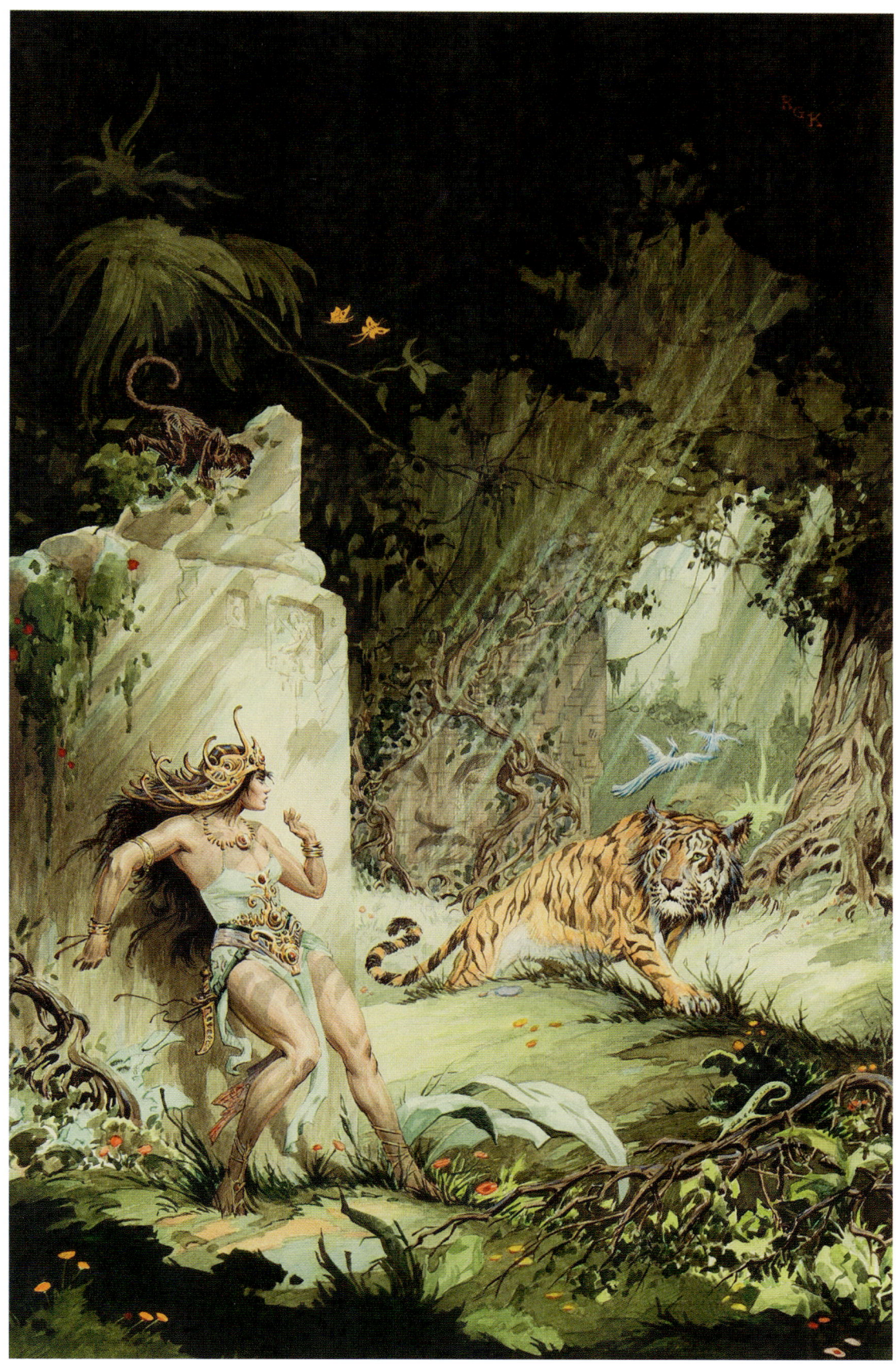

PLATE 16 (opposite).
Frank E. Schoonover
(American, 1877–1972),
A Princess of Mars,
1917, oil on canvas,
32 × 23 inches.

PLATE 17. Roy Krenkel
(American, 1918–1983),
Land of Hidden Men,
1963, watercolor with
gouache, 18½ × 11 inches.

PLATE 18. Kelly Freas
(American, 1922–2005),
Lost Tribes of Venus,
1954, oil on canvasboard,
19 × 13 inches.

PLATE 19 (opposite).
Virgil Finlay (American,
1914–1971), *Face in
the Abyss*, 1940, gouache
on illustration board,
18 × 13 inches.

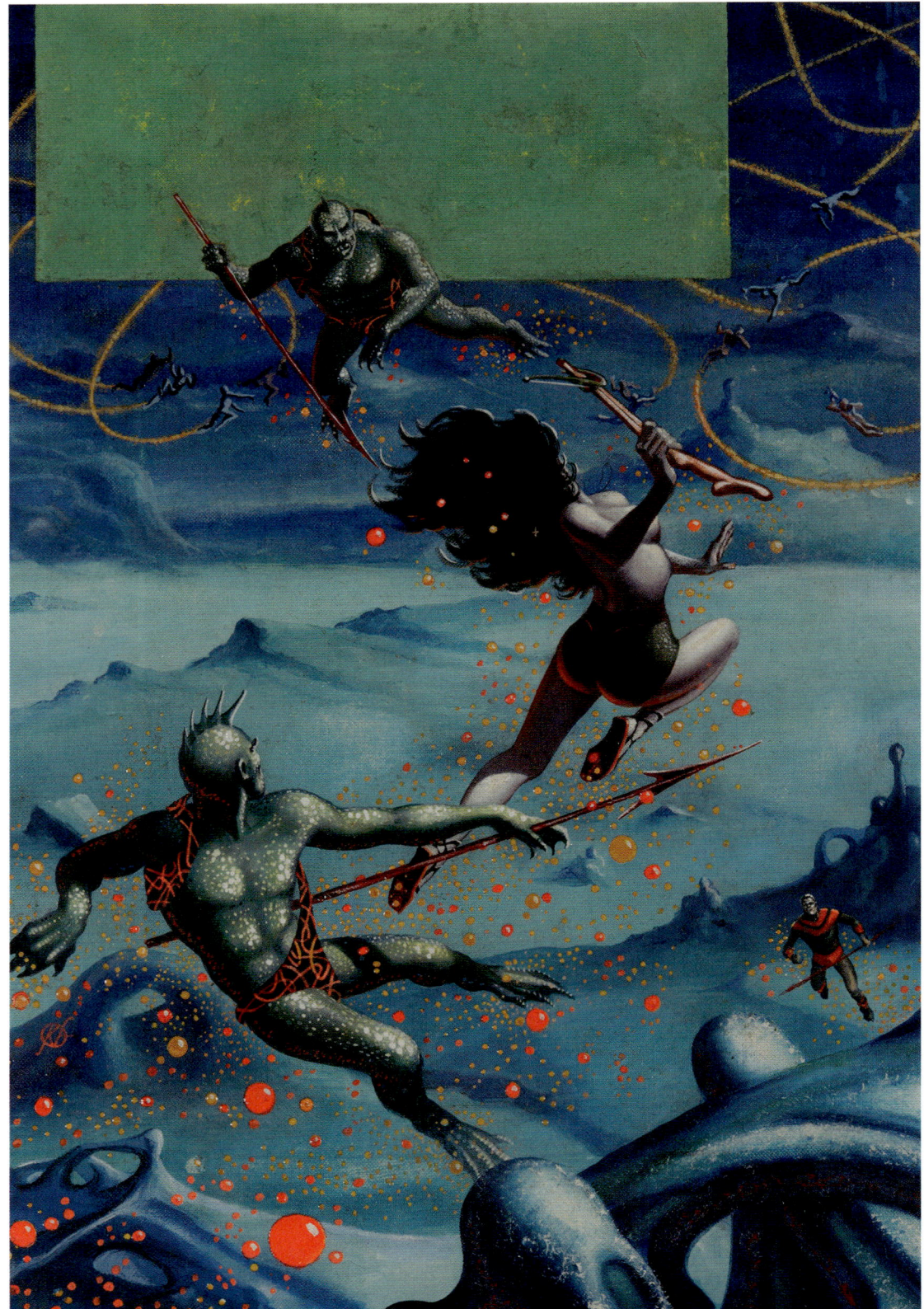

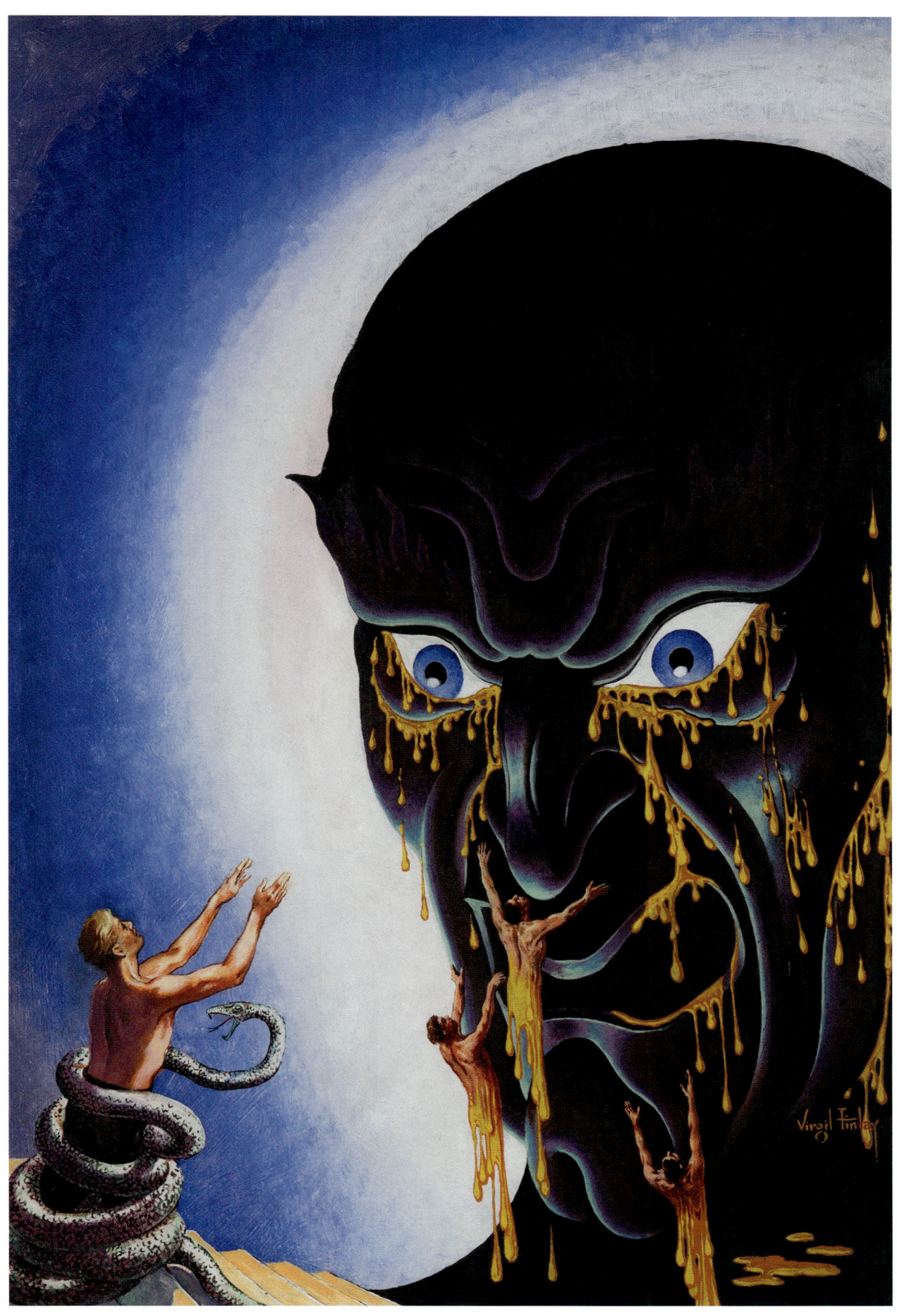

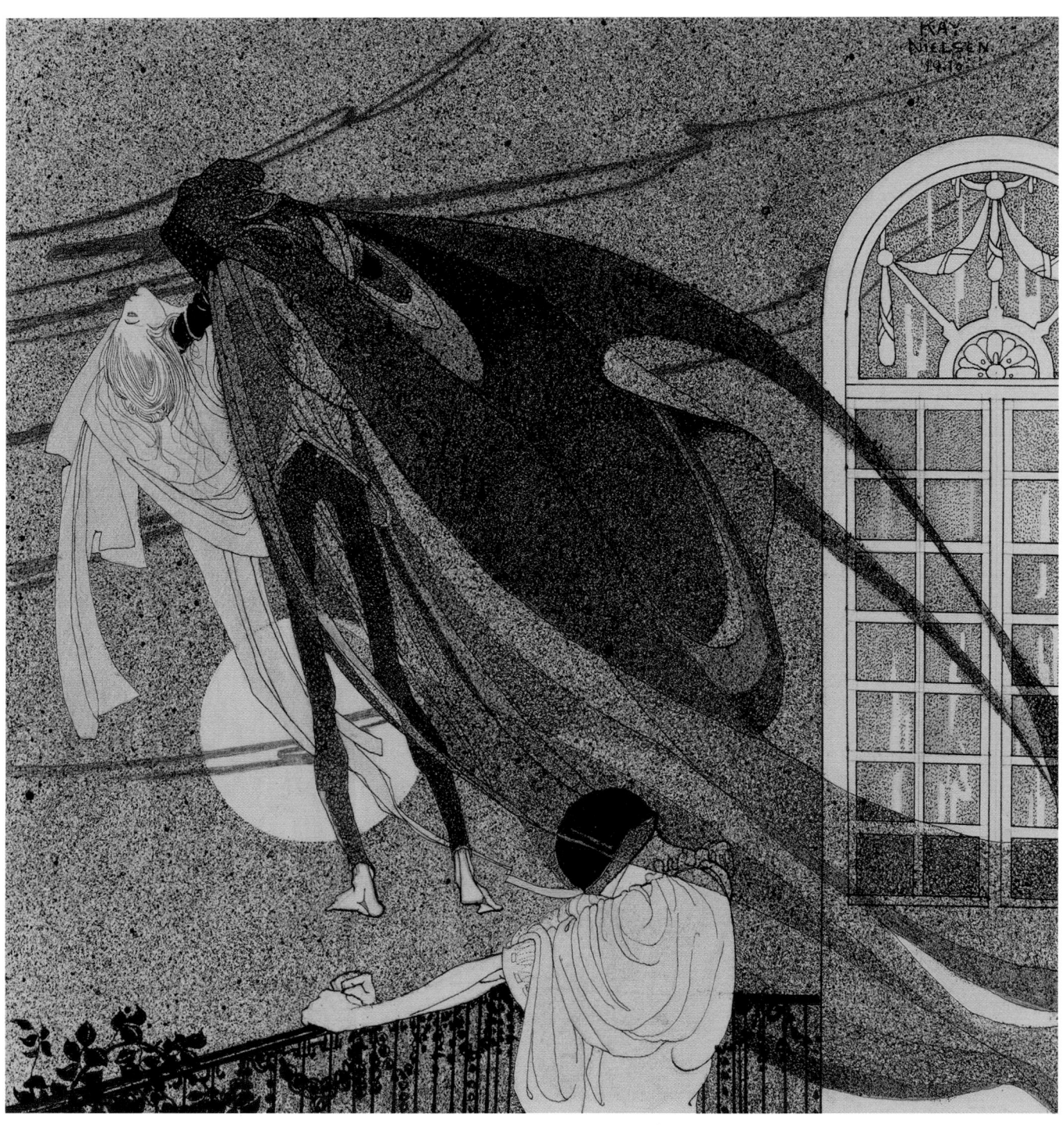

PLATE 20. Kay Nielsen (Danish, 1886–1957), *Book of Death I*, 1910, pen and ink, 8 × 8 inches.

PLATE 21 (opposite). Kay Nielsen (Danish, 1886–1957), *Book of Death II*, 1910, pen and ink, 10½ × 7½ inches.

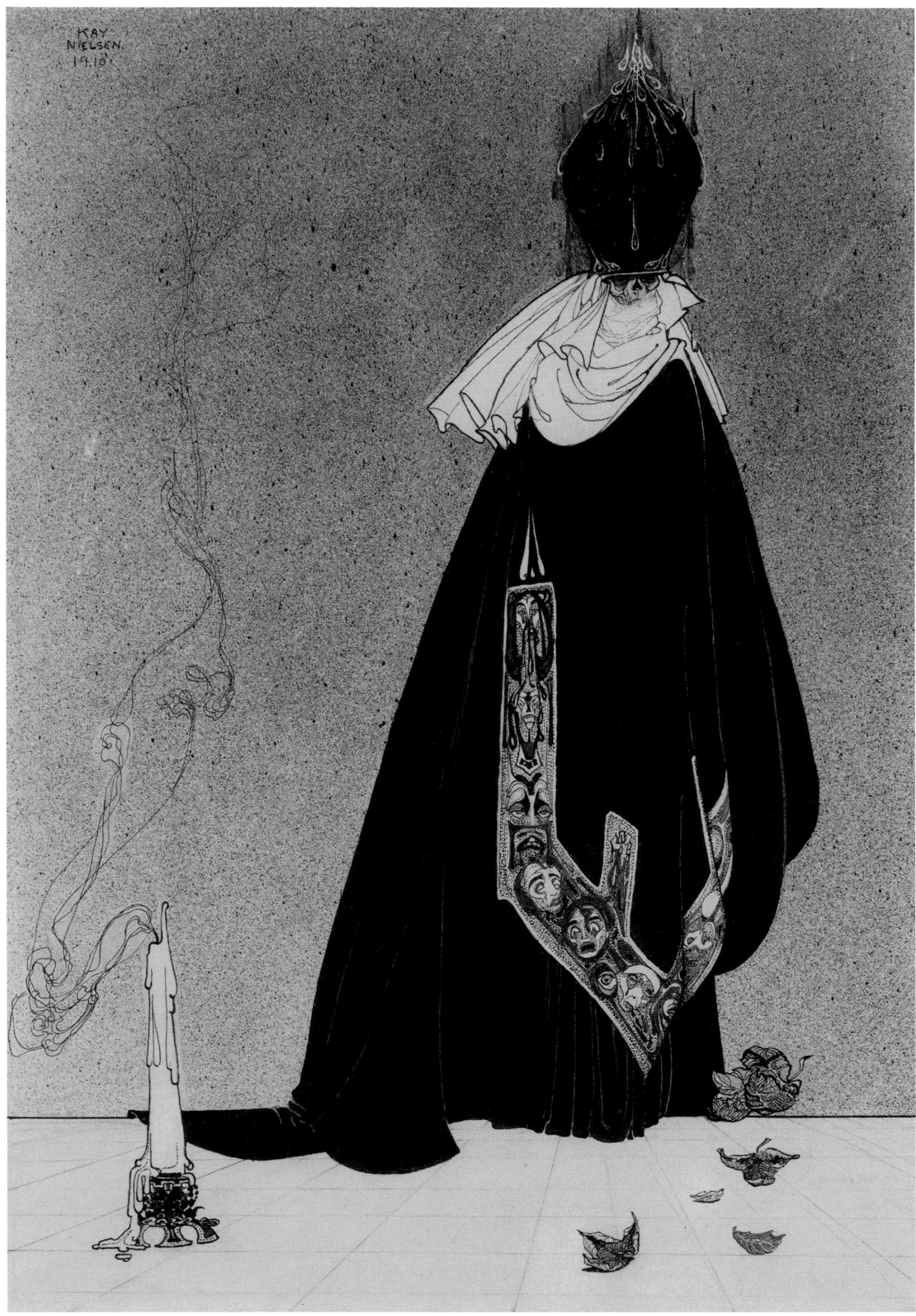

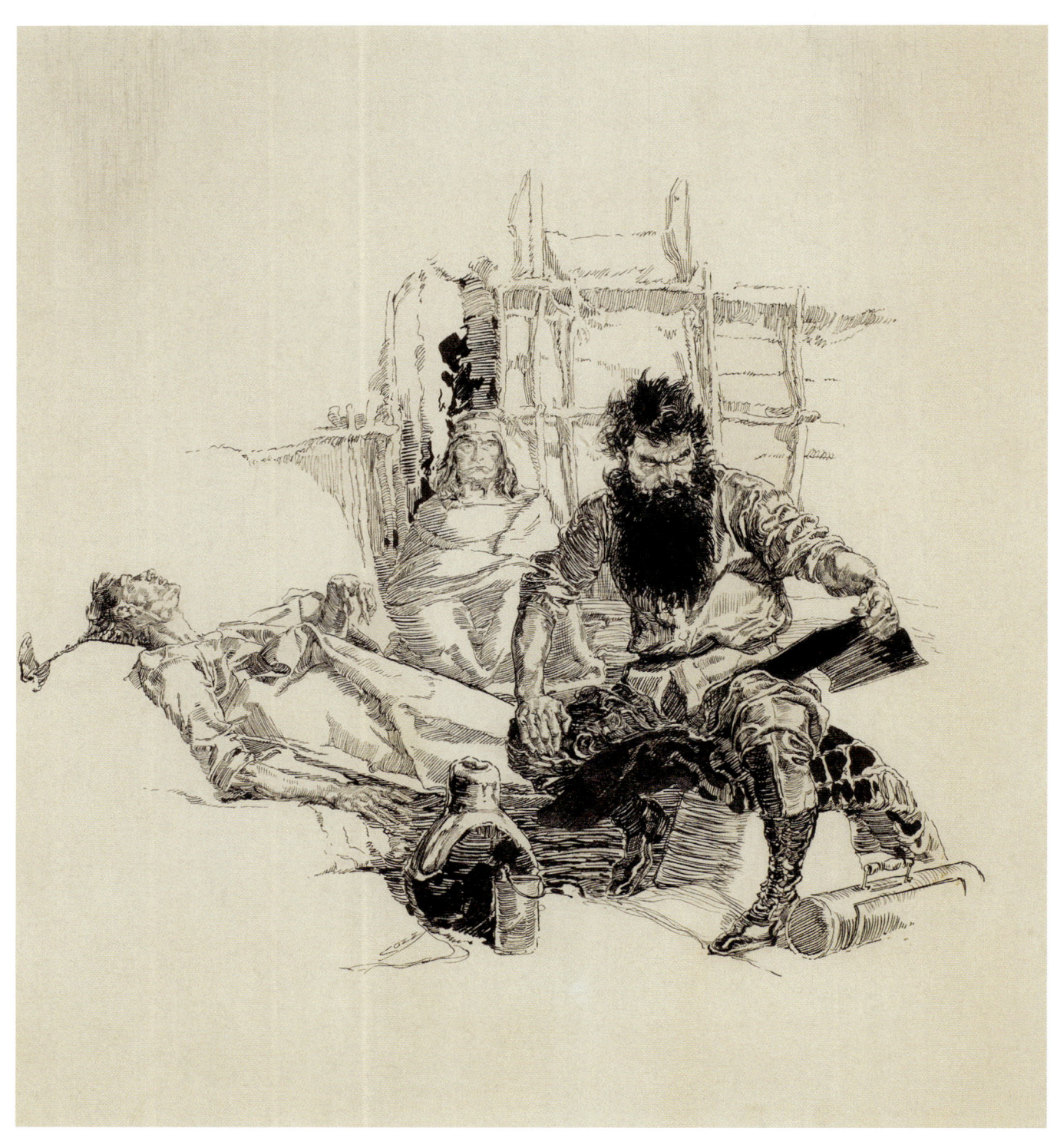

PLATE 22. Joseph Clement Coll
(American, 1881–1921), *Professor
Challenger* (*The Lost World*),
1912, pen and ink, 15½ × 14½ inches.

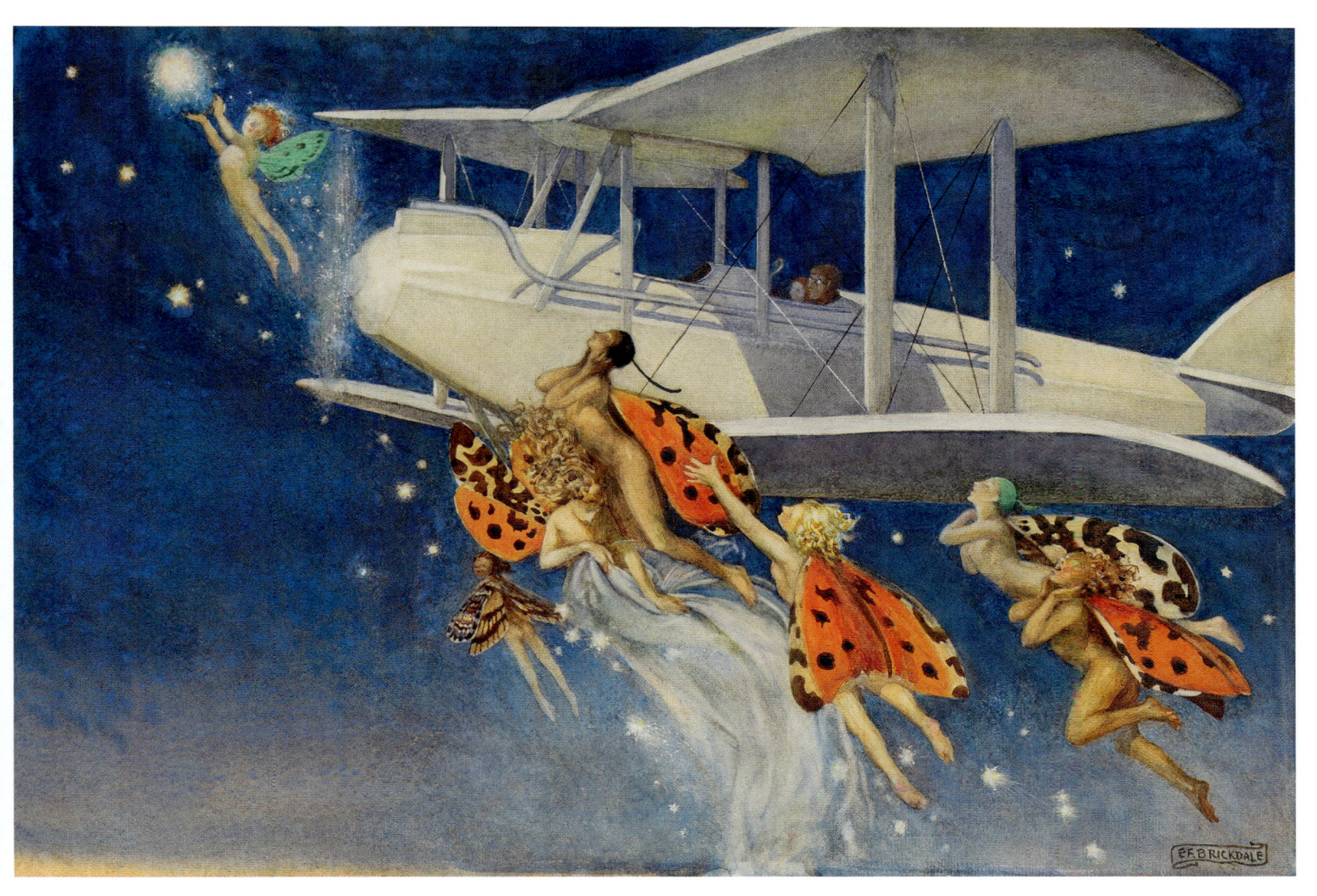

PLATE 23. Eleanor Fortescue-Brickdale
(English, 1872–1945), *The Moth*, 1917,
watercolor with gouache, on illustration
board, 11½ x 18½ inches.

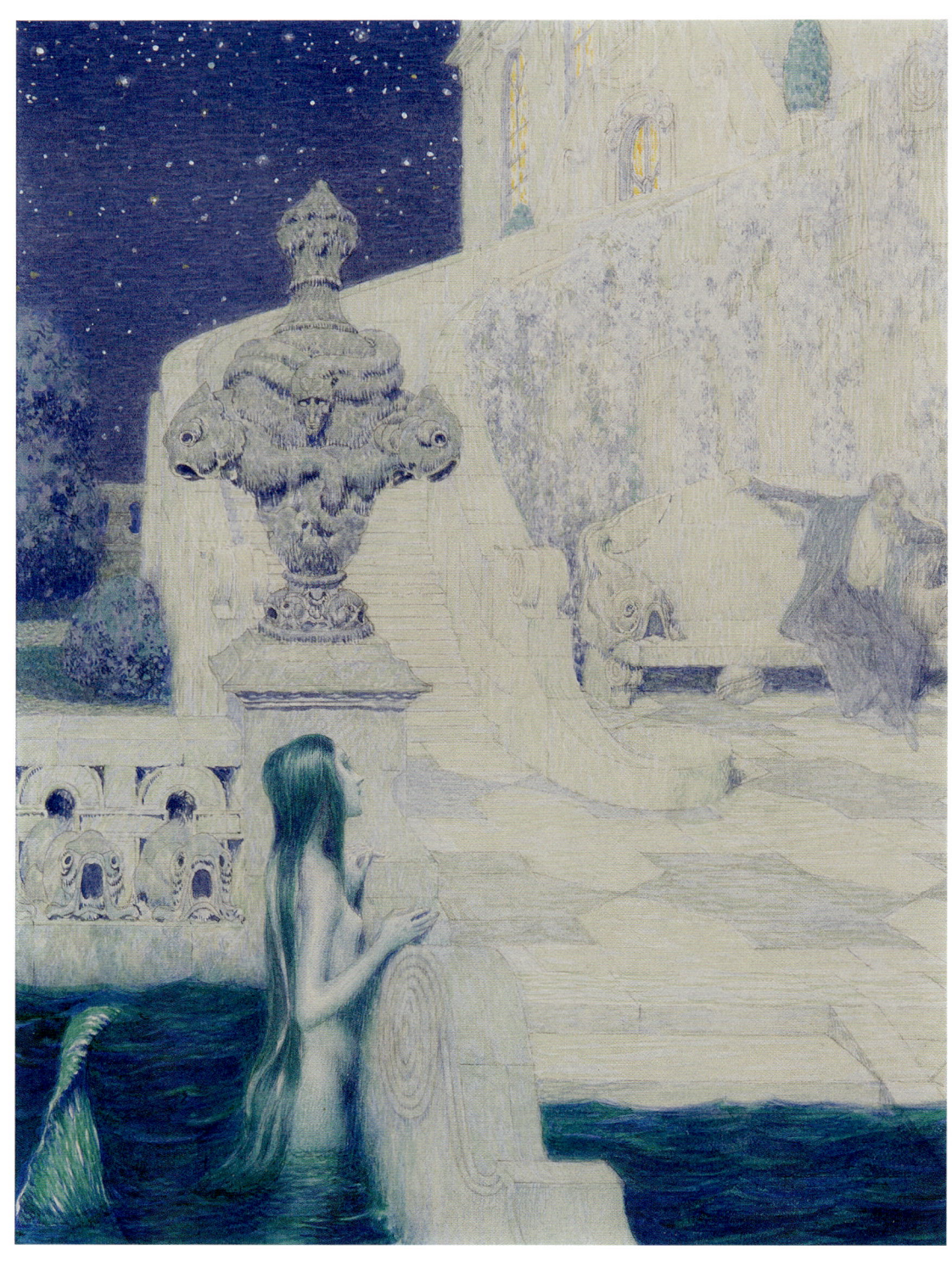

PLATE 24. Heinrich Lefler (Austrian, 1863–
1919), *The Little Mermaid (Das Meefräulein)*,
1911, pen and ink, watercolor, 9 × 7 inches.

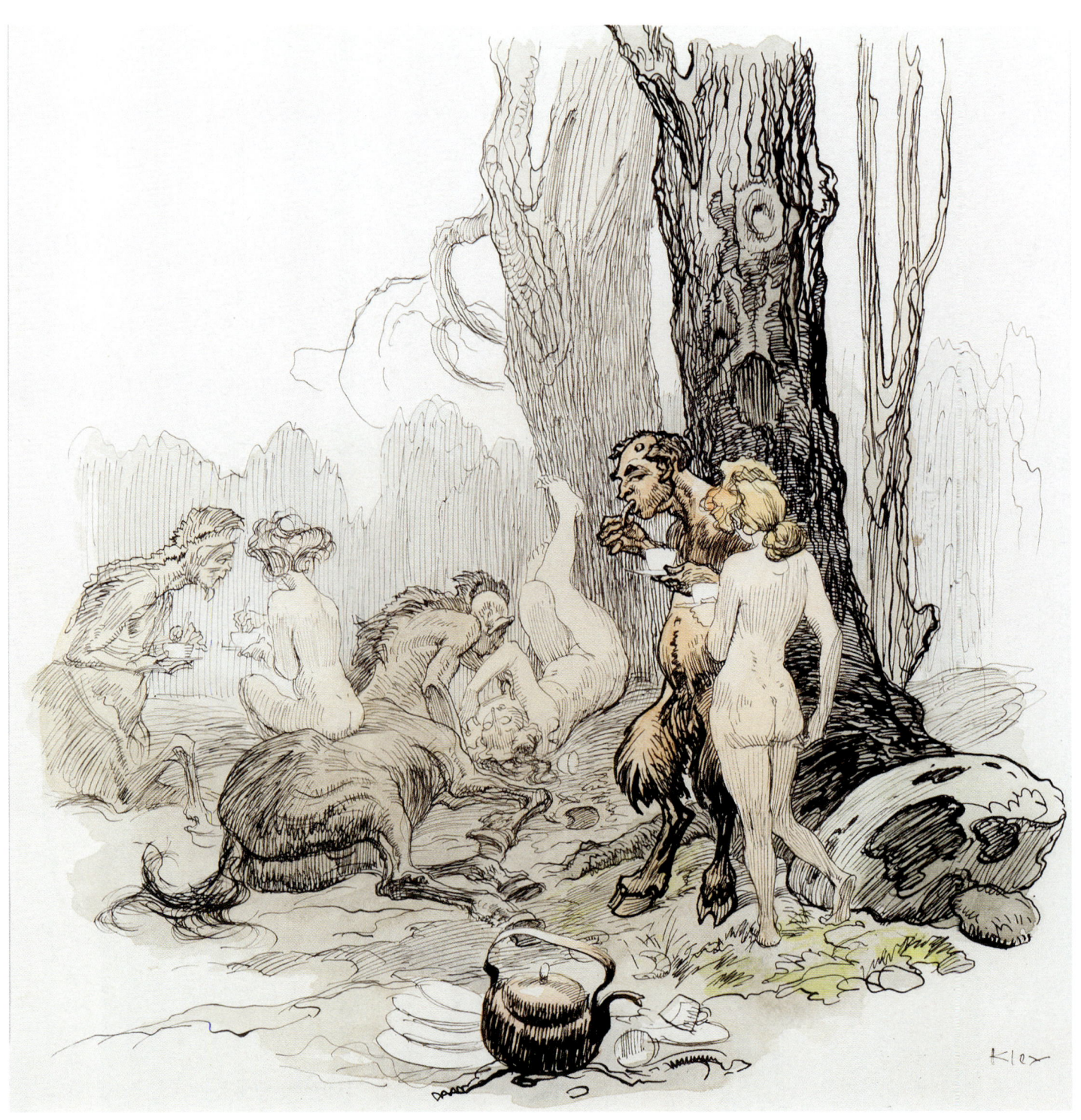

PLATE 25. Heinrich Kley (German,
1863–1945), *Picnic*, c. 1930, watercolor,
pen and ink, 9½ × 9½ inches.

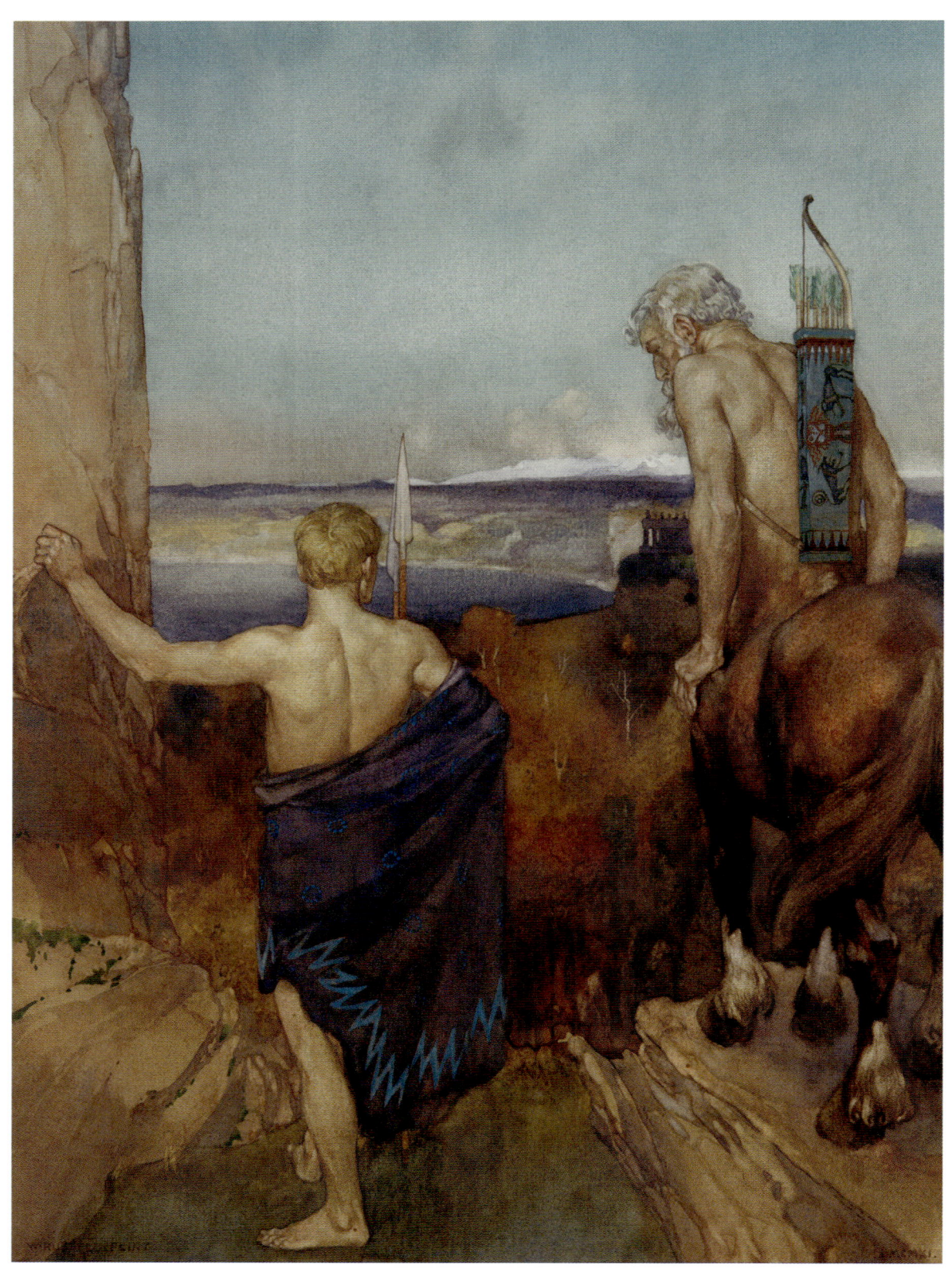

PLATE 26. William Russell Flint (Scottish, 1880–1969), *Cheiron the Centaur and Jason*, 1911, watercolor, 11 × 8½ inches.

PLATE 27 (opposite). Álmos Jaschik (Hungarian, 1885–1959), *Carnival of Souls*, c. 1935, watercolor with gouache, pencil, 9 × 5¾ inches.

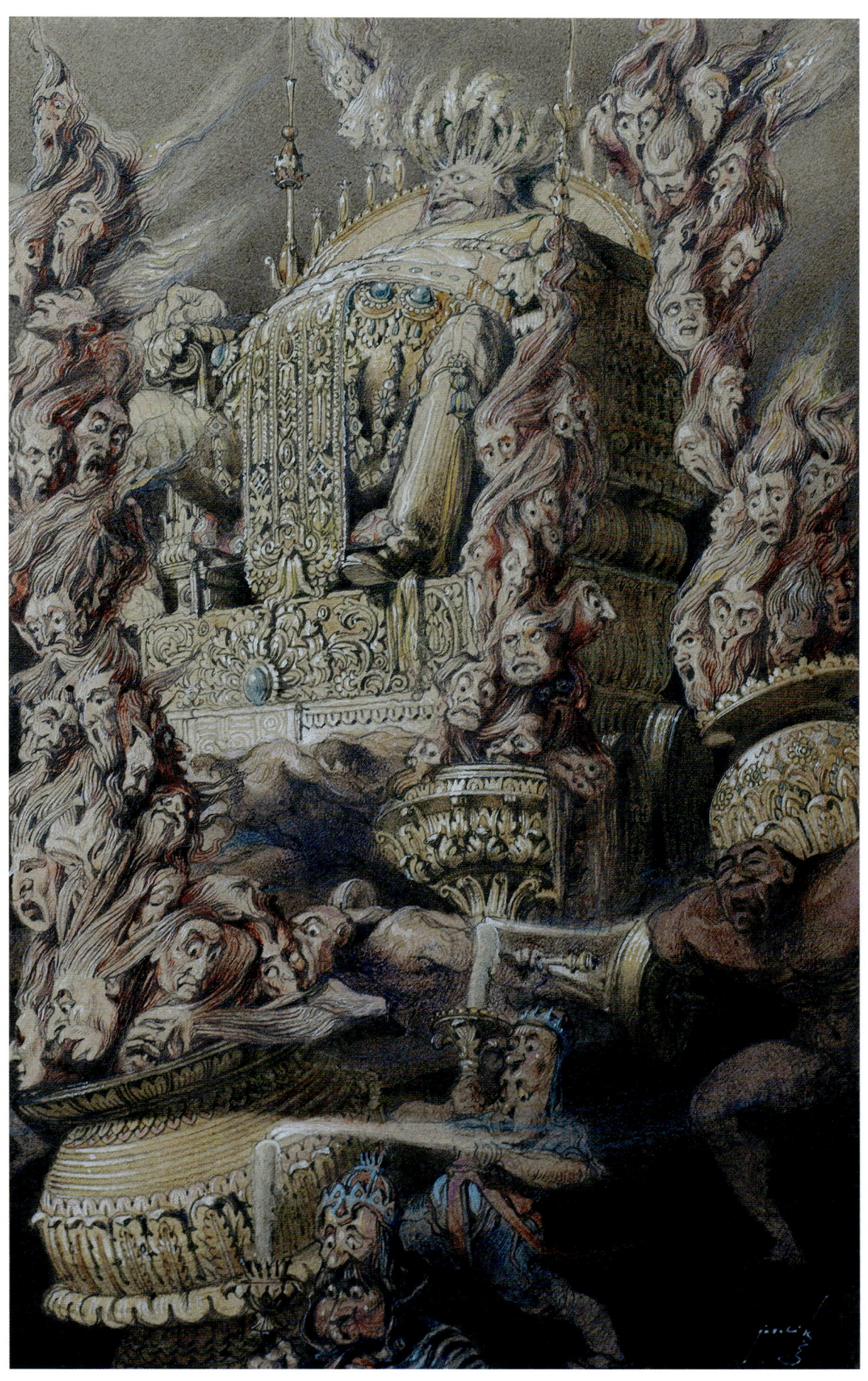

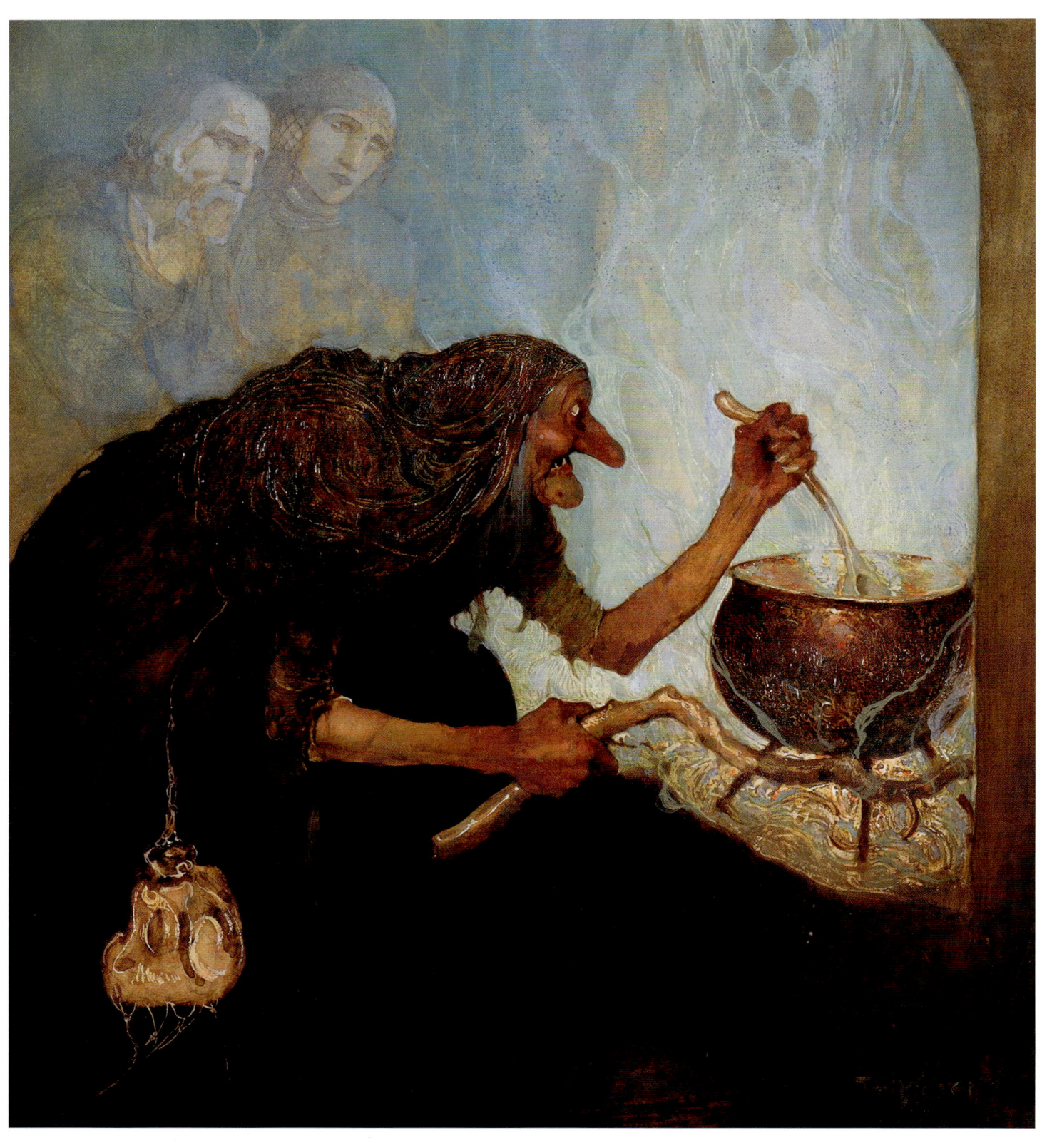

PLATE 28. Gustaf Tenggren (Swedish-American, 1896–1970), *Love In* (*Kärlekens Under*), 1922, watercolor, gouache, on illustration board, 10½ × 9½ inches.

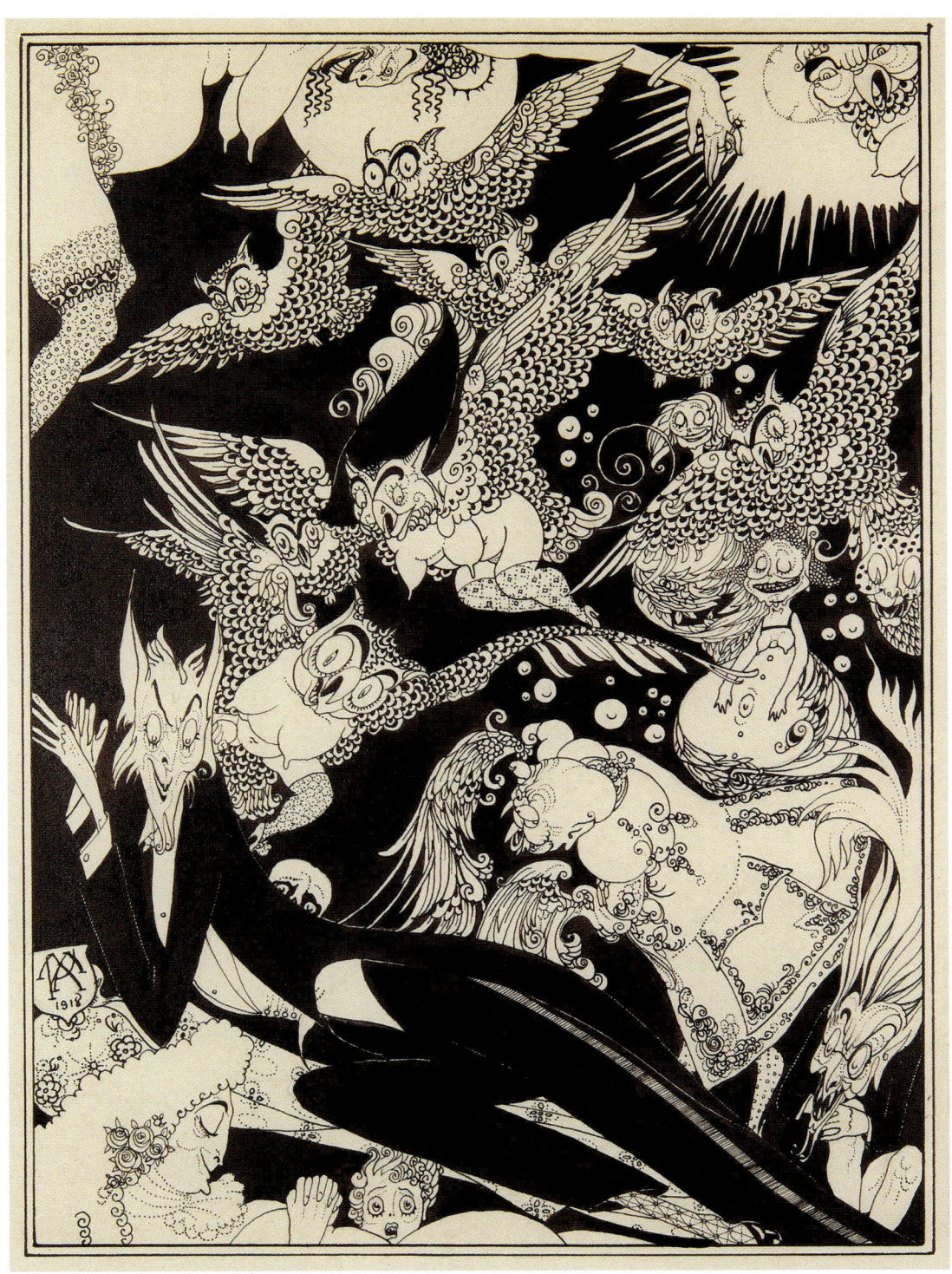

Plate 29. Paul Mak (Pavel Ivanov)
(Russian, 1885–c. 1967), *Scherzo*, 1918,
pen and ink on paper, 7½ × 5½ inches.

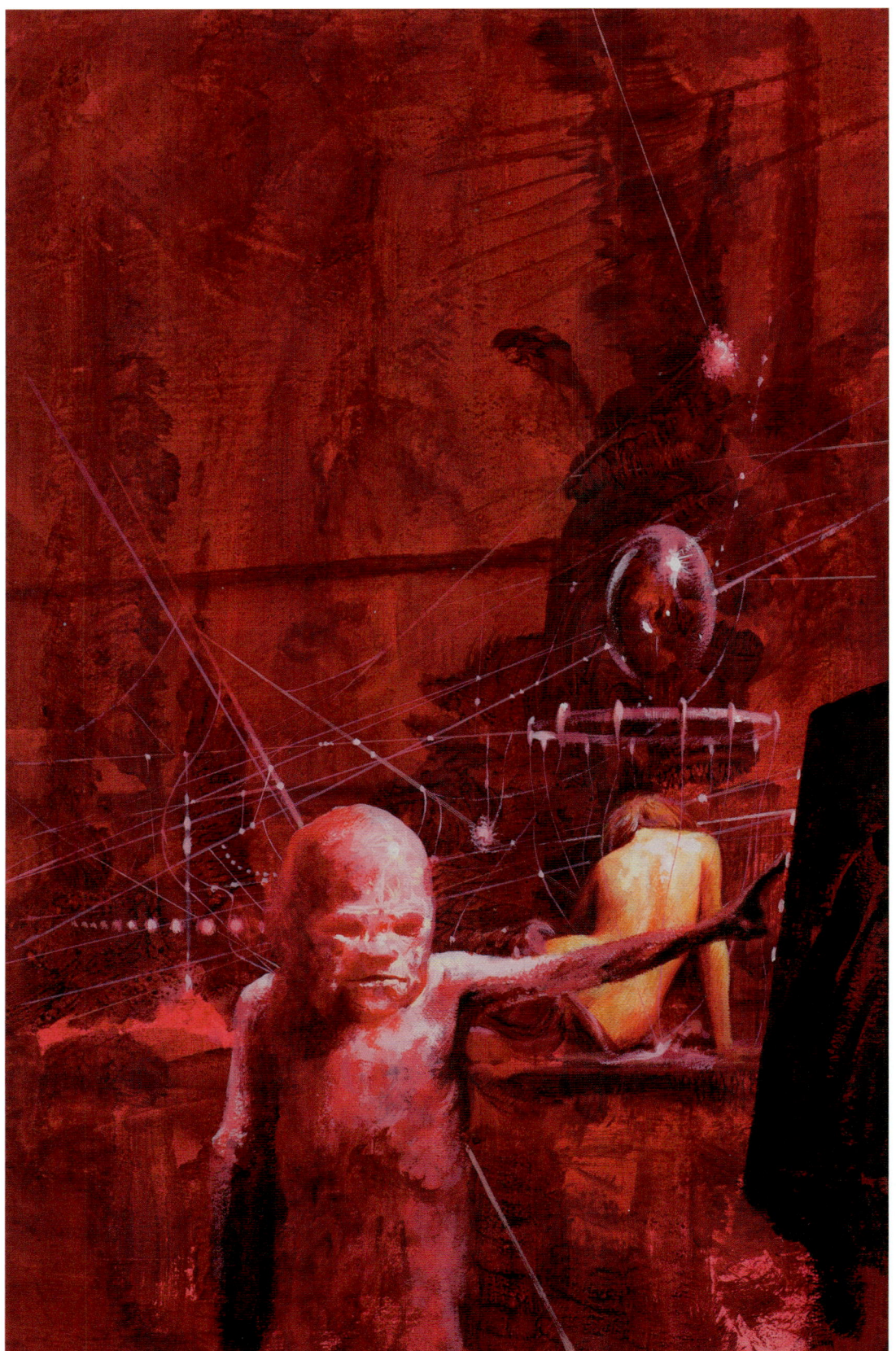

PLATE 30. John Schoenherr (American, 1935–2010), *The Heaven Makers*, 1968, acrylic on llustration board, 23 × 16 inches.

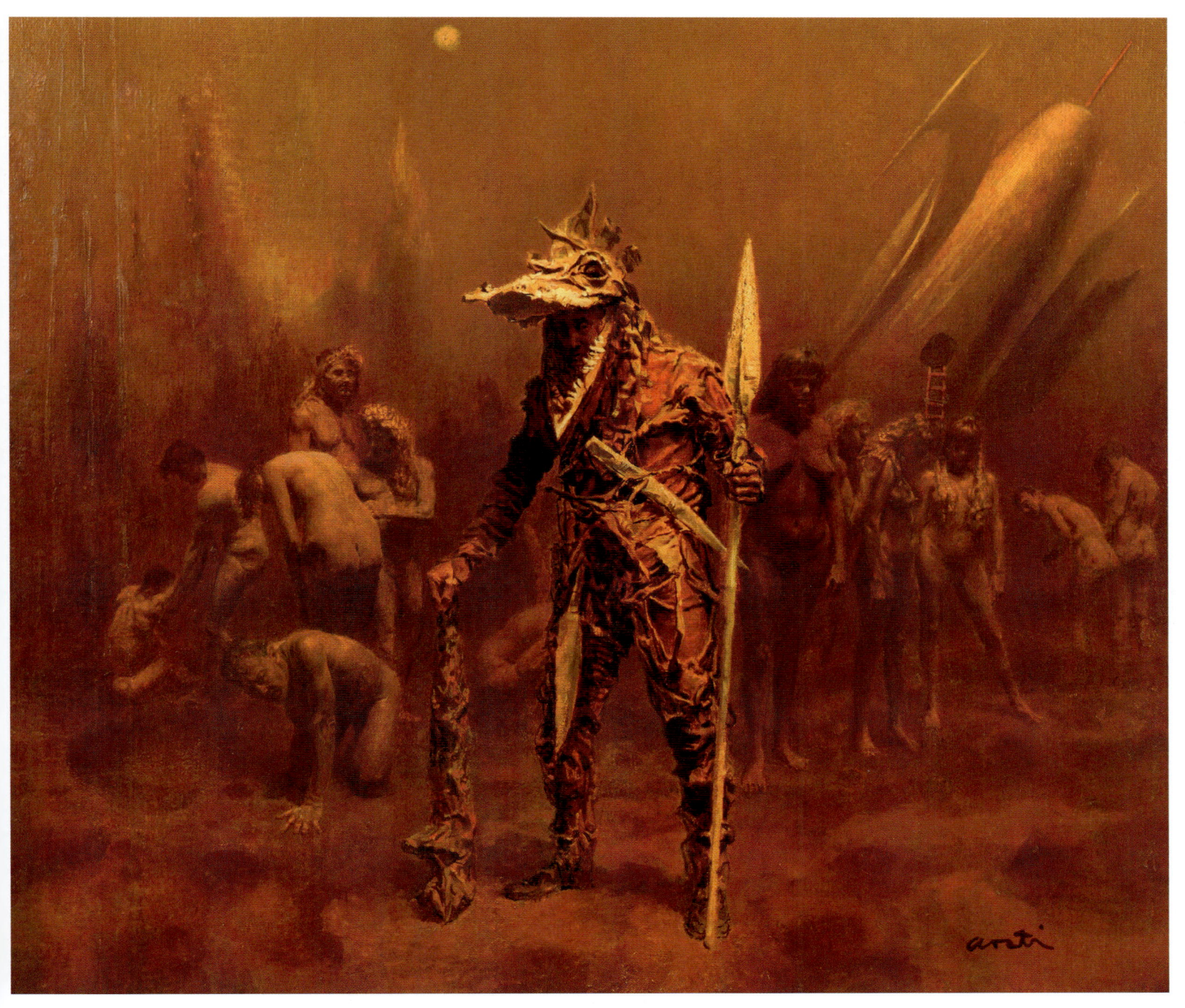

PLATE 31. James Avati (American, 1912–2005), *Deathworld 2*, 1964, oil on canvasboard, 17 × 21 inches.

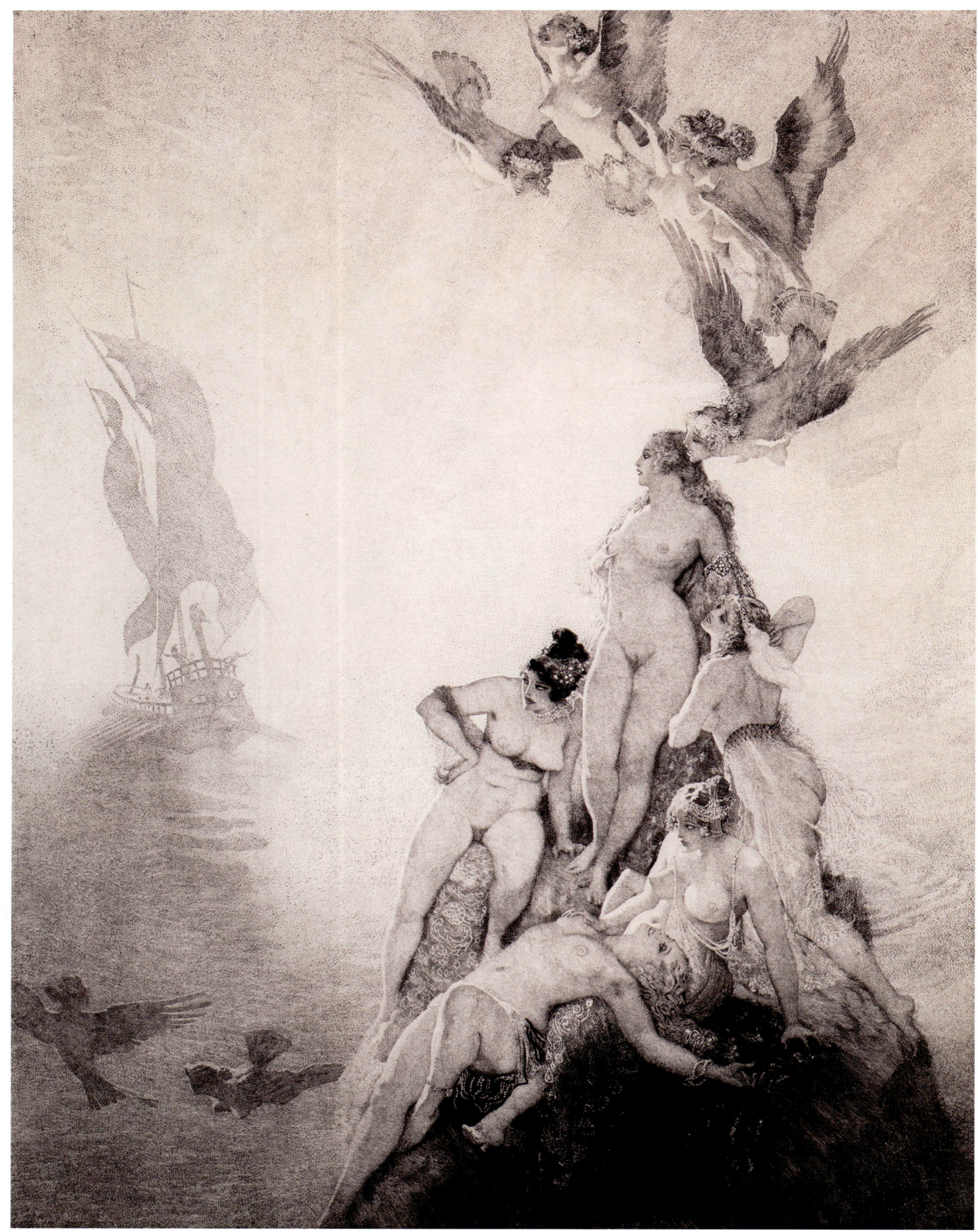

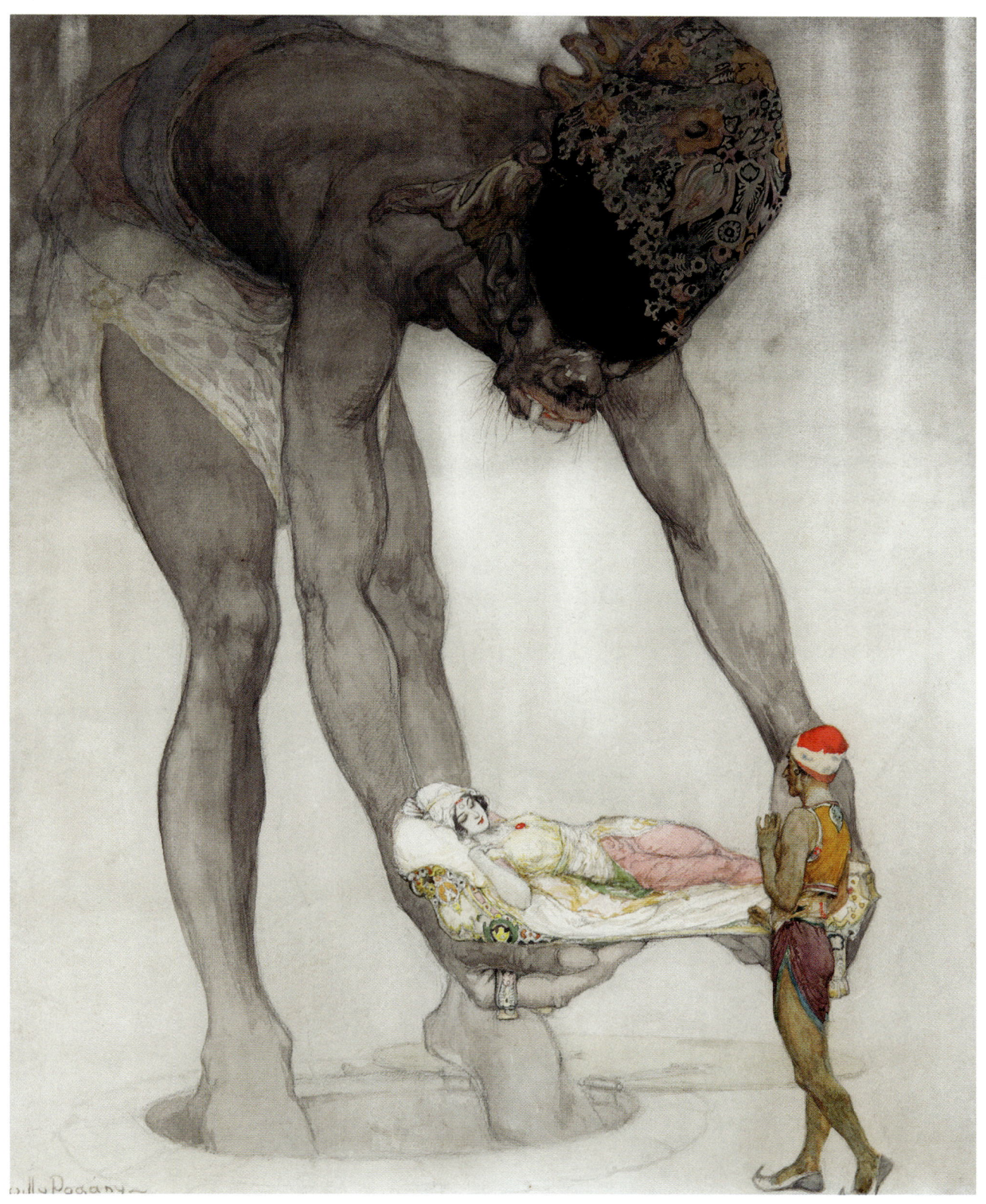

Plate 32 (opposite). Norman Lindsay (American, 1863–1919), *Unknown Seas*, 1922, etching with stippling, 17 × 13 inches.

Plate 33. Willy Pogany (Hungarian, 1882–1955), *The Sultan Misnar*, (*Tales of the Persian Genii*), 1917, watercolor, 16 × 13 inches.

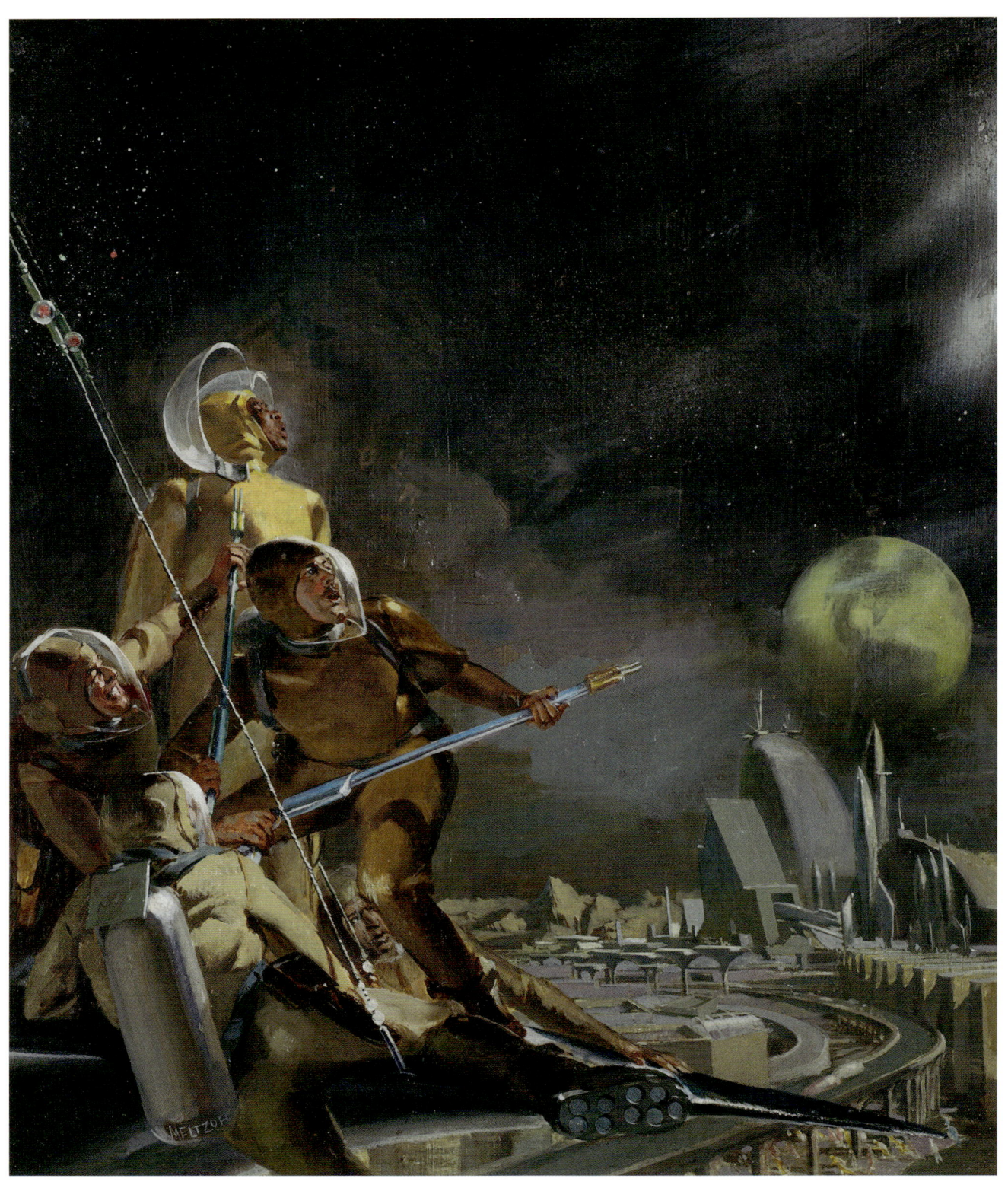

Plate 34. Stanley Meltzoff (American, 1917–2006), *The Green Hills of Earth*, 1952, oil on canvas, 20 × 18 inches.

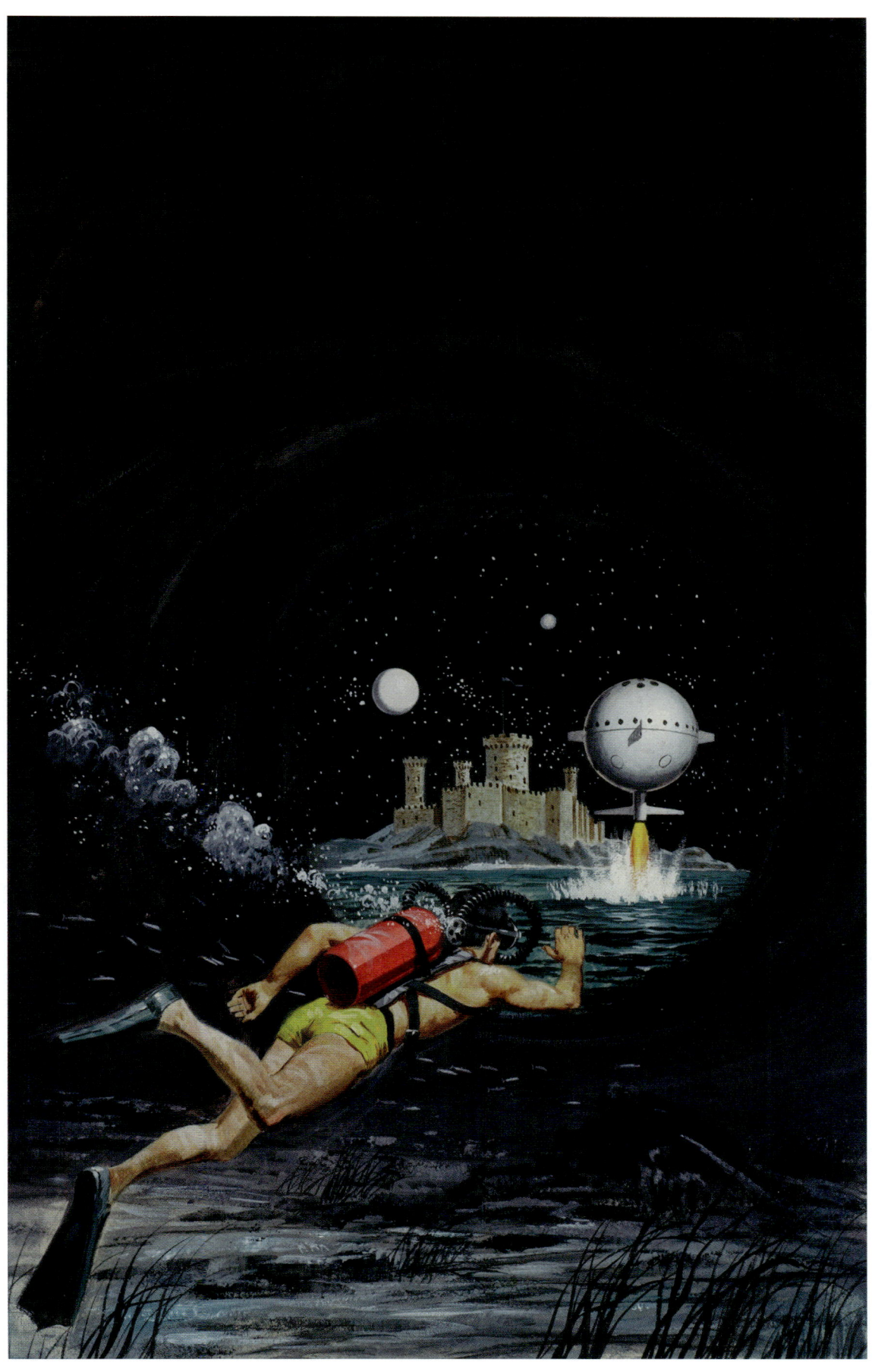

PLATE 35. Edward Valigursky (American, 1916–2009), *Key Out of Time*, 1963, gouache on illustration board, 17 × 11 inches.

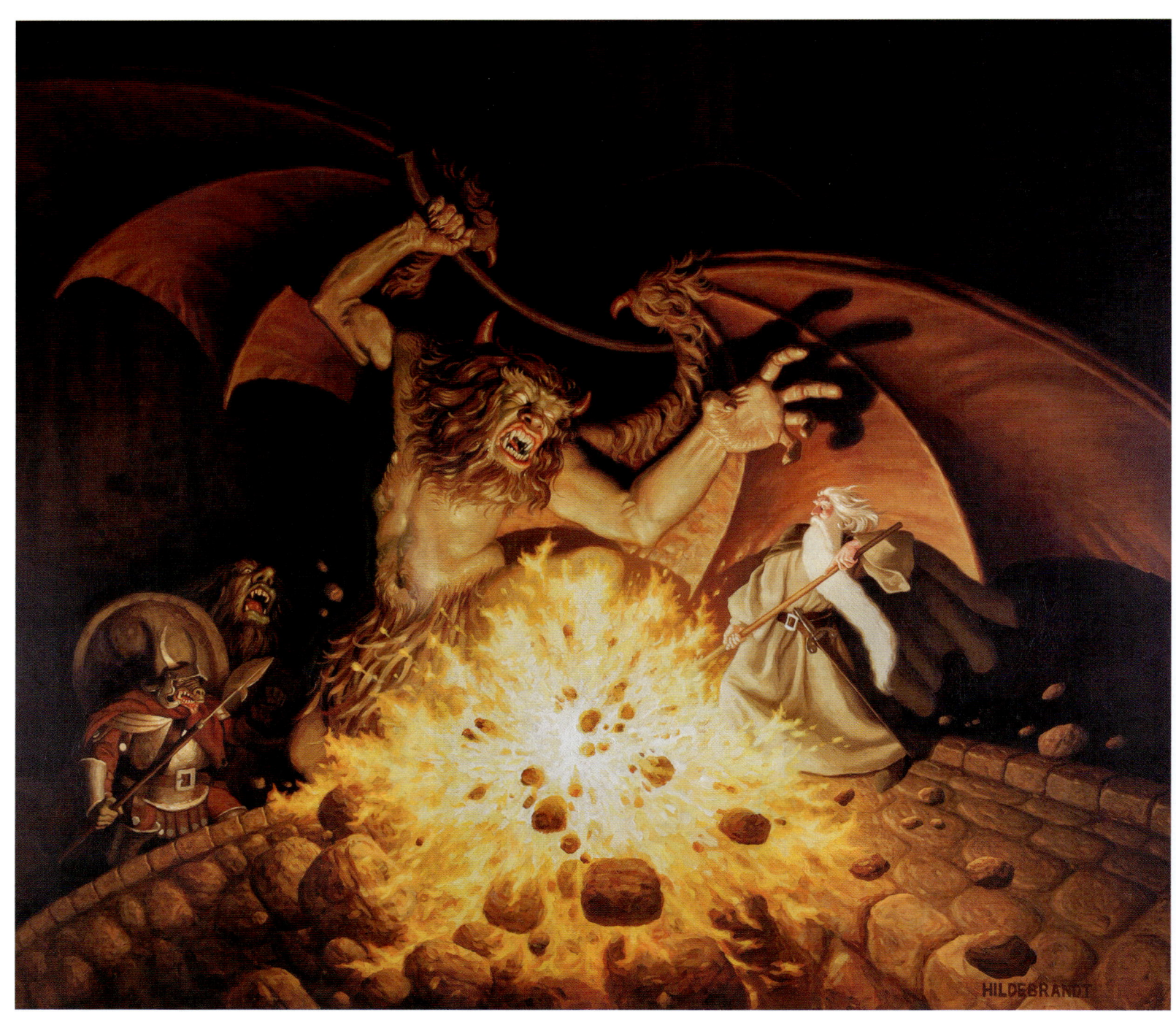

PLATE 36. Brothers Hildebrandt (American, Greg Hildebrandt, 1939–2024, and Tim Hildebrandt, 1939–2006). *The Balrog*, 1977, acrylic, 35 × 42 inches.

PLATE 37 (opposite). Michael Kaluta (American, b. 1947), *Solo*, c. 1976, pen and ink, watercolor on paper, 20½ × 15 inches.

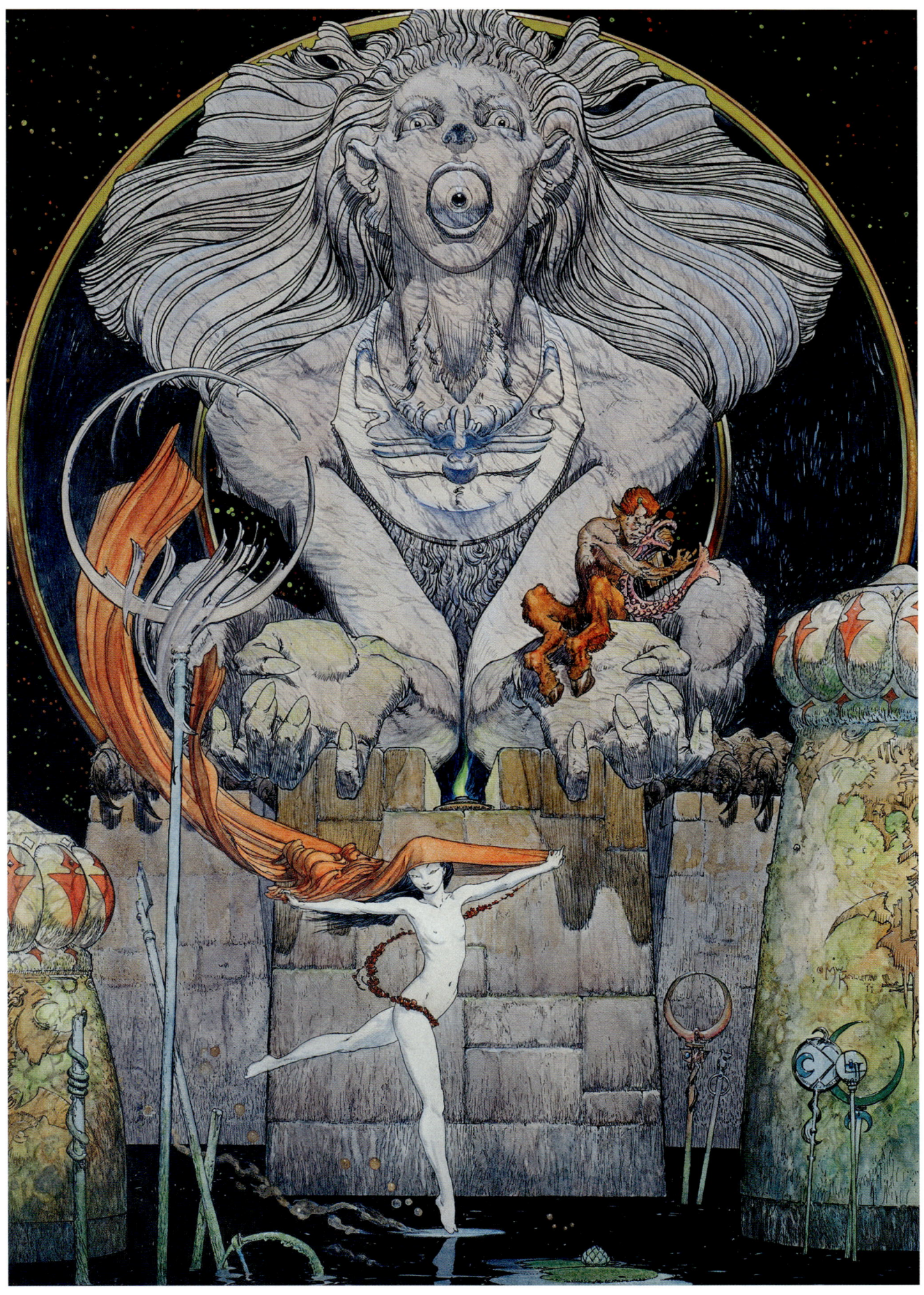

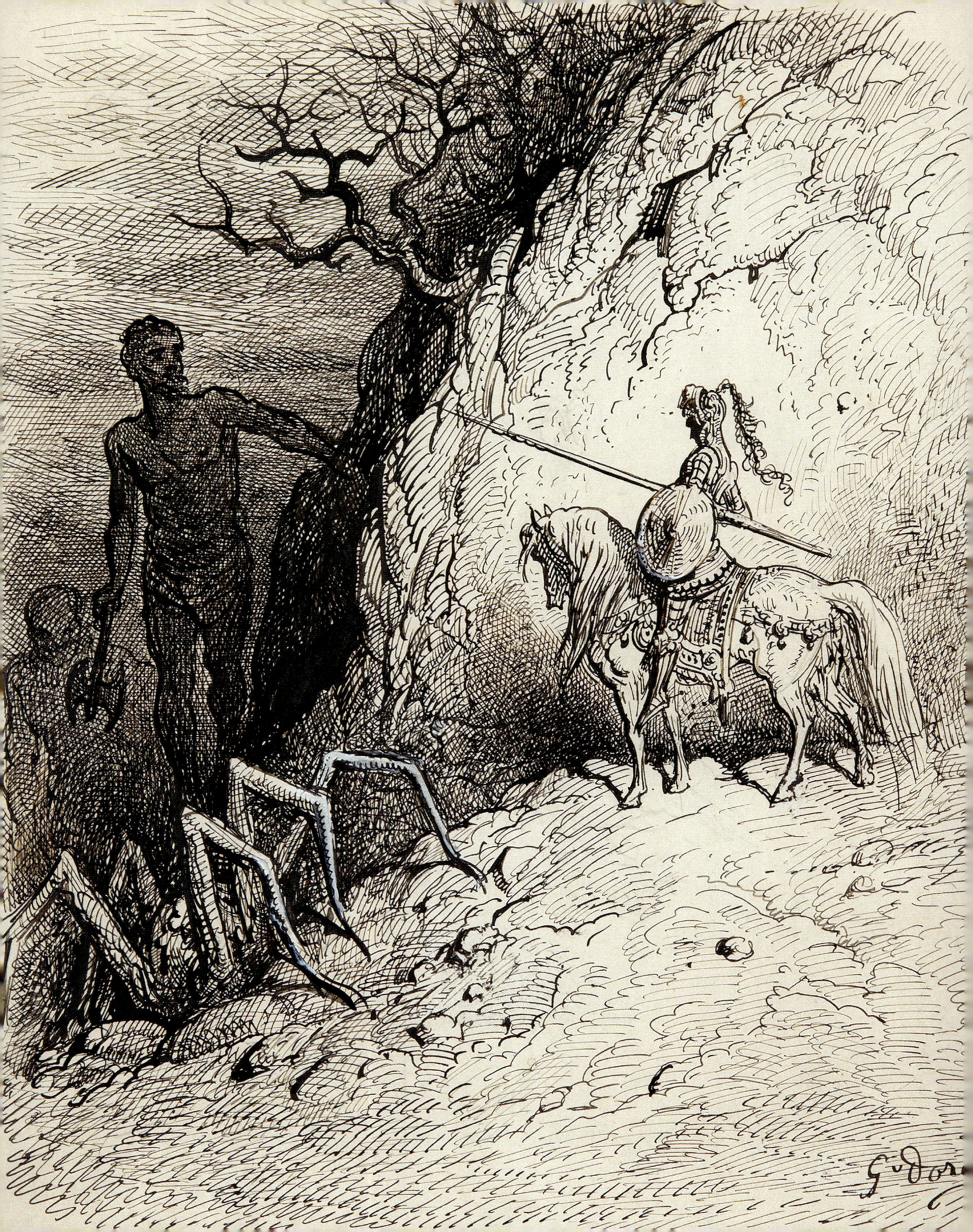

Stephen D. Korshak

ILLUSTRATIONS OF IMAGINATIVE LITERATURE FROM THE KORSHAK COLLECTION:
A Collector's Journey[1]

ORGANIZATION

The Korshak Collection spans over 160 years of illustration history and includes pioneering European and American artists in the field of fantasy illustration. Many of the works from the collection depict iconic scenes and characters from stories such as *Tarzan*, *The War of the Worlds*, *Elric*, *John Carter*, *Alice's Adventures in Wonderland*, *Allan Quartermain*, *The Lord of the Rings*, *Don Quixote* (Plate 38), *The Legend of King Arthur*, *The Little Mermaid*, *Rip Van Winkle*, *The Pit and the Pendulum*, and *The Snow Queen*, among others. As of this writing, the collection has been exhibited, in whole or in part, at twenty museums and universities in the United States, Europe, and Japan.

The Korshak Collection strives to include some of the greatest and most influential illustrators and artists in the genre of imaginative literature. There are hundreds of illustrators who have worked in this genre, so the collection is not a complete set, but a work in progress. Many of the artists in the collection are well known, and others are forgotten, while still others are simply noteworthy of attention. An emphasis has been placed on exhibiting some of the most important works from each illustrator's oeuvre and on showcasing artists from as many European countries as possible, as well as tracing the highlights of the American scene.

Subjects displayed in the collection include religion, mythology, fairy tales, legends, folklore, science fiction, and horror. The collection emphasizes adult rather than children's themes, and published illustrations over non-published. It is organized around six different areas of imaginative art: turn-of-the-century European art; early gift book illustrations; Eastern, Central, and Northern European art; Golden Age American illustrations; American pulp and paperback illustrations; and, finally, comic and gaming art. The visualizations of centaurs, satyrs, fairies, trolls, harpies, mermaids, aliens,

PLATE 38. Gustave Doré
(French, 1832–1883), *Don Quixote*,
1863, pen and ink, 10 × 8 inches.

and spaceships, among others, are an essential part of the imaginative art genre.

Book and magazine illustration artists did not work in a vacuum. Many of them had formal art school education. Contemporary art trends also influenced many of the commercial artists in the collection. The work of Aubrey Beardsley, for example, shows the influence of Japanese woodblock prints and the linear quality of Art Nouveau. Richard Powers, on the other hand, was influenced by Surrealism. Illustration artists sold their works to a wide variety of markets including those of mainstream book publishers, glossy and pulp magazines, dime novels and other, often lurid, paperbacks, and adventure novels, as well as comics, gaming, and films. Each publisher catered to different audiences and selected art based on the perceived tastes of their customers.

VISION

STEPHEN D. KORSHAK

As Jules Verne famously observed in *Around the World in Eighty Days*, what one person can imagine, others can make real. Ideas inspire and motivate people, and so too can art. The impact of science fiction on space exploration is a prime example. After the United States landed the first astronauts on the moon in July 1969, several NASA engineers were asked how they knew the mission could succeed. One apparently replied "because the science fiction illustrator, Frank R. Paul had visualized the landing years before it occurred." Whether this story is apocryphal or not, it is consistent with the widely held view that many astonishing accomplishments in the real world—including a lunar landing—are anticipated and indeed propelled by visionaries whose creations inspire imaginations and instill confidence in what human beings can achieve.

Much the same can be said of collecting. Like a creative spark, a single, inspiring vision or event can fire the imagination and lead one to new discoveries, accomplishments, and goals in the material world. The Korshak Collection began with an early, enchanting encounter with a single painting. It was literally an eye-opening experience for me—one that I remember vividly—and it launched my lifelong collecting journey. My father, Erle Korshak, had placed the J. Allen St. John illustration for *John Carter and the City of the Mummies* (Plate 39), a gift from his friend, editor Ray Palmer, in my childhood bedroom. Deeply enchanted by the image, I sought and received my father's permission to comb through the warehouse where he stored artworks and other remnants of his science fiction book publishing company, Shasta Publishers. I quickly retrieved a cache of brilliantly illustrated Shasta cover paintings. These hidden gems became the starter set for the Korshak Collection of illustration art. I collaborated with my father, and later my wife, on a forty-year treasure hunt that added numerous fantasy and science fiction works to the collection. Each acquisition has brought with it new knowledge and excitement, and I have had the good fortune to share these rewards with people all over the world, largely through presentations, museum exhibitions, and ongoing relationships with many artists, fellow collectors, and other kindred spirits.

During my collector's journey, I learned that you do not need great wealth to build a museum-quality collection. Simply purchasing various pleasing and valuable things does not make a collection or, put differently, amassing differs from collecting. In amassing, there is neither order nor purpose. Key to building a great collection is a guiding principle that organizes individual items into a set. This organizing principle is the vision for the collection, and is pursued diligently and in accordance with a personal aesthetic sensibility. Collecting requires knowledge, discipline, and decisions. What is excluded is as important as what is included.

As I gained knowledge and experience, I refined the focus of my collecting vision. Some works in the collection were essential to achieving my vision and others were not. As a result, I pruned certain items, i.e., "deaccessioned" them, and added others to the collection. My vision broadened from simply collecting Shasta illustration art covers to collecting pulp art, mainstream magazine and book illustrations, and European fantasy illustration art. Today, my vision focuses on illustrations of imaginative literature that exhibit a sense of wonder. The collection includes paintings by great illustrators, as well as by illustrators whose work exerted important influence on the field of imaginative literature.

FULFILLING YOUR VISION CALLS FOR ACTION

Developing a collecting vision is one thing; fulfilling that vision is quite another. Many collectors sit back passively waiting until items come to auction or are offered by a dealer or another collector. But what if certain pieces that you envision adding to your collection never materialize through these channels? A passive approach to collecting—watchful waiting—can diminish your acquisition prospects and slow or even halt progress toward realizing your vision. An active approach will bolster your prospects for success.

Preparation is the key because chance, whether in collecting or almost any other endeavor, favors the prepared mind. Collectors who are highly motivated, well informed, and decisive are much more likely to be successful. As I pursued my vision, it soon dawned on me, and I was repeatedly reminded, that collecting at the level I set my sights on called for a passionate commitment, becoming part of a well-informed community of collectors, honing my subject matter knowledge, paying close attention to a collecting field and its evolutionary phases, and adhering to the ethical rules of collecting behavior. Only by effectively employing these attitudes and tools, which together comprise the elements of collecting, can you fulfill a personal vision for your collection.

Each of these elements can be learned except passion, which comes from within. Once you discover and nurture it, passion helps drive you to fulfill your collecting vision. My passion propelled me to socialize and go to the sources of key works that I sought, pursuing objects that were off market. To acquire such works, I began to trade with and buy directly from other collectors. I found these collectors by attending conventions, scouring museum catalogues for lists of contributors or lenders, and meeting with artists who introduced me to collectors. In the process, I met fascinating people (some of whom became my mentors). Together we shared the same passion for collecting as well as sharing stories about collecting.

The knowledge of my field that I gained over time also helped me become an author. I wrote and published books on the art of Hannes Bok, J. Allen St. John, Frank R. Paul, and Margaret Brundage. Shasta Publishers's connections with luminaries in the field helped me accomplish my publication goals. Ray Bradbury, Sir Arthur C. Clarke, Jack Williamson, and Fred Pohl have written introductions for my books.

Socializing with renowned authors helped fuel my passion, as did the connections on a personal level with some of the important artists in this collection. I have bought important iconic pieces directly from Michael Whalen, Frank and Ellie Frazetta, and the Segrelles family heirs. In interacting with authors, artists, and collectors, I realized that they are highly dependent on each other. Words written by authors have much greater impact if they are accompanied by riveting images created by highly imaginative illustrators. Artists' reputations are established and boosted by collectors who research, acquire, and exhibit their creations. Collectors, propelled by a guiding vision for their collections, introduce or reintroduce works of individual artists to new generations of art enthusiasts who, in turn, educate and/or inspire yet another generation of authors and artists—a cycle that continues ad infinitum. Finally, the importance of museum curators and academics in contextualizing and interpreting art is not to be undervalued. My understanding of these interconnections and cycles prompted me to take the Korshak Collection on tour. One of the joys of collecting is sharing your vision with others.

All the actors with roles in collecting take the stage at different evolutionary phases of an emerging collecting market. The first-generation enthusiasts in my collecting field appeared early and formed a fan-based market. They frequently received illustration art at no charge from publishers and artists. Entrepreneurial fans appeared next. In their roles as investors and dealers, they built collections and reaped profits from the artwork they acquired. As interest in the field expanded, auction houses joined in and began selling illustration art and, as a result, prices rose rapidly. I was lucky to have experienced all three evolutionary phases of the field, as both an observer and a participant. As an observer, I met and interacted with collectors from all of these phases. Early on, I received Shasta art for free. Later, I became a dealer and entrepreneur selling some collections. Finally, as I became more financially established, I bid for paintings at auction. Knowing these evolutionary phases of a collecting market can help collectors in timing their own acquisitions.

My journey also was influenced by understanding the implicit rules and responsibilities regarding provenance, reputation, and preservation. Because collectors are temporary custodians of art, I also realized that collecting behavior entails an ethical duty to preserve and protect works in one's care wherever possible for future generations. An encounter with fake Rackham art taught me the importance of knowing the provenance of a piece and having an authenticator determine the authenticity of a work of art. Dealing with fake or stolen art can result in legal complications and damage the reputation of one's collection. All of this can be avoided by understanding that proper collecting behavior requires receiving a valid bill of sale from the seller upon purchase. Having a bill of sale, for instance, helped me win a lawsuit to regain one of Shasta's stolen paintings, the *Slaves of Sleep*.

A collector's vision is a collector's personal take on their collecting field. Of course, there are many visions of illustration art, and no one is necessarily better than any others. The Korshak Collection is a vision of the fantastic. It contains great illustrators as well as illustrators who have had a great influence specifically in imaginative literature. The contributors to this catalogue hope that studying this collection will inspire a sense of wonder in others and motivate them to pursue their own collecting vision and adventure.

LEARNING RESOURCE

We are also hopeful that the Korshak Collection can be utilized as a teaching and learning resource. Numerous exhibitions have introduced many of the artists in the collection to a new generation of collectors, artists, and fans. Because illustration helps to shape mass culture through the books, magazines, games, newspapers, comics, films, and other products it is used to market, it is worthy of academic study. The cultural influence of illustration art shows its broader influence on our society. Beyond that, we hope that the sense of wonder the collection aims to instill in viewers and in readers of this catalogue unlocks an array of possible worlds that excite imagination and curiosity. As Albert Einstein said, "The most beautiful experience we can have is the mysterious. It is the fundamental emotion which stands at the cradle of true art and science."[2] In that spirit, we look to the images in the Korshak Collection to inspire and motivate people to accomplish great achievements, as so many were once inspired by visions like those of Frank R. Paul to land men on the moon.

STEPHEN D. KORSHAK

1. I would like to thank my partners in this collector's journey: my father, Erle Korshak, who inspired me with a St. John painting and with his intellect; the love of my life, my wife Alma, who has won over so many of the hearts of the other collectors with whom we have dealt; my mother, who inspired me with her life story of grit and determination; my children, who have been inspired by the collection; my curator, Lauren Stump, who helped me and my family share the collection with the world; my mentors, Bob Weinberg, Gene Nigra, Forrest J. Ackerman, and Barry Klugerman; Stanley Grand and Daniel Pollock, who helped me organize my thoughts on collecting; all of the friends and collectors who sold art to us so it could be shared with the world; Sebastian Stelios Janelli, who introduced us to all of the great people at the University of Delaware; and the University of Delaware for having the vision to do this catalogue and beginning an academic discussion of fantasy and science fiction themes and artists. Thank you one and all!

2. Albert Einstein, "What I Believe, Living Philosophies XIII," *Forum and Century* 84, no. 4 (October 1930): 194.

Stephen D. Korshak

SHASTA PUBLISHERS

Science fiction literature first appeared in the form of serialized stories in cheap pulp magazines. But many fans wanted to have some of their favorite stories from those magazines collected into a hardcover illustrated book. In 1939, Arkham House, a specialty publisher of science fiction books, began to satisfy the demand for deluxe first editions of those stories. Soon, Gnome Press, Fantasy Press, Shasta Publishers, and other specialty publishers entered the field.

Erle Korshak (Fig. 0.1), Ted Ditky, and Mark Reinsberg (who later left the company) were the original organizers of Shasta Publishers. Shasta's first book was *The Checklist of Fantastic Literature* (1948, Fig. 0.2) by Everett F. Bleiler, with a preface by Korshak. This landmark reference book was not a reprint of earlier serialized science fiction stories but an attempt at a comprehensive list of all science fiction and fantasy books ever published up until 1948.

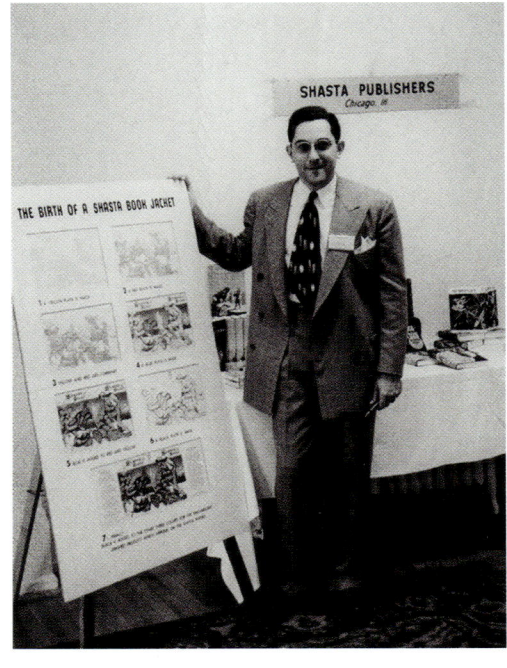

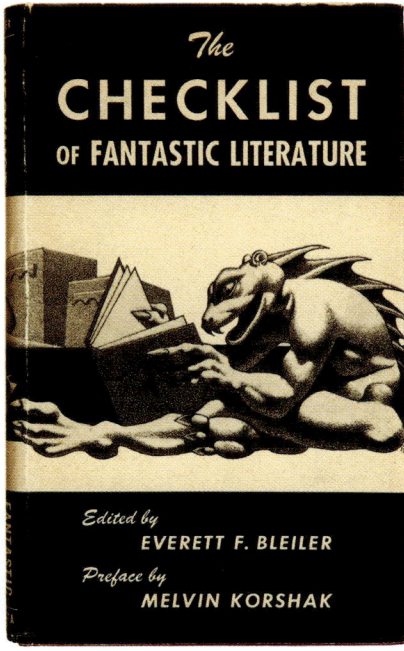

FIGURE 0.1. Erle Korshak, c. 1950, photograph courtesy of Stephen D. Korshak.

FIGURE 0.2. *The Checklist of Fantastic Literature* by Everett F. Bleiler (Chicago: Shasta Publishers, 1948).

It appeared in a small trim size so that collectors could carry it in their jacket pocket while hunting for missing books for their collections. In his book review from 1949, science writer Willy Ley described the importance of *The Checklist of Fantastic Literature* as "indispensable to librarians, book dealers, and especially antiquarians."[1]

The second Shasta book, *Who Goes There* (1948), was a collection of science fiction stories by legendary editor and writer John W. Campbell, Jr., that had originally appeared in the pulp magazine *Astounding Science Fiction*. One of the stories from Campbell's book was the basis of the 1951 film *The Thing from Another World* and the 1982 movie *The Thing*. This was followed by *Slaves of Sleep* (1948, Fig. 0.3), by L. Ron Hubbard, the founder of the Church of Scientology and author of *Dianetics*. *Slaves of Sleep* originally appeared in July 1939 in the pulp magazine *Unknown*. Other important Shasta books were future history stories of Robert A. Heinlein, including *The Man who Sold the Moon* (1950), *The Green Hills of Earth* (1951), and *Revolt in 2100* (1953), and Alfred Bester's *The Demolished Man* (1953), considered by some critics as one of the greatest science fiction books of all time. Shasta also published important books by A.E. van Vogt, Fredric Brown, L. Sprague de Camp, S. Fowler Wright, and Stanley Mullen during the same period.

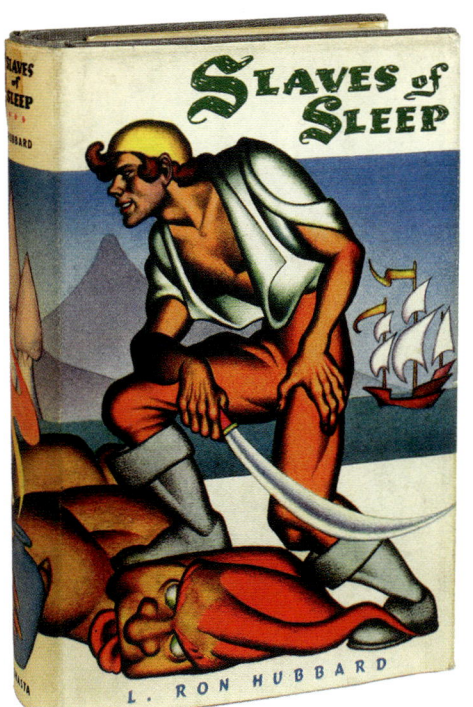

The slogan of Shasta was "Books of Lasting Significance." In furtherance of that goal, Shasta used an involved four-color printing process that, along with stunning artwork by Hannes Bok and Hubert Rogers, produced some of the finest color dust jackets ever printed in the early science fiction specialty press field. Additionally, the papers used, as well as the book bindings themselves, were of high quality. Shasta, like many fellow specialty press publishers, began to sell paperback reproduction rights to major publishers including Pocket Books and others. These New York publishing companies, along with science fiction book clubs, soon went directly to the authors to sign their books outright and outbid the specialty press publishers with higher royalty payments based on their large distribution models. In a sense, the niche specialty press publishers had unwittingly subsidized their own demise by bringing the major publishing companies into the field.

Sensing this changing trend, Shasta attempted to become a general press publisher. It had plans to publish explorer Vilhjalmur Stefansson's *Survival*

FIGURE 0.3. Hannes Bok (American, 1914–1964), cover illustration for L. Ron Hubbard, *Slaves of Sleep*, 1948, Shasta Publishers, Chicago, Korshak Collection.

and a book by A. Reynold Morse on supernatural and science fiction author M.P. Shiel, among others. Before Shasta could publish these books, it first distributed the *Westmore Beauty Book* (1956) by the first family of Hollywood makeup artists. The book described makeup techniques used to make actresses appear more beautiful. However, production costs for the book were enormous and, after Perc Westmore became ill, book sales collapsed, and Shasta closed its doors.

In 2008, Erle and Stephen D. Korshak resurrected Shasta as Shasta-Phoenix Books of Lasting Significance (Fig. 0.4). Shasta-Phoenix's first book, *The Paintings of J. Allen St. John: Grand Master of Fantasy* (2008), was done in conjunction with Vanguard Productions. This was followed by Shasta-Phoenix's first solo book *From the Pen of Paul: The Fantastic Images of Frank R. Paul* (2009). This color art book on the father of science fiction illustration art included essays by Stephen D. Korshak, Arthur C. Clarke, Jerry Weist, Roger Hill, and Gerry de la Ree. Shasta-Phoenix also published *The Alluring Art of Margaret Brundage: Queen of Pulp Pinup Art* (2013), again in conjunction with Vanguard Productions.

Art used in some of the beautiful dust jacket cover designs for Shasta books is included in the Korshak Collection. In today's science fiction book market, there are many new and different ways to publish a book, but many collectors still desire a deluxe first edition hardcover book with a stunning cover jacket. It seems that books of lasting significance are as important in today's market as they were at the time of the original specialty press science fiction publishers.

1. Willy Ley, review of *The Checklist of Fantastic Literature,* by Everett F. Bleiler, *Astounding Science Fiction,* July 1949, 142.

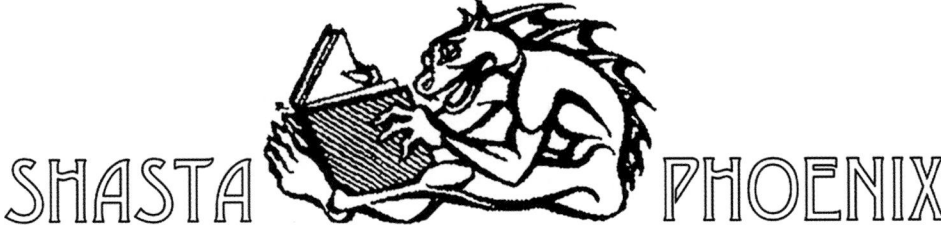

FIGURE 0.4. Shasta Phoenix Insignia,
n.d., Courtesy of Stephen D. Korshak.

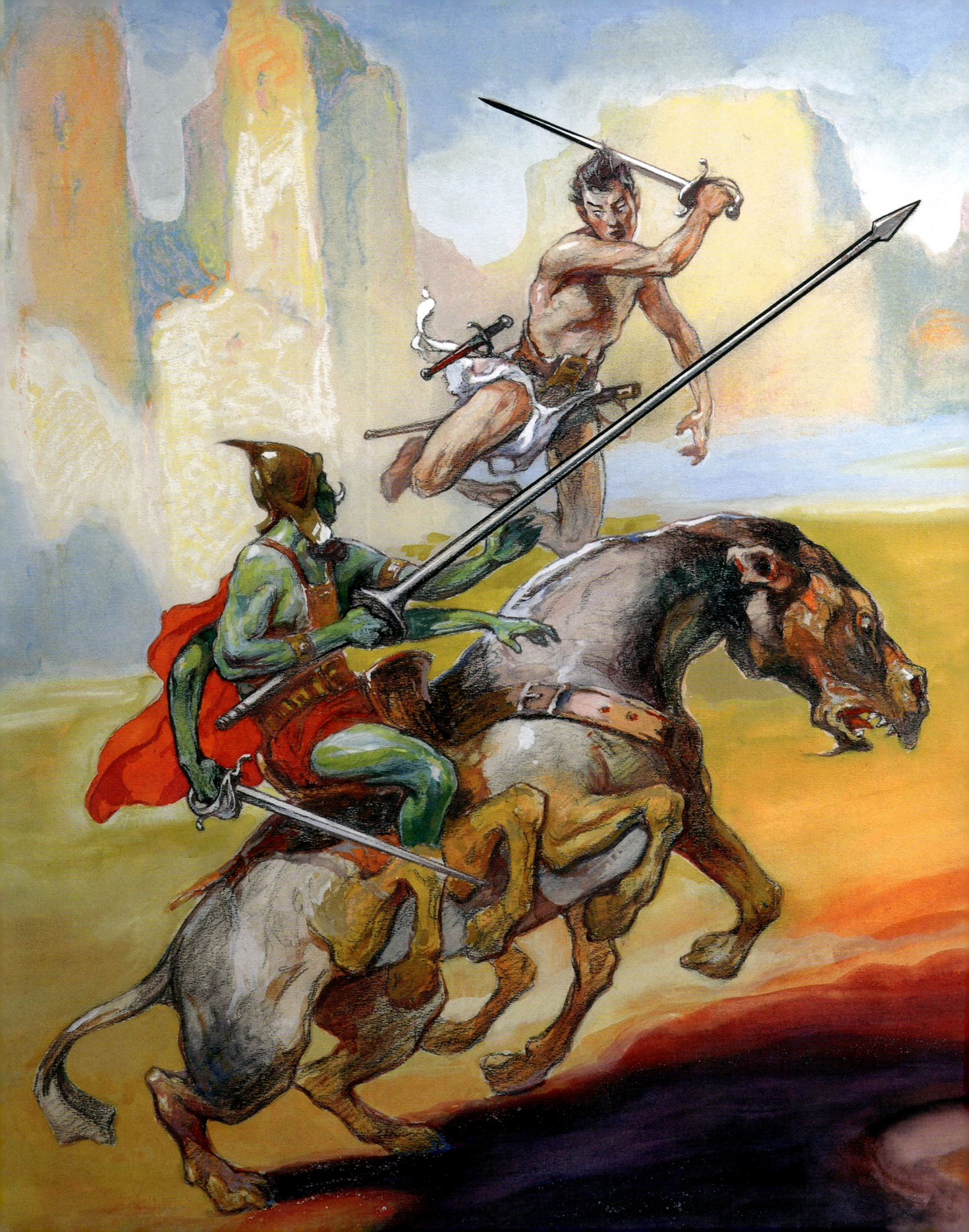

David M. Brinley

THE KORSHAKS: A Legacy of Influence

When Steve Korshak was a young boy, his father Erle hung a vibrant J. Allen St. John illustration with the foreboding title of *John Carter and the City of Mummies* (Plate 39) above Steve's bed that enticed, inspired, and carried his imagination away along with John Carter, Warlord of Mars. Six-legged beasts, four-armed glossy green aliens, and exotic locales awaited! Beginning with the retrieval of two unpublished Hannes Bok book cover illustrations from Erle's famous Shasta Publishers archives, Steve and his wife Alma (as well as Erle prior to his passing) have been on an astonishing treasure hunt for the most iconic science fiction and fantasy illustrations for over forty years, and are still going strong.

The educated curation of these iconic twentieth-century illustrations to create a landmark collection has taken ingenuity, patience, negotiating skills, and immense luck along the way. While many of the artists in the collection are household names in the realm of illustrators of imaginative literature, all comprise a fascinating group that have created, inspired, or touched nearly all modern illustration art, therefore influencing future art, as well. Highly regarded as the godfather of fantasy art in America, St. John inspired famous disciples such as Roy Krenkel, who in turn mentored the genre grandmaster Frank Frazetta. St. John's painterly renderings and heroically grand gestures spark the imagination. In having the opportunity to know Steve, it has been enlightening to hear and ruminate on the inspiring story of how *John Carter and the City of Mummies* planted the inspirational seed within him. The passion Steve has for collecting this art is as palpable as the public's collective love for these images.

As an artist and illustrator, many points of view both formally and conceptually influence my desire to create new images. Why do artists have this drive and how does it work? Unpacking the way other artists work inspires me and new generations of artists, from writers to image-makers. Studying the variety of artists and work in Steve's collection has opened my eyes even further to less familiar European and American artists and the expressive possibilities within my own new art. Discussing the importance of visual

PLATE 39. J. Allen St. John
(American, 1872–1957), *John Carter
and the City of Mummies*, 1941,
gouache on paper, 18 × 13 inches.

literacy, language, and communication with Michael R. Whelan for the catalogue has been an absolute honor.

As American artists collaborated with writers and publishers of horror, crime, war, sports, sex, Western, and other niche stories, their techniques evolved with printing processes. As the "slicks" hosted more highbrow and, in many cases, more traditional content throughout the decades, pulp magazines were ephemeral and devoted to cheap production costs. Even their distinctive acidic odor and tan hue—derived from the wood pulp used to make their unrefined paper—creates sensory memory if you collect enough of them.

The Korshak Collection repositions the role of narrative artists and illustration in twentieth-century art history. The featured artists have been compelled to tell stories in different mediums in many cultures, times, and places. Their work is made to reflect and retell narratives that, in many cases, have influenced a number of profound artists over the decades not only in the field of fantasy and science fiction publishing, but also in genres of popular culture, such as experimental films, comic books, and major motion studio pictures—most of which are not what we have historically referred to as fine art. Being boxed in by traditional concepts of what is and isn't fine art can become rather tedious. In people's daily lives, they interact with all sorts of popular storytelling visual forms. The visual vocabulary developed by the artists in the Korshak Collection is still used today throughout the vast worlds of contemporary art, animation, and film. Disparate influences make for a rich and, in many cases, far quirkier approach.

In addition to St. John, Spanish painter and illustrator José Segrelles also inspired Krenkel and Frazetta to blaze new trails in beautiful figurative works. But Segrelles's influence extended to filmmaker Guillermo del Toro, Steven Spielberg, and a powerful contingent of Hollywood concept and film production artists. Looking at Segrelles's *War of the Worlds* (Plate 46), it is difficult to believe that it was created nearly one hundred years ago, as it appears to be a climactic modern scene in its composition, design, and execution. American artist Hannes Bok was the epitome of a fine art illustrator due to his uncompromising personal vision, and he was a fascinating man to study. He was consumed with developing a individualized aesthetic and unique visual expression in his work with publishers, a predicament at once inspiring, at times frustrating, and yet, for me as an artist, relatable. Ironically, Segrelles and Bok have largely been forgotten, but this is changing. Thanks to the passion of others to share their legacy, influence, and artistry, this catalogue and exhibitions of the Korshak Collection can play a role in reviving serious scholarship on such artists.

DAVID M. BRINLEY

Being a lifelong student of illustration and collector of related ephemera, it has been heartening to learn more about many of the artists in the collection directly from Steve Korshak, why he was drawn to them, and how artistic styles and approaches spread internationally. Even if the artists were not aware of each other at the time they created their pieces, it is interesting to compare composition, color choices, subject matter, and the artists' own image-making tenets to reconsider what we thought were idiosyncratic tendencies in their work.

As an educator, I believe it is invaluable for future generations of students to be aware of and learn from this important art collection and the history it represents. Fostering new passions in other, particularly younger, people to find the meaning in these works of art is exciting. This collection comes from such a place of passion and understanding, as well as love. What began as an initial selection of artworks very personal to one family, the Korshak Collection of illustrations of imaginative literature has grown to become the definitive collection of science fiction and fantasy art illustration due to the curatorial care and educated interpretation of Erle and Steve Korshak.

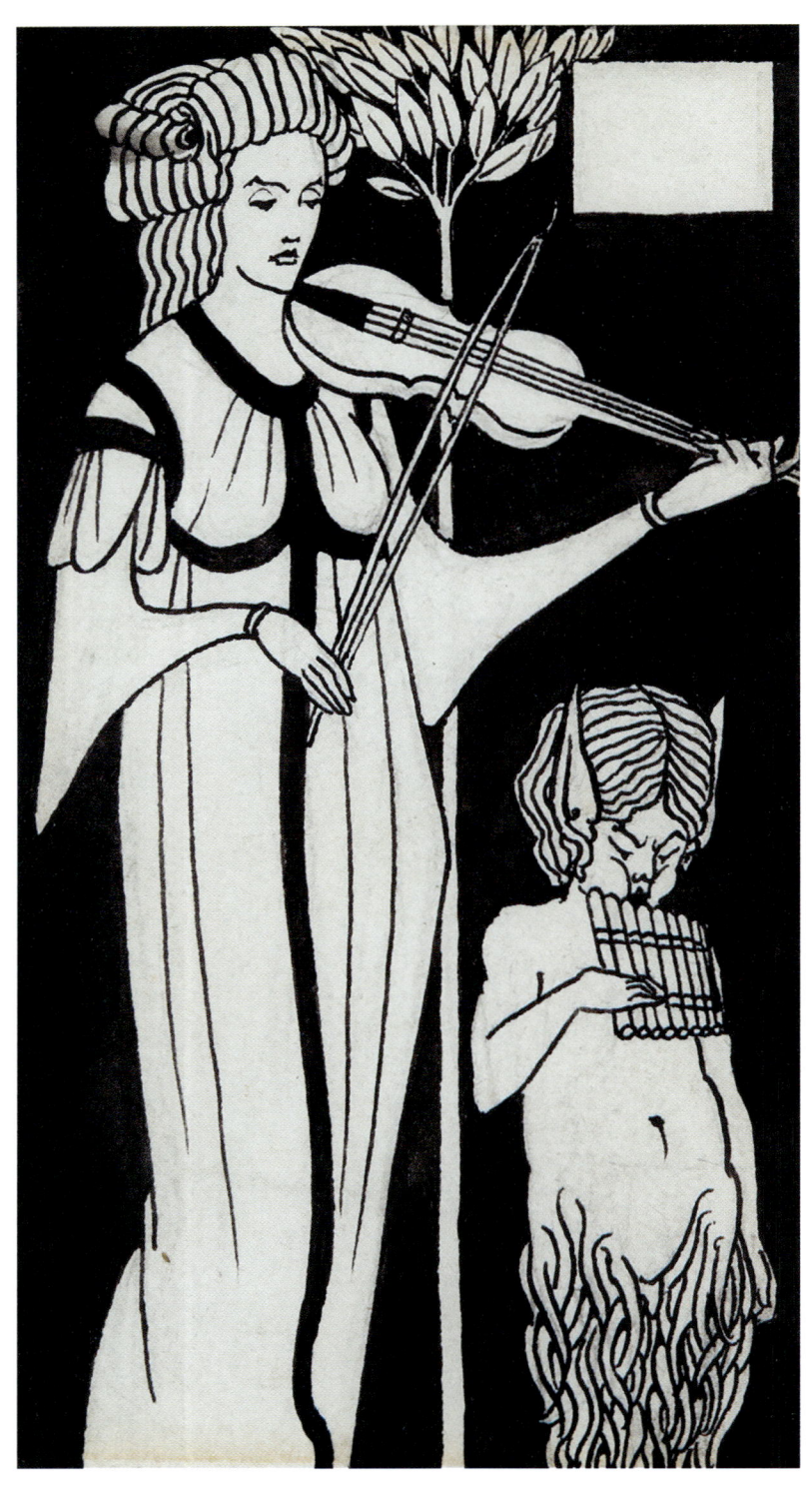

PLATE 40. Aubrey Beardsley (British, 1872–1898),
Le Morte d'Arthur, or *Woman Playing the Violin*
and Satyr Playing the Pipes for Le Morte d'Arthur,
1894, pen and ink on paper, 5 × 3 inches.

Margaret D. Stetz

AUBREY BEARDSLEY:
The Illustrator Who Would Not "Illustrate"

In a volume that celebrates the Korshak Collection's assemblage of important illustrations, the presence of Aubrey Beardsley (1872–1898), through his 1893 pen-and-ink drawing *Le Morte d'Arthur* (Plate 40), may be somewhat problematic. Beardsley is widely recognized as among the most innovative artists ever to create images to accompany printed texts. During the short period that he did so—from 1893 until his untimely death from tuberculosis a mere five years later—he produced an enormous body of black-and-white work of lasting significance, and fulfilled commissions for a variety of notable British publishing firms of the 1890s. Such firms included that of J.M. (Joseph Malaby) Dent, which issued *Woman Playing the Violin and Satyr Playing the Pipes for Le Morte d'Arthur*, now in the Korshak Collection under the abbreviated title *Le Morte d'Arthur*. From the start, his groundbreaking style influenced illustrators around the globe, and it continues to do so even today. This impact remains especially strong in the field of fantasy—on figures, for example, such as the American writer and artist Audrey Niffenegger (b. 1953). The illustrations for her own books, including *The Three Incestuous Sisters* (2005), are filled with self-conscious Beardsleyan echoes, and she has spoken openly about her fascination with his art, which she has likened to that found in the modern Japanese comics known as manga.[1]

Yet Beardsley chafed at being called an illustrator. For him, this label represented an implicit assumption, which he rejected, that the visual art he supplied for a book was somehow dependent upon or subordinate to the literary text it accompanied. On being appointed to the art editorship of the *Yellow Book* by John Lane, co-proprietor with Elkin Mathews of the London-based Bodley Head firm, Beardsley made clear his own vision for this new periodical as a home for autonomous images. The published prospectus for the inaugural issue of April 1894 announced boldly and unambiguously, "The pictures will in no case serve as illustrations to the letter-press, but each will stand by itself as an independent contribution."[2] Such a statement defied the established practice of Victorian magazine publishing as a whole, even as it reflected Beardsley's determination to raise his own status and that of his contemporaries in the visual sphere to the same heights that authors enjoyed.

This attempt to elevate the reputation of artists working in the world of print culture was no anomaly in his career. Whenever he was allowed to control how his role in a book would be identified, he insisted upon a different designation from the usual phrase "illustrated by," trying out several alternatives along the way. As Nicholas Frankel reports, he "went to considerable pains to avoid the term *illustration*: *Salome* [1894] was 'pictured' by Beardsley, its title-page tells us; *Morte d'Arthur* [1893–94] was 'embellished' by him; and

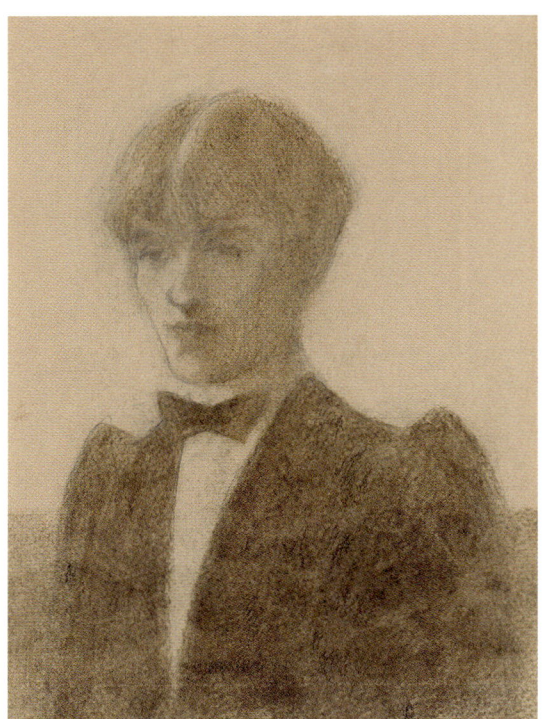

when Beardsley's publisher [Leonard Smithers] sent him page proofs for *The Rape of the Lock* [1896], Beardsley cancelled the word 'illustrated' on the title-page and replaced it with the phrase 'embroidered with nine drawings by Aubrey Beardsley'" (italics in original).[3] In every case, Beardsley was in search of words that emphasized his equality with the author as the creator of the material form in which a literary text appeared.

Most interesting, perhaps, was his choice of the verb "embroidered" for his contributions to the edition of Alexander Pope's 1712 mock-heroic comic poem *The Rape of the Lock*. Although the word had connotations of ornamenting and exaggerating, it also suggested more literal meanings. Embroidery, of course, was a decorative art with strongly feminine associations. The Arts and Crafts movement, led by William Morris (1834–1896) and his late Victorian circle, had argued for the dignity and value of handiwork of many sorts, but embroidery was often denigrated nonetheless—viewed as an occupation for middle- and upper-class ladies who, confined to domestic spaces, filled their otherwise empty hours by sewing.

A maverick in terms of crossing conventional gender lines, both in his life and in his art, Beardsley had no hesitation in aligning himself with femininity. Among his widely circulated self-portraits was a drawing in pencil, charcoal, and crayon that appeared in the journal *The Sketch* in April 1894 (Fig. 1.1). Titled *The Art Editor of the Yellow Book*, it featured Beardsley wearing what Linda Zatlin, author of the catalogue raisonné of his work, has called "a jacket … reminiscent of a woman's leg-of-mutton sleeves and décollatage," and sporting a hairstyle that signaled "the importance of androgyny to him"; this

FIGURE 1.1. Aubrey Beardsley (British, 1872–1898), *The Art Editor of The Yellow Book*, 1894, pencil, charcoal, and crayon on paper, The Mark Samuels Lasner Collection, University of Delaware Library, Museums and Press.

enabled him "to toy with the viewers by pushing the boundaries of what was publicly acceptable" in terms of gender presentation.[4]

He was just as eager to push boundaries when depicting images not of himself, but of fantasy figures, as in *Le Morte d'Arthur*. To say this image was not an "illustration" of the text by Sir Thomas Malory (ca. 1415–71) about the questing Knights of the Round Table would be an understatement. Into the medievalist realm of King Arthur, Beardsley introduced a series of visual anachronisms that challenged readers who expected representations closely tied to Malory's prose narrative. Certainly, in terms of the imaginary, the satyr was no more or less real than the character of Sir Lancelot. Yet, such a creature belonged to an entirely different cultural landscape—i.e., to the world of Classical mythology. Equally fantastic, however, was the figure of a woman with a violin, an instrument not invented until the sixteenth century and as much out of place in Malory's story as an electric light bulb would have been.

Beardsley's decision, moreover, to put a violin in the hands of a woman was no neutral choice. As Paula Gillett makes clear in *Musical Women in England, 1870–1914* (2000), until late in the nineteenth century, the Victorians remained opposed to women playing this stringed instrument. Unlike the piano, which was favored for middle- and upper-class ladies, the violin not only carried Satanic associations, but also required an immodest display of the performer's body, especially by focusing attention on the region of her bosom.[5] For just such reasons, Beardsley not only depicted a violin-playing woman, but also drew her wearing a dress that emphasized the outline of her breasts—thus offering an open challenge to contemporary standards of gendered decorum.

Potentially offensive, too, to a Victorian audience were some of the other details in this pen-and-ink drawing. Beardsley's satyr is composed of multiple phallic images. These include, of course, his pointed ears and the pipes into which he blows, which visually echoes the twisting and tubular shapes of the "hair" on his nether parts. Equally suggestive is the tree that sprouts upright behind the two figures, along with the woman musician's headdress, composed of a series of forms that mirrors the satyr's pipes. In Classical Greek imagery, satyrs were often distinguished by their standing phalluses— something that Beardsley dared not show directly and that the publisher would never have countenanced. During the course, however, of executing his commission from Dent, Beardsley developed the artistic practices that he would soon perfect in his work for Lane and Mathews, such as in Oscar Wilde's *Salome* (1894), as he defiantly pushed the envelope as far as possible in terms of erotic imagery that covertly, if not overtly, violated taboos. Here, for instance, the satyr also seems to be a mere child—closer, in some ways, to a Pan-like figure—but is sexualized nevertheless, despite being underage.

By the time Beardsley prepared the prospectus in 1893 for *Le Morte d'Arthur*, which was meant to advertise this mock-medieval production, there was as much of the "mock" (as in mockery) in it as of the medieval. The drawings he turned out featured the gratuitously lascivious and often slyly comic displays of nudity that soon would become signature characteristics of his art. In an image, for instance, that once again relied more on the inspiration of Ancient Greek mythology than of Arthurian legend, Beardsley combined the sort of entangled branches familiar from the work of Edward Burne-Jones (1833–1898) with a series of naked satyrs—this time, with mature bodies that sport, in some cases, pendulous breasts (Fig. 1.2). Indeed, one of those branches rises from between a satyr's legs in an unmistakable erection, making it obvious that Beardsley's interest here was less in focusing on the Grail than on the groin.

As he incorporated this daring content, Beardsley also drifted further from the Pre-Raphaelite–influenced style that, in 1892, had won him the commission for *Le Morte d'Arthur* in the first place. He owed the arrangement with J.M. Dent to his friendship with London bookseller and photographer Frederick H. Evans. It was Evans who had put forward Beardsley's name when Dent, under the spell of the beauty of the Kelmscott Press books issued by William Morris, was in search of a cut-rate version of Burne-Jones to illustrate his own edition of Malory's text. At that early stage in his career (and when a mere twenty years old), Beardsley was every bit as enchanted as Dent by the pseudo-medieval glories of the volumes on which Morris and Burne-Jones had collaborated, and was eager to imitate the look of them. So inexperienced was he, however, that he produced a design for the front wrapper of the parts issue that contained such basic errors as a misspelling of the title *Le Morte d'Arthur* as *La Mort Darthure* (Fig. 1.3).

Although Dent's payment for the numerous designs that Beardsley supplied was less than it would have been had he engaged Burne-Jones or another established artist, it was still munificent by Beardsley's standards. With the contract in hand for work that would carry him well into the following year, Beardsley was able in 1892 to quit the job that he loathed, a clerkship in a London insurance office. This commission came not merely at an opportune time, but also not a moment too soon, for he was already suffering from the effects of the tuberculosis that would kill him at the very young age of twenty-five. Thanks to Dent, he was at last free to pursue his

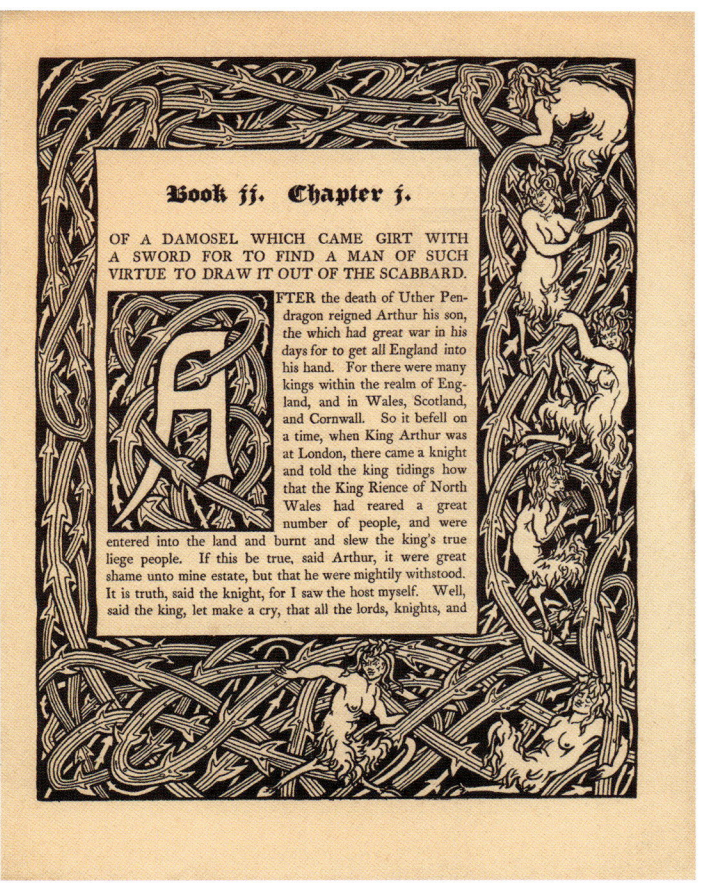

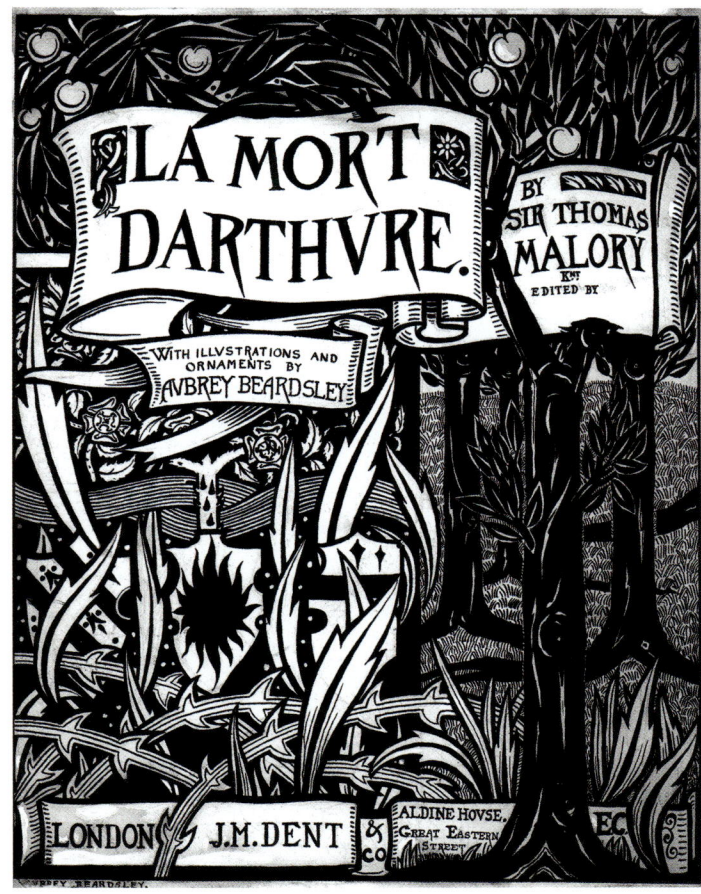

FIGURE 1.2. Aubrey Beardsley (British, 1872–1898), *Prospectus for Sir Thomas Malory, The Birth, Life, & Acts of King Arthur, of His Noble Knights of the Round Table, Their Marvellous Enquests and Adventures, the Achieving of the San Greal, and in the End, Le Morte d'Arthur . . .*, London: J.M. Dent, 1893, The Mark Samuels Lasner Collection, University of Delaware Library, Museums and Press.

FIGURE 1.3. Aubrey Beardsley (British, 1872–1898), *La Morte Darthure* [misspelling of *Le Morte d'Arthur*], London: J.M. Dent, 1893.

own Holy Grail—art as a profession—and to do so while he was still physically able.

While fulfilling his obligation to Dent and turning out hundreds of drawings—scores of images of figures, along with many designs for borders and other decorative elements—Beardsley, however, grew restless. An autograph manuscript of reminiscences by his mother, Ellen Pitt Beardsley, attests to the fact that "Aubrey hated working to order" and had to be pushed to complete what was legally required of him.[6] As his striking image in the Korshak Collection demonstrates, he was eager to move beyond illustration per se and to begin creating visual works that stood on their own—ones that reflected the fantasies emerging from his own imagination and, increasingly, from the influence not of an ornate Pre-Raphaelitism, but of the simplicity and starkness he admired in Japanese prints. Looking now at this important drawing helps us to understand Beardsley as a young artist who, like the woman with half-closed eyes playing her violin and the youthful satyr intent upon his reedpipes, was already moving to a music all his own.

MARGARET D. STETZ

1. Matilda Battersby, "Audrey Niffenegger on Art, Writing and Aubrey Beardsley as a Manga Illustrator," *Independent* (UK), September 30, 2011.

2. Aubrey Beardsley, *Prospectus for the Yellow Book: An Illustrated Quarterly, Volume I, April 1894* (London: Elkin Mathews and John Lane, 1894). The Mark Samuels Lasner Collection, University of Delaware Library, Museums and Press, Newark, Delaware.

3. Nicholas Frankel, *Masking the Text: Essays on Literature & Mediation in the 1890s* (High Wycombe, UK: Rivendale, 2009), 156.

4. Linda Gertner Zatlin, *Aubrey Beardsley: A Catalogue Raisonné,* vol. 2 (New Haven, CT: Yale University Press, 2016), 68.

5. Paula Gillett, *Musical Women in England, 1870–1914: Encroaching on All Man's Privileges* (New York: St. Martin's Press, 2000). For information about nineteenth-century women who played the violin, see "Woman and the Devil's Instrument," 77–108, and "The New Woman and Her Violin," 109–40.

6. Ellen Pitt Beardsley, *Aubrey Beardsley,* autograph manuscript, 1921. The Mark Samuels Lasner Collection, University of Delaware Library, Museums and Press, Newark, Delaware.

Ashley Rye-Kopec

"A HINT AND AN OPPORTUNITY":
Goblins, Fairies, and Mysterious Creatures in Arthur Rackham's *The Sleep of Rip Van Winkle*

On Tuesday, March 7, 1905, the *Manchester Courier* announced Arthur Rackham's newest project with a brief note: "'Rip Van Winkle' is the subject of fifty water-colours by Mr. Arthur Rackham, A.R.W.S., shortly to be on view at the Leicester Galleries. No story could offer better subjects to an artist of Mr. Rackham's peculiar gifts, and those who have been privileged to see his pictures regard them as the best work he has yet done."[1] The next week, the newspaper again addressed Rackham's exhibition at the Leicester Galleries. This longer account provides insight into the suitability of the *Rip Van Winkle* story for Rackham's "peculiar gifts": "Mr. Arthur Rackham, though he has been before the public for a comparatively brief period, has made his mark as an original and attractive illustrator. His inventive powers and a habit of thought that is partly fantastic, partly imaginative, are peculiarly suitable to the illustration of fairy tales and stories. His series of pictures of 'The Ingoldsby Legends' and 'Grimm's Fairy Tales' have been highly successful, and now at the Leicester Gallery Mr. Rackham is exhibiting a collection of delightfully quaint and delicate drawings illustrative of 'Rip Van Winkle.'"[2]

The *Manchester Courier*'s assessment of *Rip Van Winkle* was prescient: it is widely acknowledged as the project that catapulted Rackham to fame. Yet, as the *Courier* writer noted, the story also offered a subject especially suited to "an artist of Mr. Rackham's peculiar gifts." Indeed, Washington Irving's short story provided a multitude of avenues for Rackham's imaginative imagery. First published in 1819, the story revolves around its title character, who, after drinking liquor from mysterious mountain-dwellers, falls into a twenty-year slumber. Set in the Kaatskill (Catskill) mountains in New York, the tale includes strange characters, an inexplicable event, and a spooky environment. Yet, while Rackham clearly took inspiration from Irving's mysterious text, he also asserted his independence from it—and in doing so, ultimately reinterpreted the core event in the story.

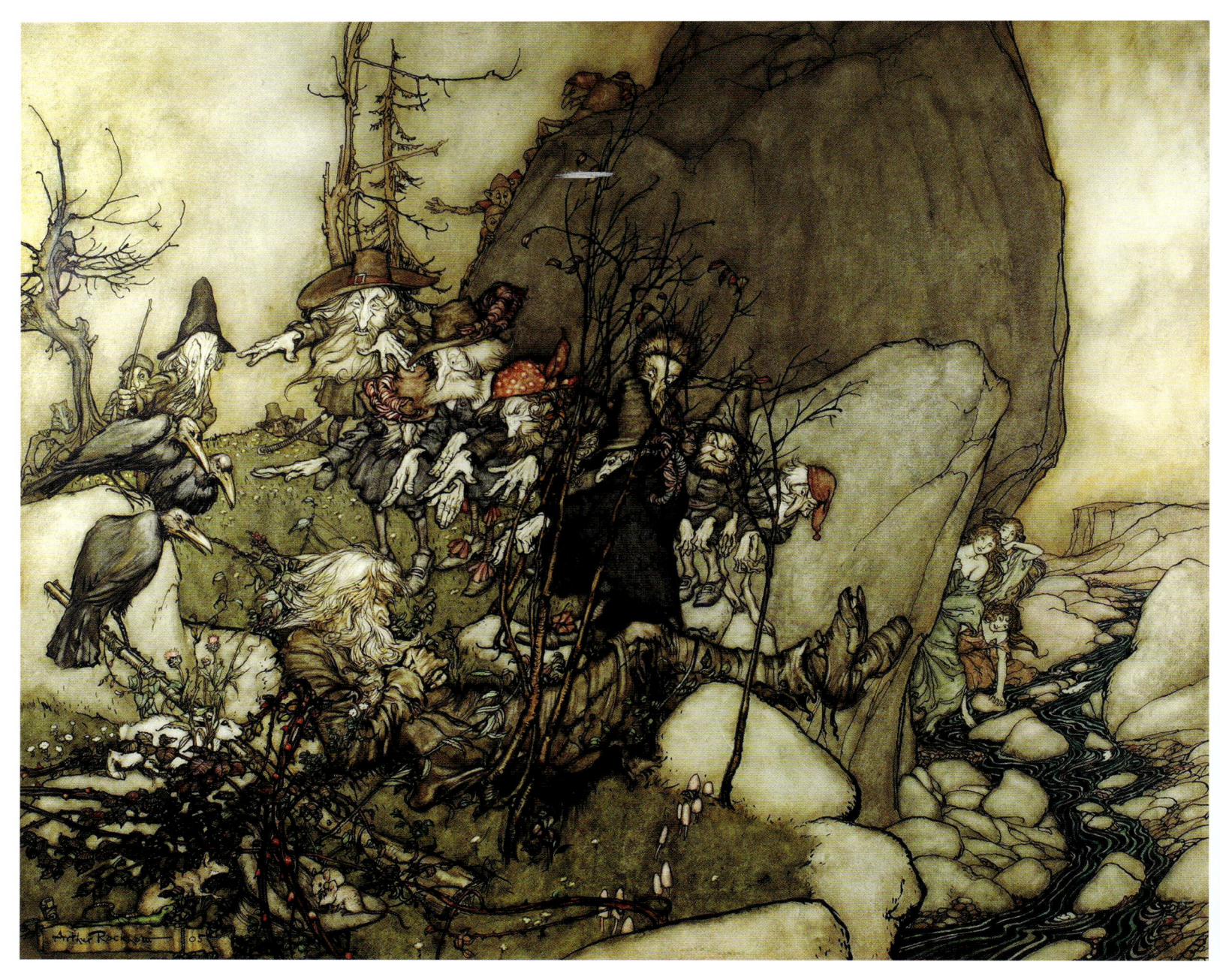

PLATE 41. Arthur Rackham (British, 1867–1939), *The Sleep of Rip Van Winkle*, 1905, pen and ink, watercolor on paper, 11¼ × 14 inches.

Rackham's creative approach to the illustrations for *Rip Van Winkle* can be seen particularly clearly in the original watercolor for *The Sleep of Rip Van Winkle* (Plate 41) in the Korshak Collection. This picture is one of only two of Rackham's illustrations produced for the *Rip Van Winkle* volume that does not refer to a direct quotation from Irving's text. (The other is a portrait of Rip's daughter and grandchild.) It is also the only illustration to depict a scene that the text does not describe—in the story, Rip falls asleep and then awakens, unaware of the time that has passed—but is the event around which the entire story revolves. And in Rackham's rendering, the artist allows his creativity to flourish, with limited direction or constraint from the source material, depicting the central event in a way that emphasizes his commitment to mysterious subjects.

When Rackham undertook the *Rip Van Winkle* project, he had been working as an illustrator for over a decade and had provided illustrations for over fifty titles.[3] Yet, whether illustrations of books or popular periodicals, his previous artworks were often black-and-white line drawings with occasional color images interspersed throughout some of the longer texts. Irving's story was a much more substantial project: Rackham produced fifty-one color illustrations for it, plus three line drawings and one decorative initial. The tale contains less than five-thousand words, meaning that, on average, there is an illustration by Rackham for every hundred words of Irving's text.

The exhibition and publication history of Rackham's *Rip Van Winkle* illustrations indicates how the artworks were simultaneously connected to and independent from Irving's text. The commission for the illustrations came from Ernest Brown & Phillips, art dealers who operated the Leicester Galleries in London.[4] The dealers purchased the original watercolors plus the publishing rights, which they then sold to the publishing firm of William Heinemann. In March of 1905, the watercolors were exhibited at the Leicester Galleries, where they were available for sale, a pattern that would be repeated in Rackham's other illustration projects in the future. For Ernest Brown & Phillips, the strategy was a profitable one—contemporary accounts noted that all of the original illustrations for *Rip van Winkle* were sold—but it also benefited both the publisher Heinemann and Rackham himself.[5] The exhibition served as a precursor to the 1905 publication of both the standard and deluxe editions, raising awareness and driving up interest in the lavishly illustrated book. And for Rackham, the widely publicized and generally well-reviewed exhibition provided an opportunity for viewers to experience his watercolors independent from Irving's text.

In that text, Irving introduces Rip, an amiable, albeit lazy, man who lives in a village at the foot of the Kaatskill mountains. To avoid his disagreeable wife, Rip endeavors to spend as much time as possible away from his home. One autumn day, he takes his rifle and his dog Wolf, wanders through the mountain woods, and encounters a strange man wearing clothing "of the antique Dutch fashion."[6] The man is struggling to carry a large keg of liquor on his own, so Rip offers assistance, and the pair slowly make their way up the mountain. There, they encounter even more odd-looking men playing a game of nine-pins. After surreptitiously drinking several flagons of the liquor he had helped carry, Rip falls into a deep sleep. When he awakens, he discovers a rust-encrusted gun in place of his well-oiled rifle, and his dog is nowhere to be found.

While climbing down the mountain, Rip discovers changes to the landscape, including the presence of a large stream where there had previously been an empty gully. The changes are even more pronounced when Rip arrives in his village: the inhabitants are unfamiliar, his house is falling apart and apparently abandoned, the village inn has been renamed, and the portrait of King George III on its sign has been replaced by a portrait of a man called George Washington. After encountering his now-adult children, Rip realizes that his night sleeping on the mountain lasted twenty years. Although the village inhabitants initially view Rip with suspicion (particularly after he proclaims himself a loyal subject of the king), they eventually determine that he is who he claims to be. And after consulting Peter Vanderdonk, "the most ancient inhabitant of the village, and well versed in all the wonderful events and traditions of the neighbourhood," they determine that Rip is telling the truth.[7] The Kaatskills, readers learn, have always been a source of mystery.

The Sleep of Rip Van Winkle, the illustration in the Korshak Collection, depicts the central event in the story. Rip Van Winkle lays sleeping atop some large rocks on a craggy outcropping near a deep-blue stream. The depiction of Rip indicates that he has already been asleep for many years. His clothes are tattered and his boots are coming apart, exposing his toes. His hair is long, white, and disheveled; the same is true of his beard. His eyes are closed and his hands rest on his torso, one atop the other as if he was a corpse.

Rackham's image conjures a mysterious environment in which a range of living things exert power over the sleeping man. Rip's body is partly hidden behind large, scraggly branches, and vines wind their way around his legs, as if holding him prisoner. Mice nest in his hat and a bird perches on the end of his rifle, both of which are seemingly trapped under the vines. Two other birds sit on a large boulder, peering down their beaks at the sleeping man. Nine squat, goblin-like men stand around Rip, staring and extending their hands in his direction. One of the men holds what appears to be a wand in his right hand. He also wears a pointed hat that suggests he may be some kind of sorcerer. More men are visible in the distance, and a few elfin creatures observe the scene from behind a large boulder. On the right side of the picture, a trio of fairies huddles together near a stream. Hidden from the group in the center of the image, they peek around a boulder, their expressions a mix of curiosity and concern.

Although Irving does not explicitly identify the cause of Rip Van Winkle's twenty-year slumber, his story suggests that the alcohol Rip helped carry up the mountain played a role. When Rip awakens and begins to note the differences from what he thought was the day before, he blames the liquor he consumed. When viewing the much-changed village, he again points to the alcohol as the source of his confusion, pondering how the contents of the flagon had addled his mind. The story's final lines likewise point to alcohol's role, when Irving writes that "it is a common wish of all hen-pecked husbands in the neighbourhood, when life hangs heavy on their hands, that they might have a quieting draught out of Rip Van Winkle's flagon."[8]

Yet while the text points to the old Dutch gin that he sneakily imbibed as the source of Rip's decades of slumber, in *The Sleep of Rip Van Winkle*, Rackham instead emphasizes the mysterious setting of the mountain and the supernatural powers of those who inhabit it. This can be seen most clearly in the group of small goblin-like creatures who surround the sleeping Rip.[9] Irving characterizes the men Rip encounters on the mountain as short, and he notes that at least one of the men has a prominent nose—both factors seem to have influenced Rackham's illustration. However, the presence of robes, hats, and a wand, which are commonly associated with wizardry, is entirely due to Rackham's imagination. The specific portrayal of the goblin-men is likewise unique: they stare directly at Rip, as if required to do so in order to effectively cast a magical spell.

The presence of other fantastical beings further establishes Rackham's creative interest in depicting supernatural figures. In the background, peering over some rocks, we find different magical creatures—possibly elves. These otherworldly beings do not appear to be involved in the process of keeping Rip asleep. Instead, their presence simply reinforces the sense of mystery that characterizes Rackham's illustrations. The fairies play a similar role to establish the Kaatskill mountains as a region of wondrous supernatural power.

Both the elves and the fairies remain in the distance; like the picture's viewers, they observe the events surrounding Rip. Ultimately, Rackham uses the generally fantastical setting of Irving's story to populate his images with a wide range of mysterious and magical beings.

Critics particularly appreciated Rackham's handling of the mystical aspects of the story. *The Athenaeum* commended Rackham's drawings, noting that they were "of remarkable merit, both in conception and execution. Especially is this true of the pictures representing the supernatural features of the story. That much-overworked adjective 'weird' faithfully describes many of them, and they cannot be other than a delight to all lovers of true art."[10] *The Studio*, too, commended the "weird" quality of Rackham's imagination: "Mr. Arthur Rackham's talent is displayed to great advantage in his illustrations to Irving's well-known story. His weird imagination, his free and admirable line work, his appreciation of colour harmony, combined with a careful study of costume and character associated with 'colonial' times in America, have resulted in a series of pictures altogether removed from the commonplace."[11]

ASHLEY RYE-KOPEC

The slight differences in *The Athenaeum*'s and *The Studio*'s use of the term "weird" to refer to Rackham's *Rip Van Winkle* project are informative. While *The Athenaeum* writer found Rackham's illustrations of the story's supernatural elements appropriately, and delightfully, "weird," *The Studio* pointed not to Rackham's drawings, but to the artist's own "weird imagination" as a key factor that contributed to the creation of a group of unusual images.

Indeed, part of Rackham's effort to remove his art from the commonplace involved letting his imagination roam freely, rather than limiting himself to a narrow interpretation of the text he was illustrating. As *The Academy* explained, "Indeed, of Mr. Rackham … it might be said that 'he draws just what he chooses, taking from his author's text nothing more than a hint and an opportunity.'"[12] Perhaps nowhere is this more clear than in *The Sleep of Rip Van Winkle*, where Rackham transformed an account of a man's seemingly magical liquor-induced slumber into an opportunity to imagine the presence of goblins, fairies, and other mysterious creatures.

1. "Art and Artists," *Manchester Courier*, March 7, 1905, 10.

2. "Our London Correspondence," *Manchester Courier*, March 13, 1905, 6.

3. Fred Gettings, *Arthur Rackham* (London: Studio Vista, 1975), 109.

4. James Hamilton, *Arthur Rackham: A Life with Illustration* (London: Pavilion, 2010), 68.

5. "The Talk of the Office," *Country Life in America* 40, no. 2, December 1906, 142.

6. Washington Irving, *Rip Van Winkle, with drawings by Arthur Rackham, A.R.W.S.*, First American ed. (New York: Doubleday, Page & Co., 1905), 22.

7. Irving, *Rip Van Winkle*, 51.

8. Irving, *Rip Van Winkle*, 57.

9. Contemporary critics used a range of terms including goblins, gremlins, and gnomes to describe the mysterious figures Rackham included in his *Rip Van Winkle* illustrations.

10. "Illustrated Books," *The Athenaeum*, November 25, 1905, 730.

11. "Rip Van Winkle," *The Studio* 36 (1906): 279.

12. "Mr. Rackham's Color Drawings," *The Academy*, April 1, 1905, 371.

Amanda T. Zehnder

THE BLUE OF DEEP WATER AND THE BLUE OF A WINTER NIGHT'S SKY: The Poetry of Word and Image in the Art of Edmund Dulac

Blue above and blue below. The color suffuses the two watercolors by Edmund Dulac (1882–1953) in the Korshak Collection. Blue evokes deep water in *The Tempest "Full Fathom Five"* (Plate 42), made in 1908 as an illustration for William Shakespeare's play *The Tempest* from the early 1600s. In contrast, blue conjures an enchanted cold night sky in the *The Snow Queen* (Plate 43), created in 1910 as an illustration for Hans Christian Andersen's celebrated mid-nineteenth-century children's story with the same title. Dulac's predilection for the color, especially early in his career, has long been noted by critics and scholars.[1] Water versus air, stasis versus activity, malevolence versus beauty—the use of blue in these two watercolors marks several similarities and differences notable between them that provide insight into Dulac's approach to creating imagery that conveys a story's aura. His ability to produce exquisite visual expressions that relate to words inspired early reviewer Evelyn Marie Stuart to call him "a poet of the brush."[2]

The Tempest "Full Fathom Five" and *The Snow Queen* date from the pre–World War I period in Dulac's career when he was rising rapidly to prominence. Edmond Dulac was born in Toulouse, France, and had a formal art education in France at the Ecole des Beaux-Arts and briefly at the Académie Julien before he emigrated to England in 1904. There, he changed the spelling of his first name to the more British "Edmund" and became a naturalized British citizen in 1912. The year 1905 proved to be seminal as Dulac launched his career. He received his first major commission from the publisher J.M. Dent to illustrate the complete novels of the Brontë sisters, a starting point in a long artistic rivalry between Dulac and Arthur Rackham.

The watercolors by both artists in the Korshak Collection provide a window into this competitive period between the artists and their publishing houses. Dulac's preference for blue in his early career helped to create a contrast with Rackham's frequent use of earth tones, found in all three watercolors

Plate 42 (opposite). Edmund Dulac (British, b. French, 1832–1953), *The Tempest "Full Fathom Five,"* 1908, watercolor, gouache, and ink on paper, 17 × 11½ inches.

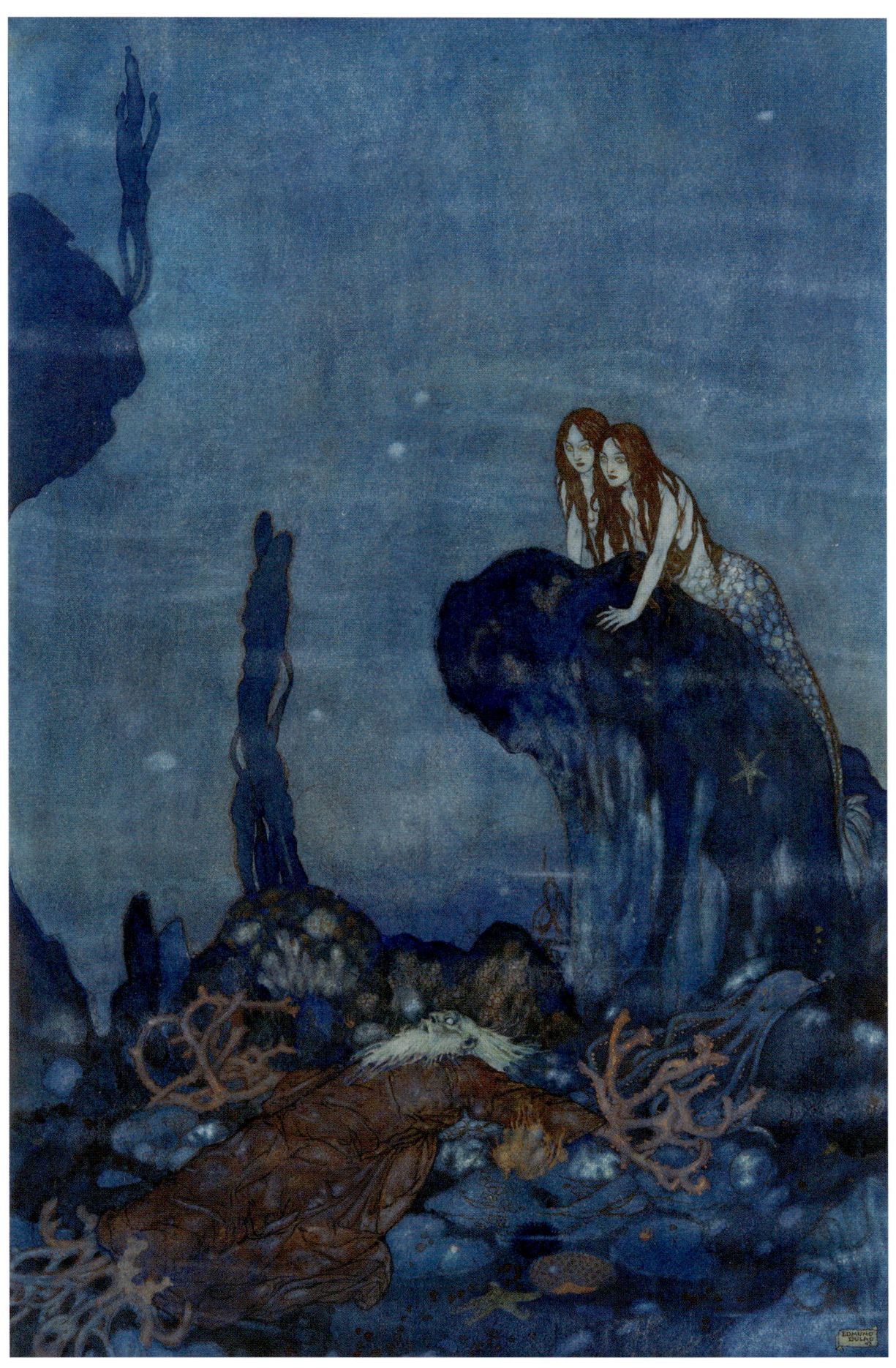

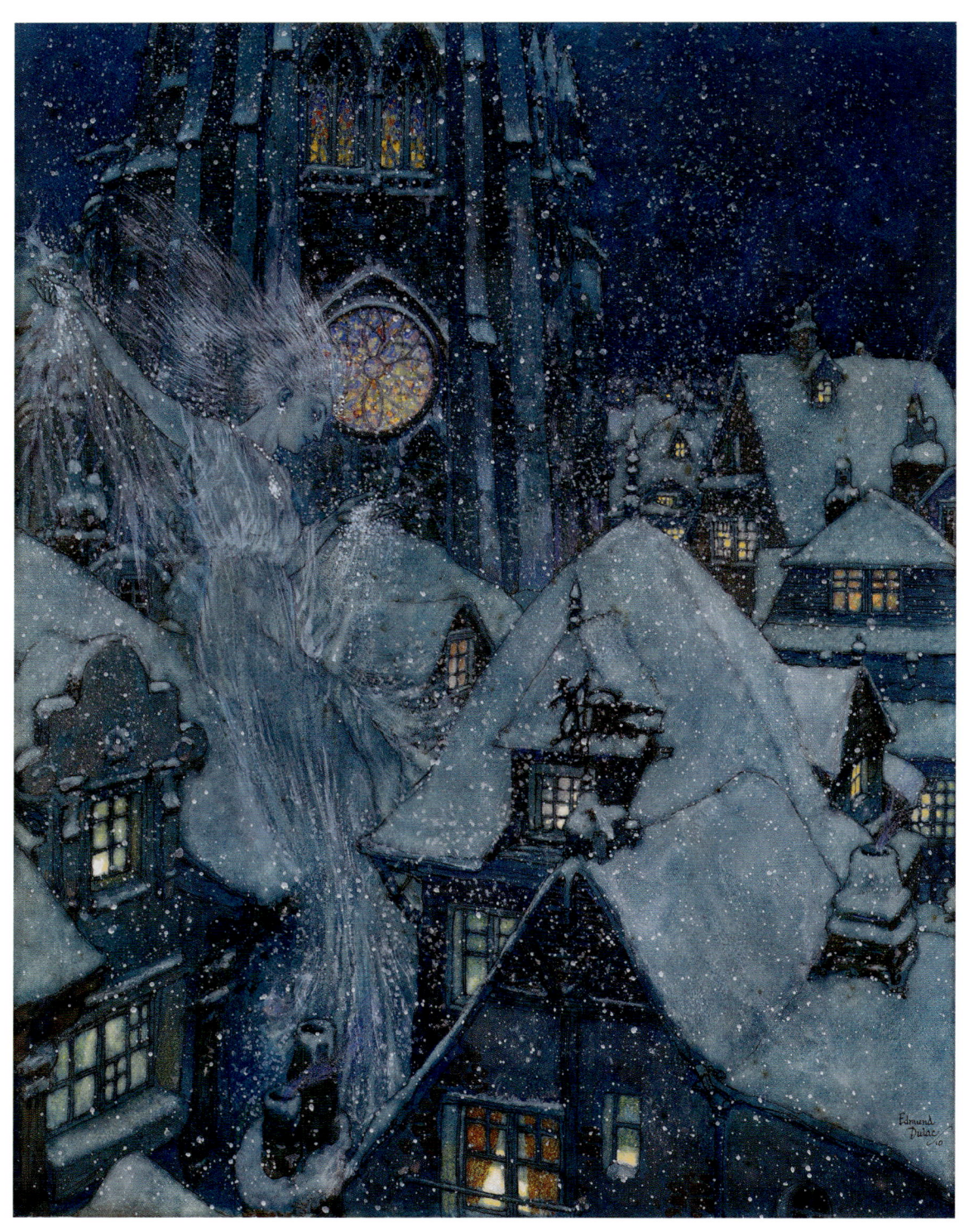

PLATE 43. Edmund Dulac (British,
b. French, 1882–1953), *The Snow Queen*,
1910, watercolor, gouache, pen and ink
on paper, 12³/₈ × 10 inches.

by Rackham in the collection. Both Dulac and Rackham became major forces as illustrators in the British publishing world, particularly in the gift books market. Gift books were lavish productions often marketed to children, and often gifted as holiday items. Publishers sought sophisticated illustrators to create compelling imagery to be reproduced as full-color plates, employing newly emerged technology, to complement the texts of the volumes.[3] In 1905, Rackham produced the illustrations for the groundbreaking full-color edition of Washington Irving's *Rip Van Winkle*, published by William Heinemann. The Korshak Collection includes a watercolor (Plate 41) for the *Rip Van Winkle* project, the subject of the previous essay. With Rackham signing on with Heinemann, rival publishers Hodder and Stoughton—who had once worked with Rackham—sought a new relationship with an equally captivating artist, and, upon the recommendation of colleagues from the Leicester Galleries in London, they chose Dulac.[4]

The partnership between Dulac and Hodder and Stoughton was long and successful. Dulac produced one gift book each holiday season for the publisher between 1907 and 1918, which totaled more than 270 color plates, among them the most famous images from Dulac's career.[5] The publication of each holiday gift book would typically correspond with an exhibition of watercolors by the book's illustrator at the Leicester Galleries. Both of the Dulac watercolors in the Korshak Collection were displayed at the Leicester Galleries in this manner, and the original exhibition labels for *The Snow Queen* have been preserved alongside the work itself.

Seeing Dulac's illustration *The Tempest "Full Fathom Five"* for one of Shakespeare's most fantastical plays, filled with spirits and magic, and his illustration for Andersen's famously mysterious and imaginative fairytale "The Snow Queen" together in one collection provides graceful and lyrical examples of how his artistic sensibility was well-suited to the fantasy genre for which he became most renowned. Dulac's way of interpreting the world around him was also reflected in his social circles of artists, dancers, and poets—including his longtime best friend, poet W.B. Yeats. Dulac's keen sensitivity to the relationship between language and image was key to his success as an illustrator. While he had the facility to create beautiful art based on words, he could also use language to evoke visual images. Scholar Colin White recounted Dulac's reactions to views he encountered during a Mediterranean trip with his wife and seven friends in 1913, noting Dulac's capacity to "paint in words, and the verbal equivalents he chose for his colour combinations, confirming his leanings towards the exotic and sensuous."[6] The trip began on September 1 with a departure from Marseilles to Corsica, and Dulac brought two sketch-books with him where he recorded his impressions of the scenery on the voyage through drawings and written reflections. When writing about the sunset and the water in the Straits of Bonifacio, he indulged in lush musings on color, "The sea is shimmering like golden moiré … a slight mist on the horizon, ahead cerulean. Behind us the sun is being wrapped up in a changing cloth of gold, deep orange and light metallic green dropping purply incense. On the side the foam makes designs of molten lapis lazuli." On the clear waters in Taormina, he remarked that "the shadows in it are blue. Blue—the *only* blue, a blue that makes you drunk."[7]

Access to the original watercolors provides an opportunity to observe the delicacy of Dulac's manual skill, which was the basis to produce lush illustrations for publication while employing well-known advances in color illustration technology in the early twentieth century.[8] Experiencing the watercolors in person also allows the viewer to note the extreme subtlety of some aspects of his compositions. For example, when seen from across a room, the figure of the title character in *The Snow Queen* is barely noticeable and mainly appears to be a misty part of the night sky. She becomes more and more apparent to the viewer as they move closer. This is something a reader, with a close-up view of the published illustration, might not realize.

Color was the dominant element in Dulac's compositions, downplaying the role of line work. In watercolor, he layered washes to create a diaphanous impression of depth—famously noted in his nocturnal skies.[9] This relates to the sky in *The Snow Queen*, and the creation of a murky sense of depth is also relevant to the depiction of water in *The Tempest "Full Fathom Five."* Dulac's gauzy washes of color combined with spidery, whisper-thin outlines lend a dreamlike air to both the scenes.

In *The Tempest "Full Fathom Five,"* the blue water forms nearly the entire flat background of the composition. It is an image of stillness filled with an initial sense of tranquility. The two mermaids to the right are at rest on an outcropping of rock. They gaze down upon a bearded man lying splayed out and motionless on the seafloor, thirty feet below the surface. The mermaids are beautiful, but their wide, staring eyes also are unsettling, appearing entranced. The sense of quietude becomes disturbing upon recognizing that the man's limbs have transformed into tendrils of coral and the stasis depicted is the stillness of death as the man's pearly eyes stare upward toward the water's surface above the frame of Dulac's composition. Instead of decomposing, his body is transforming into elements from the sea.

Understanding some of these visual details relies on the viewer having familiarity with *The Tempest*.[10] Or, Dulac relies on his audience to be reading the play alongside the images. This calm yet macabre image is also one of deception in the form of the spirit Ariel's song from Act I, Scene II, misleading Ferdinand into believing his father, King Alonso, has drowned in the shipwreck caused by the tempest conjured by the magician Prospero. This is only an illusion, however, since on another part of the island King Alonso is alive himself in a state of worry that his son Ferdinand has drowned. The following three lines are printed on the tissue that protects the tipped-in full-color plate 13 in the 1908 Hodder and Stoughton gift book. It rests in the volume between pages 34 and 35.

> *Ariel: Full fathom five thy father lies;*
> *Of his bones are coral made;*
> *Those are pearls that were his eyes:*

The remainder of Ariel's song adds more details that inform Dulac's visual interpretation. The song continues:

> *Nothing of him that doth fade*
> *But doth suffer a sea-change*
> *Into something rich and strange*
> *Sea-nymphs hourly ring his knell:*
> *Burthen Ding-dong.*
> *Hark! Now I hear them,—Ding-dong, bell.*[11]

Just as *The Tempest* "*Full Fathom Five*" watercolor is part of a broad visual history related to Shakespeare, *The Snow Queen* watercolor exists within a tradition of numerous illustrators who have tackled Andersen's classic story, beginning with Vilhelm Pedersen, the illustrator of the first edition. "The Snow Queen," written in Danish and published in 1844, is a long story, laid out in seven parts. It has an impressive legacy of inspiring subsequent works of art, literature, and film. Notably, the title character in "The Snow Queen" is seen as a model for C.S. Lewis's character of the White Witch from the 1950s series *The Chronicles of Narnia*, and more recently, Disney's 2013 animated movie *Frozen* drew loose inspiration from Andersen's story.[12] Dulac's illustration was made for the Hodder and Stoughton 1911 gift book *Stories from Hans Andersen*, dating to 1910, as it was made in advance as part of the production process.

The story of "The Snow Queen" examines good and evil, and is a meditation on the nature of human perception. In the first part, a demon (sometimes

EDMUND DULAC

87

translated as "goblin") creates and unleashes an evil mirror upon humanity that causes anyone who gazes into it to perceive only the grim side of life. The evil mirror then shatters into a billion tiny pieces, some of which become lodged in unlucky people, altering their personality and perception of the world in a negative way. A young boy, Kay, ends up with slivers of this evil mirror in his eye and heart. Because of his distorted perception, he is lured to run away with the Snow Queen to her frozen palace. At its core, the story traces a perilous quest undertaken by his friend, a little girl named Gerda, as she attempts to rescue him.

While the Snow Queen is the title character, she is only encountered in the second and seventh sections. Dulac's watercolor is an illustration for part of the text from the "Second Story: About a Little Boy and a Little Girl." It references these lines: "Many a winter's night she flies through the streets and peeps in at the windows, and then the ice freezes on the panes into wonderful patterns like flowers."[13] In this section, the Snow Queen is further portrayed as being like a queen bee surrounded by snowflakes that resemble a swarm of bees. Her garments are described as white and gauzy, as if millions of star-like snowflakes are joining together to form a veil. She is beautiful but frightening, with sparkling eyes and a gaze that is never at rest. The white speckles in the watercolor depicting the stars mingled with the snowflakes, in stark contrast to the dark blue of the surroundings, provide a good example of Dulac's famous technique, seen in a range of illustrations, in which he used small dots of contrasting or bright colors against darker backgrounds to create sparkling, jewel-like highlights.[14]

In contrast to the stillness that pervades Dulac's watercolor for *The Tempest*, this illustration is filled with dynamism. The movement includes the swirling and swarming snowflakes that accompany the delicate and intimidating Snow Queen as she flies into the scene from the upper left. The compositional device of a strong diagonal line emphasizes the Snow Queen's descent with flying hair as she will flit from window to window to peer inside. The diagonal line begins with the tip of the Snow Queen's outstretched hand, runs through her angled shoulders, and continues along to the roofline of one of the buildings below. The various steeply pitched roofs of the densely packed buildings add to the sense of an up-and-down visual movement as the viewer's eye dances from angle to angle and on into the distance. The contrast between the cold, blue outside and the warm yellow windows of the buildings has the impact of emphasizing the chilliness of the scene. This contrast between cold and warm is a recurring, metaphorical theme throughout the story of "The Snow Queen," and Dulac successfully conveys the sense of this broad motif in his illustration of a specific moment in the narrative.

Both images by Dulac in the Korshak Collection have a long track record of being reprinted and used in a range of contexts. One of the more unusual examples of this was the use of both *The Snow Queen* and *The Tempest "Full Fathom Five"* as illustrations in a deck of tarot cards, printed by Lo Scarabeo in 2020, that employ images from across Dulac's career for each card. *The Snow Queen* was used for the Five of Coins and *The Tempest "Full Fathom Five"* was used for the Eight of Swords.[15] The use of Dulac's work in this context is likely inspired by the mystical, sensuous, and fantastical subject matter for which he is most famous. Also in the year 2020, Dulac was inducted into the Society of Illustrators Hall of Fame.[16] It was Dulac's ability to create refined imagery that responds to and reinterprets the subject matter of texts from different eras, while maintaining his own distinctive vision, that has earned him a place among the most successful and impactful illustrators of the early twentieth century.

1. In her 1910 review of Dulac's illustrations for *The Rubáiyát of Omar Khayyam*, Evelyn Marie Stuart described sapphire and greenish blues as the artist's favorite colors and mentioned his tendency to create "pronounced blue studies." Stuart, "Edmund Dulac—Poet of the Brush," *Fine Arts Journal* 23, no. 2 (August 1910): 96, 100. More recently, Colin White has gone so far as to call the earlier years of Dulac's career his "Blue Period" in *Edmund Dulac* (New York: Charles Scribner's Sons, 1976), 56.

2. Stuart, "Edmund Dulac," 87.

3. For good descriptions of the new halftone and color printing methods that became available in the early twentieth century and facilitated the production of richly illustrated gift books, see Stuart Sillars, "Shakespeare in Colour: Illustrated Editions, 1908–14," *The Yearbook of English Studies* 45 (2015): 218, and White, *Edmund Dulac*, 23.

4. Stephen D. Korshak, "Hall of Fame 2020, Edmund Dulac," *Society of Illustrators: 62nd Annual of Illustration* (New York: Society of Illustrators, 2020), 20–21.

5. Jeff A. Menges, "Introduction," in *An Edmund Dulac Treasury: 116 Color Illustrations*, ed. Jeff A. Menges (Garden City, NY: Dover Publications, 2011), vi.

6. White, *Edmund Dulac*, 65.

7. White, *Edmund Dulac*, 64.

8. Brian Sanders, "Introduction," in *Dulac*, ed. David Larkin (New York: Charles Scribner's Sons, 1975), 6.

9. "Dulac built up his skies from layers of related colours dabbed on with a large brush, lightly blotting each section before applying the next to produce a soft mottled surface resembling shot silk. He had been using this technique for plane surfaces ever since *Stories from The Arabian Nights* [1907]" (White, *Edmund Dulac*, 61).

10. Peter Whitfield, *Illustrating Shakespeare* (London: The British Library, 2013), 129.

11. William Shakespeare, *William Shakespeare's Comedy of The Tempest with illustrations by Edmund Dulac* (London: Hodder and Stoughton, 1908), 35–36.

12. See "The Snow Queen," *Beyond Frozen: Education Resources,* https://www.frozeneducation.co.uk/beyond-the-story/inspiration/the-snow-queen/.

13. Hans Christian Andersen, *Stories from Hans Andersen with illustrations by Edmund Dulac* (London: Hodder and Stoughton, 1911), 11.

14. White, *Edmund Dulac,* 28–29.

15. Giacomo Gailli, *Edmund Dulac Tarot,* ed. Pietro Alligo (Turin, Italy: Lo Scarabeo, 2020).

16. At the time of Dulac's induction into the Society of Illustrators Hall of Fame, Stephen Korshak contributed an article to the society's publication, the *62nd Annual of Illustration,* as part of the recognition that came along with bestowing this posthumous honor. Korshak, "Hall of Fame," 18–23.

Rachael Kane

KNIGHTS OF OLD:
Władysław Benda's Skeletal Hussars

Entrenched deep in the fabric of history and storytelling, images of warfare and soldiers are a mainstay in any collection of illustrations. From high fantasy to historical fiction, famous warriors advance across the pages of books, literary magazines, and periodicals, eternally caught in the midst of great battles. For many European viewers in the twentieth century, these fictitious skirmishes often reflected real-life events, serving as a method of processing the escalating intensity of contemporary warfare. Illustrators and authors alike frequently shared their experiences with violence through their artwork, embedding their own understandings of armed conflict deep in the artistic canon. This cultural engagement with combat prompted many artists to engage with propaganda and art styles that validated or criticized their increasingly militarized societies. For Władysław Benda (1873–1948), creating war- and military-related artwork served as a political outlet, allowing him to express his Polish identity and support the Polish military during World War I. His large charcoal drawing included in the Korshak Collection, *The Army of the Dead* (Plate 44), deals with many of these ideas, placing a skeletal band of mounted soldiers amidst an intense battle. Despite having immigrated to America in 1898, Benda remained devoted to his homeland, often lending his renowned artistic skill to campaigns for voluntary enlistment in and financial donations to the Polish armed forces. Completed in 1917, *The Army of the Dead* offers both a call to arms for Polish recruitment as well as a morbid commentary on the destruction of the Great War.

Although considered a leading figure of the Golden Age of American Illustration, Władysław Teodor Benda was born in 1873 in Poznań, a Polish city then in the German Empire. Part of a creative family, Benda began formal art classes at age five before enrolling in a technological school as a young adult. In reaction to increasing tensions between Polish and German cultural groups, Benda's family moved to Krakow, where he continued his education at the Krakow Academy of Fine Arts. There, he studied the work of Polish masters including Florian Cynk, Władysław Łuszczkiewicz, and Izydor Jabłoński,

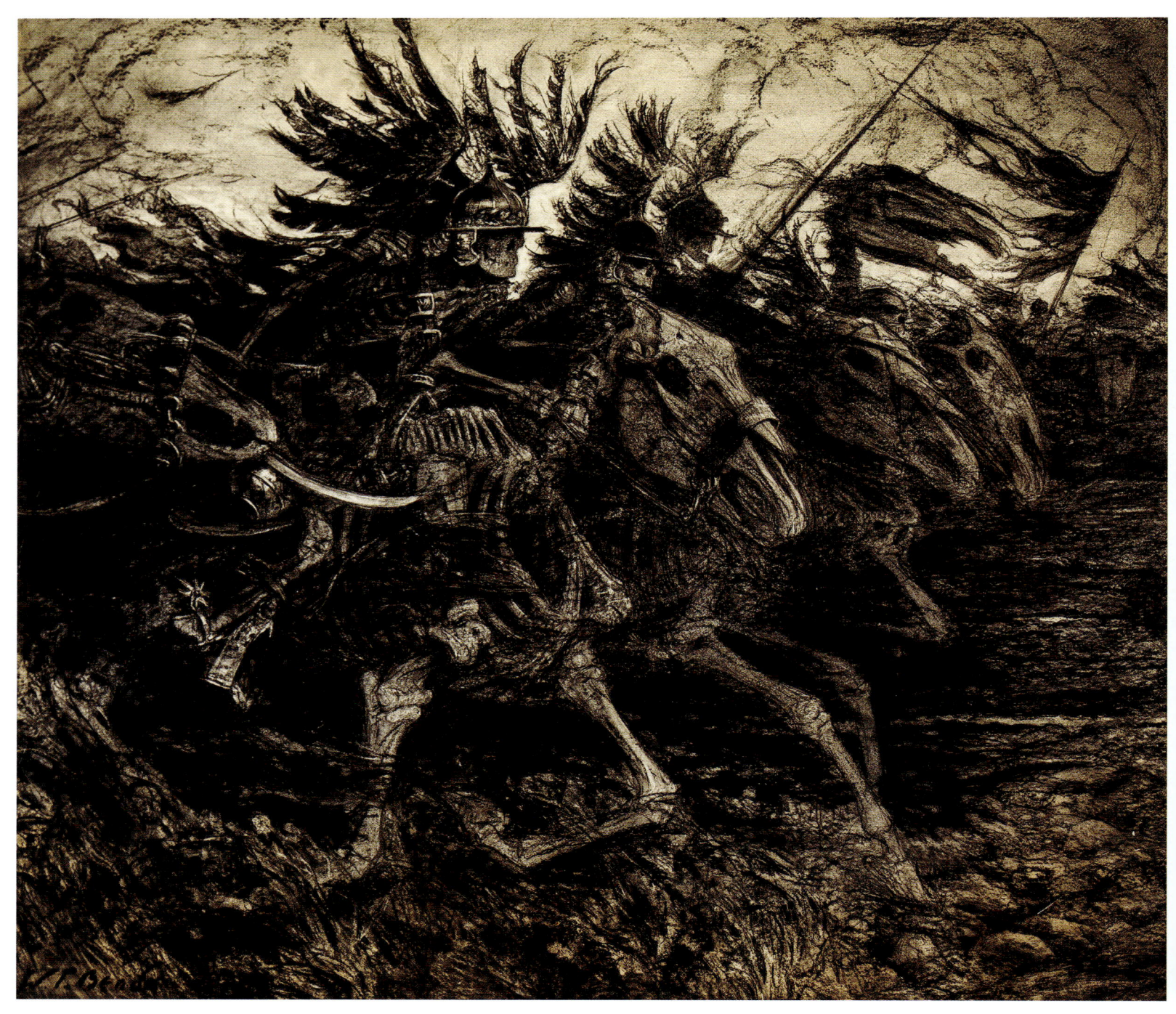

PLATE 44. Władysław T. Benda (Polish, 1873–1948), *The Army of the Dead*, 1917, charcoal on paper, 29¼ × 34 inches.

aligning himself with the rich artistic traditions of his native region. After a brief period of study at the Vienna School of Fine Arts, his family moved to the United States in 1898 as the conflicts between Prussian, Russian, and Polish powers continued to escalate.[1] They joined Benda's aunt, stage actress Helena Modrzejewska, in the wilds of California, where he assisted her with props for her stage work. In 1905, he moved cross-country to study at the Arts Student League of New York.[2] Under the tutelage of Robert Henri and Edward Penfield, Benda interpolated his Polish fine art pedagogy through the American Ashcan School, creating a distinctive style.[3] A notably successful illustrator, Benda drew advertisements, book illustrations, and magazine covers for publications like *Collier's, Cosmopolitan, The Saturday Evening Post,* and *Hearst's International Magazine* (Fig. 4.1).[4] Joining the Society of American Illustrators in 1907 and the Architectural League in 1916, Benda integrated into the New York art scene, gaining U.S. citizenship in 1911.

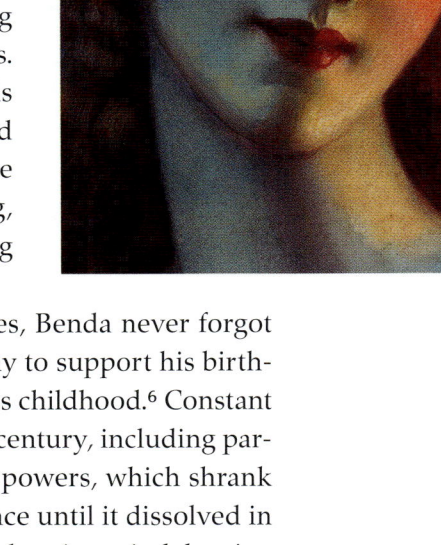

Later in his career, Benda returned to the theater, producing grotesque and surreal papier-mâché stage masks; this work is now his primary artistic legacy (Fig. 4.2). Benda's art, both in illustrations and masks, plays with proportions by elongating facial features and creating exaggerated silhouettes, producing highly emotive works. He referenced the European mannerism typical of his training while integrating Polish, Eastern European, and American symbolism and motifs.[5] Regardless of the media he was working in, Benda produced captivating, imaginative figures that span across genre, enchanting audiences both on paper and on stage.

Despite spending most of his life in the United States, Benda never forgot his Polish roots, often using his artistic practice as a way to support his birthplace. However, there was no Polish state during Benda's childhood.[6] Constant warfare plagued the region throughout the eighteenth century, including partitions of territory by Russian, Prussian, and Austrian powers, which shrank the Polish-Lithuanian Commonwealth's area of influence until it dissolved in 1795.[7] This level of conflict continued through the Napoleonic period, leaving the region in tumult all the way up until World War I. The political and geographic changes to the German, Russian, and Austro-Hungarian regimes at the end of the war resulted in the establishment of a new, independent Polish state. The region experienced massive loss of life, property, and natural resources

FIGURE 4.1. Władysław T. Benda (Polish, 1873–1948), *Head of Girl With Long Blonde Hair*, c. 1923, Library of Congress.

leading up to and during the war; by 1917, when *The Army of the Dead* was dated to, the devastation experienced in Poland spanned the physical, emotional, and psychological.

Like many Poles, Benda lived in exile from his familial home, experiencing the horrors of warfare secondhand. Polish American artists, including Benda, as well as similarly displaced illustrator Witold Gordon, used their professional expertise to bolster American interest in the war effort on the European continent, while also processing the deep sense of loss at the unprecedented violence. Their sincere pleas for support helped build American sympathy, reaching the public through creative expressions that revealed both their political leanings as well as their emotional response to the injury of Polish cultural communities and ancestral lands.

Taking a closer look at *The Army of the Dead* reveals telling details that indicate both Benda's interest in his heritage as well as his complex feelings about the war effort. Like many fantasy illustrations, this work holds roots in reality. For Polish people and military history aficionados alike, this image recalls the famed Winged Hussars, a Polish-Lithuanian cavalry unit whose successful

RACHAEL KANE

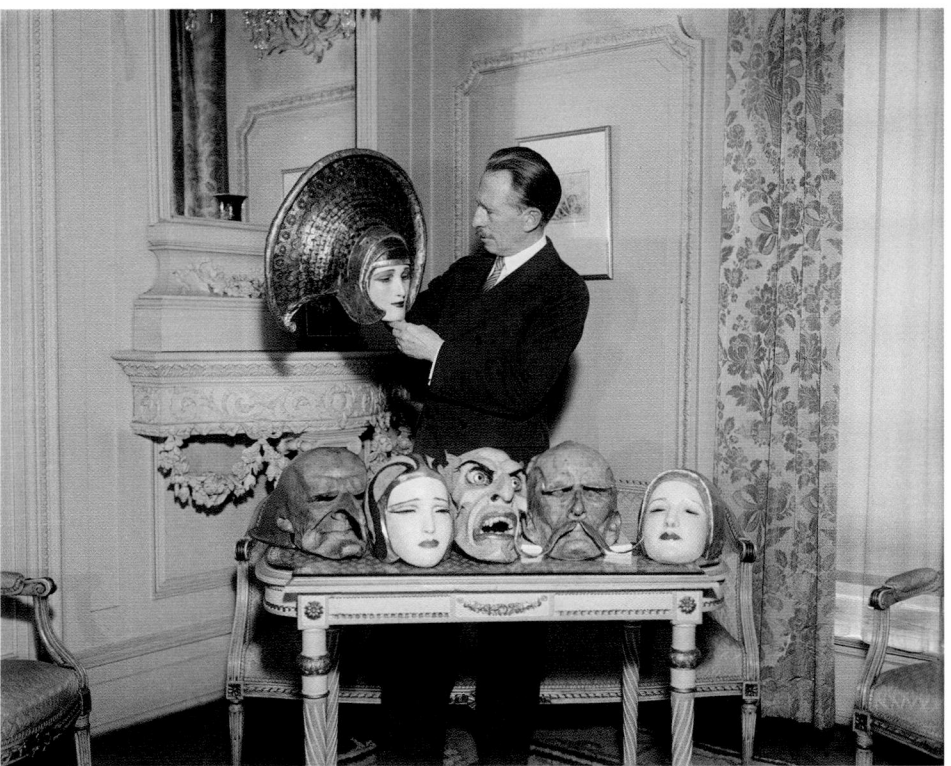

Figure 4.2. Harris & Ewing,
Polish Artist Władysław T. Benda with His Masks, 1931, Library of Congress.

campaigns inspired generations of the region's soldiers, transitioning from a purely historical group into a folkloric national symbol. Instantly recognizable, the Winged Hussars are frequently indexed in art with large, feathered wings mounted to either the back of their body armor or their mount's saddle (Fig. 4.3). Other typical features include a Hungarian-style breastplate, a kopia lance, a saber or broadsword, and a distinctive Ottoman-style helmet, typified by long face guards and a rounded top with a point. English-language sources often describe the helmet as a lobster-tail burgonet, or visored helmet.[8]

The soldiers' most striking feature, the wings, were a real part of the mounted unit's standard battle armor. They did not serve a practical purpose, but instead intimidated the enemy as the mounted force charged onto the battlefield. Often made from large bird feathers, the wings quickly became an iconic feature of their armor. While there are certain typical features in the images of the Winged Hussars, they are depicted with a range of details to their armor and weapons depending on the time period and event portrayed. Despite this mutable quality, these details almost always take inspiration from Ottoman or Turkish design, often found in the helmet or hat design, clothing, horse tack, or armor. Although the exact origin of such design is unknown, it is likely related to the public perceptions of the strength of the Ottoman military.[9] The Hussars gained notoriety during a time rife with Orientalist fascination in the region. This included an interest in the long, successful military history of the Ottoman Empire, feeding the public imagination around a new, impressive Polish-Lithuanian armed cavalry unit.

The Hussars were established in the early sixteenth century and remained active for more than one hundred years, fighting for the Polish-Lithuanian Commonwealth in a remarkable number of conflicts. Perhaps most well known for turning the tide during the Siege of Vienna in 1683, the Winged Hussars proved effective against skilled military forces until their disbandment in 1776.[10] Despite the Turkish influences in their helmets, their success against the Ottoman Empire's armies was lauded by poets and folklorists. The combination of their genuine skill and their fantastical armor choices created a public interest in and adoration of the Winged Hussars, building a popular culture concept that quickly joined the ranks of Polish folklore.

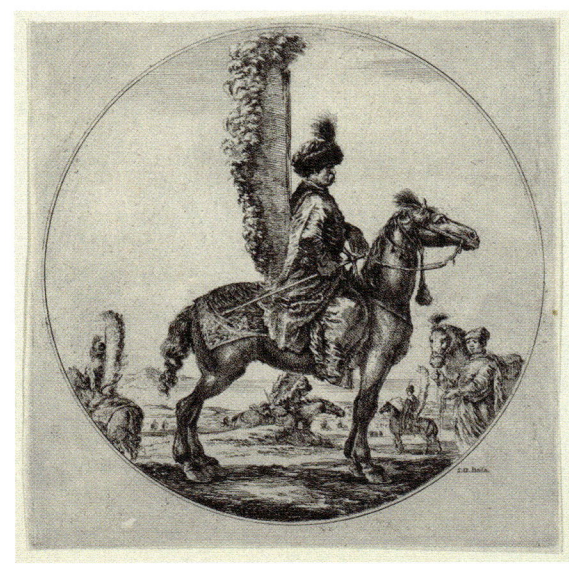

WŁADYSŁAW BENDA

FIGURE 4.3. Stephano della Bella, *Polish Hussar in profile facing right with wings attached to his back, a circular composition*, from *"Figures on Horseback"* (*Cavaliers nègres, polonais et hongrois*), c. 1648–53, Metropolitan Museum of Art.

While the unit did not exist in twentieth-century warfare, they became a mainstay of Polish nationalist imagery, often associated with calls for military support and victory. Usually, the Winged Hussars are depicted in their prime, rather than skeletal as they are seen in Benda's work. As a direct reference to death, the inclusion of the morbid, skeletal warriors in *The Army of the Dead* calls to something beyond the nationalist rhetoric of the Winged Hussars' military might, perhaps examining the increasingly pressing horrors of the battlefield, the center of the devastation of World War I. While the Winged Hussars were commonly associated with wartime nationalism, their skeletal bodies offer insight into the anxieties and fears associated with total warfare.

Benda was no stranger to the war from abroad. He regularly drew propaganda of a variety of types for the American Committee on Public Information (CPI) and the Polish Military Commission, while also producing films and other media as a form of aid.[11] In the United States, World War I yielded a significant increase in government-funded propaganda aimed toward aiding the war effort, both at home and abroad. Many prominent illustrators lent their talents to promoting food rationing, war bond purchases, and nationalist ideologies. Although founded in 1917, after Benda created *The Army of the Dead*, the Division of Pictorial Publicity (DPP), a subdivision of the CPI run by renowned illustrator Charles Dana Gibson, focused specifically on poster and illustrated print propaganda.[12] Like many other members of the Society of Illustrators, Benda worked through this committee to produce patriotic material. The work of the DPP was considered a success, both as a nationalist support during the war and as an artistic exploration of American visual culture and iconography.

In addition to the United States, many countries relied on poster propaganda during this period, lending visibility to national war machines. While prominent visual campaigns emerged across Europe, the lack of a centralized Polish government resulted in a corresponding lack of nationalized propaganda. However, there were a number of well-known artists who did create war-related art that gave voice to individual fears and frustrations, including Józef Mehoffer, Wojciech Weiss, and Stanisław Wyspiański. Despite the violent intensity of life in the region, the Young Poland (Młoda Polska) movement gained momentum during this period, reimagining popular European art movements such as Art Nouveau with distinctly Polish design elements, symbols, and themes.[13] With the term "Young Poland" appearing in 1898 in conjunction with a major exhibition of Polish illustration, Benda would have felt the rise toward this unified movement without witnessing its manifestation before his emigration. However, during his time in Krakow, he would have encountered the work of the movement's leaders, potentially including the artists mentioned above, as well as Władysław Podkowiński, Olga Boznańska, Jacek Malczewski, and Teodor Axentowicz. During the Interwar period, this movement contributed to a strong nationalist poster and propaganda tradition, fueled by increasing tensions between Bolsheviks and the Polish state during the buildup to the Polish-Soviet War of 1919 to 1921.

While much of Benda's work was designed to promote American military interests, many themes and motifs from Polish propaganda appeared in his work, including the Winged Hussars, often captured riding out into battle. Although they are rarely shown flying in other media, Benda depicted them in flight at least once, comparing them to airplanes, a key tool in the development of twentieth-century warfare. Seen in Fig. 4.4 from the Smithsonian's National Air and Space Museum, the flight of the Hussar is accompanied by the caption, "Poland's Warriors of the Air. Like Knights of Old, Defend the Freedom of the World." By referencing the legend of the famed Winged Hussars, this image unites historical and contemporary ideas under the guise of a fantastical flight, creating a compelling and contextually rich war relief poster.

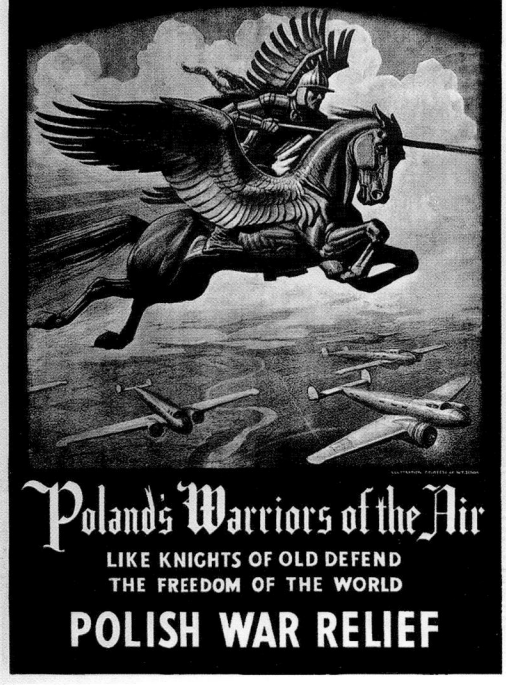

Fantasy images and folklore figures appear occasionally in wartime posters, often calling on popular histories and shared beliefs to motivate relevant efforts. In a similar approach, wartime posters from England frequently featured Saint George slaying the dragon as in Christian legend as an example of bravery in hopeless situations, and French and American propaganda occasionally depicted Joan of Arc to suggest the need for self-sacrifice during times of struggle. Such popular images can be rooted in history or entirely fictional, but they retain the very real power of public recognition, using heroic figures to encourage support for ongoing military campaigns. Calling on shared stories about legendary figures like the Winged Hussars remained a useful tactic for Benda and others who intended to create powerful wartime propaganda.

Despite Benda's frequent contributions to pro-military publications and posters, *The Army of the Dead* was not used in his most significant propaganda posters.[14] However, a somewhat similar drawing did enter production,

FIGURE 4.4. Władysław T. Benda (Polish, 1873–1948), *Poland's Warriors of the Air*, c. 1917, Smithsonian National Air and Space Museum.

retaining the imagery of the mounted cavalry without the skeletal forms.[15] The altered version produces a vastly different effect, using the more traditional symbolic imagery of the Winged Hussars rather than employing the morbid effect of the sketched version. While compelling, this image lacks the imaginative quality of the drawing in the Korshak Collection. Given the existence of an alternative version, it is worth considering why Benda chose to depict the Hussars as skeletal warriors in *The Army of the Dead*. Ultimately, the skeletal hussars never appeared in broad publication, and Benda's wartime work focused on his more typical romantic images of Polish people, and the occasional depiction of the Winged Hussars as a cultural reference (Fig. 4.5).

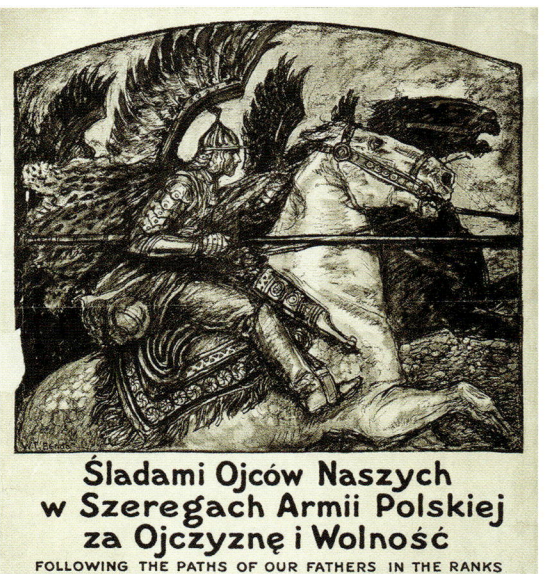

Although some of Benda's other work features fanciful clothing or costumes, there is little evidence that he made other pieces with similar darkly imaginative themes. Yet, while most of Benda's propaganda work is deeply couched in nationalist pride, *The Army of the Dead* nods toward a more complex set of emotions, tinged with the horror and fear of warfare.

As suggested earlier, the skeletons in the image may simply reflect the massive loss of life experienced during this time period in the Polish region. Modern estimates place the death toll around 450,000 Poles during World War I, with far more injured during the fighting.[16] Especially from afar, this may have provoked a more morbid outlook for Benda, leading to the choice to opt for a darker imagining of the war. However, armies of the dead are not an uncommon theme in literature and art history, from Norse and Teutonic mythology through twelfth-century folklore in medieval Europe. Often drawn from disquieted souls, the idea of an ancient army of dead soldiers pervades cautionary historical tales in Europe. Rarely viewed as a source of heroic rescue, these revenant hordes tend to lend themselves to discussions of morality, the Christian afterlife, and harrowing retellings of historical events, often serving as a reminder of the potential for eternal punishment that awaits in the afterlife.[17]

The icon of the army of the dead has phased in and out of popularity over time, but there are other examples of it associated with the horrors of twentieth-century warfare, including, most famously, the arrival of a heroic army of the dead in the final volume of J.R.R. Tolkien's *Lord of the Rings* trilogy. The depiction of death has changed immensely in response to the changing types of warfare.

Figure 4.5. Władysław T. Benda (Polish, 1873–1948), *Following the paths of our fathers in the ranks of the Polish army for motherland and freedom*, c. 1914–18. Library of Congress.

Relevant to the time period of Benda's work, the Battle of Osowiec Fortress occurred in the Polish region in 1915. Infamously, German forces used a deadly concoction of gas as a weapon against Russian combatants. Benda would have encountered images of mutilated, death-like forces during this battle, which was often termed the "Attack of the Dead Men."[18] Many artists tackled this topic, often calling up deeply disturbing images of the incident and others like it.

Benda was no exception, falling in with a number of artists whose work changed as they processed the haunting toll of total warfare, including the introduction of flight and aerial bombing as widespread military tactics. These new realities brought about new fears and new cultural imagery that shifted the visual concept of war. Perhaps the clear invocation of the past, both through the use of Winged Hussar imagery and the literal interpretation of the risen dead, was a call to the ancestors, an attempt to bring their military success and famed bravery to bear on the unimaginable atrocities of early twentieth-century warfare.

In contrast to the clean, beautifully rendered images of finished propaganda posters, Benda's *The Army of the Dead* relies on the emotional tension of raspy charcoal lines and rough shading to communicate a less idealized version of the Great War. While Benda's pride in his birthplace explains his interest in creating war relief posters, there are elements of his drawing that reach toward a more macabre expression of his feelings about the conflict. Benda created a sizable canon of pro-Polish imagery in which he primarily focused on images of women and children, or of contemporary Polish soldiers, rather than mythologized combatants. However, despite the disbandment of the Winged Hussars more than two hundred years prior to World War I, they came back into fashion as a symbolic element, allowing for their legendary quality to inspire a new generation of soldiers during a traumatic war. The introduction of aerial battles and bombing campaigns called for the soaring figure of a mounted winged warrior coming to protect the interests of the land.

While fantasy illustrations often serve to explore the varied realms of human imagination, they also represent the tangible world around the artist. Embedded in swirls of charcoal, the hopes and fears of one Polish American artist took form, giving voice to the complex feelings and harsh realities facing many during the World War I period. By invoking these "Knights of Old," Benda gave his audience a familiar icon, grounded in the beliefs and traditions of the Polish people, and capable of inspiring a critical, contemporary call-to-arms.

WŁADYSŁAW BENDA

1. Mark B. Pohlad, "The Man Behind the Masks: W. T. Benda," *Illustration Magazine*, no. 13 (Spring 2005): 4–35.

2. Władysława Jaworska, *Polish Masters from the Kosciuszko Foundation Collection* (New York: The Foundation, 1995).

3. Pohlad, "The Man Behind the Masks."

4. Walt Reed, *The Illustrator in America*: *1860–2000*, 3rd ed., The Society of Illustrators (New York: Hearst Books International, 2001).

5. Much like the exaggerated quality typical of Mannerist artists, Benda relied on elongated proportions, asymmetrical compositions, and intricate details to communicate a sense of dramatic tension in his work. Irena Piotrowska, "Benda Masks and Their Ancestors," *The Polish Review* 3, no. 1/2 (1946): 39–41.

6. Omer Bartov, *Tales from the Borderlands: Making and Unmaking the Galician Past* (New Haven, CT: Yale University Press, 2022).

7. M.B. Biskupski, *The History of Poland* (Westport, CT: Greenwood Press, 2000).

8. Richard Brzezinski and V. Vukšić, *Polish Winged Hussar, 1576–1775*, Warrior 94 (Oxford: Osprey, 2006).

9. Jan K. Ostrowski, ed., *Art in Poland, 1572–1764: Land of the Winged Horsemen* (Alexandria, VA: Art Services International, 1999).

10. Paul Hulsenboom, "A Hero and His History: The Branding of Jan III Sobieski and His Letters in the Northern Netherlands during the Early Nineteenth Century," in *Branding Books Across the Ages: Strategies and Key Concepts in Literary Branding,* ed. Helleke Van Den Braber, et al. (Amsterdam: Amsterdam University Press, 2021), 83–108.

11. Joseph T. Hapak, "Film in the Service of Polish Independence," *Polish American Studies* 44, no. 1 (1987): 25–37.

12. Eric Van Schaack, "The Division of Pictorial Publicity in World War I," *Design Issues* 22, no. 1 (Winter 2006): 32–45.

13. David Crowley, *National Style and Nation-State: Design in Poland from the Vernacular Revival to the International Style* (New York: Manchester University Press, 1992).

14. Although difficult to definitively prove that the image was not circulated, the Korshak Collection claims this within the original entry for the artwork in their object description. Additionally, it does not appear in any of the collections of Benda's posters accessible to the public.

15. Władysław T. Benda, *Following the paths of our fathers in the ranks of the Polish army for motherland and freedom,* 1917, Library of Congress, 2002708898.

16. Robert Bideleux and Ian Jeffries, *A History of Eastern Europe: Crisis and Change* (London: Routledge, 1998).

17. Nancy Mandeville Caciola, *Afterlives: The Return of the Dead in the Middle Ages* (Ithaca, NY: Cornell University Press, 2017).

18. Alexander A. Cherkasov, Alexander A. Ryabtsev, and Vyacheslav I. Menjkovsky, "'Dead Men Attack' (Osovets, 1915): Archive Sources Approach," *European Researcher* Series A.2, no. 12 (December 2011): 1577–82.

Lauren Stump

JOSÉ SEGRELLES: The Spanish Master
of Mystical and Fantastical Illustration

*Segrelles journeyed in the innermost recesses of his soul and returned
to enrich our all too prosaic lives with a bouquet of inspired imagery—
exotic blossoms plucked from The Tree of Dreams.*

—*Barry Klugerman,* Introducing José Segrelles *(1999)*[1]

Valencian artist José Segrelles (1885–1969) contributed significantly to the genre of fantasy illustration, although these contributions have remained largely unexplored in modern surveys of the genre. His artwork was an expression of various connections between artistic tradition and technological innovation, between the Old World and the New, and between the world we inhabit and the imagined worlds of stories and dreams. In his prolific career as an illustrator, Segrelles's work embraced a broad spectrum of largely narrative themes in which he experimented with unorthodox perspectives and theatrical lighting effects. This work was unapparelled in its ability to incite suspense and drama, bringing a sense of otherworldliness to familiar stories. Executed with brilliant respect for the luminosity available to watercolor, Segrelles's paintings once captivated readers in Europe and the United States. Unfortunately, though, his influence on the fantasy genre is underrepresented given his lack of exposure in contemporary circles outside of his native Spain.

Born in the small town of Albaida, Spain, in 1885, the third of twelve children, Segrelles spent his youth in a traditional Spanish setting centered upon the community of the church in which his father ministered.[2] He took to both artistic and musical expression with great conviction, both drawings of his own making and music being the constant background in his childhood home. Segrelles showed an impressive aptitude for the arts before the age of ten and was sent to Valencia for formal artistic education at the San Carlos School of Fine Arts. There, he received lessons from Joaquín Sorolla, a celebrated Spanish Luminist and Impressionist, whose work left a formative impression on the artist's own. Like Sorolla, also an artistic prodigy,

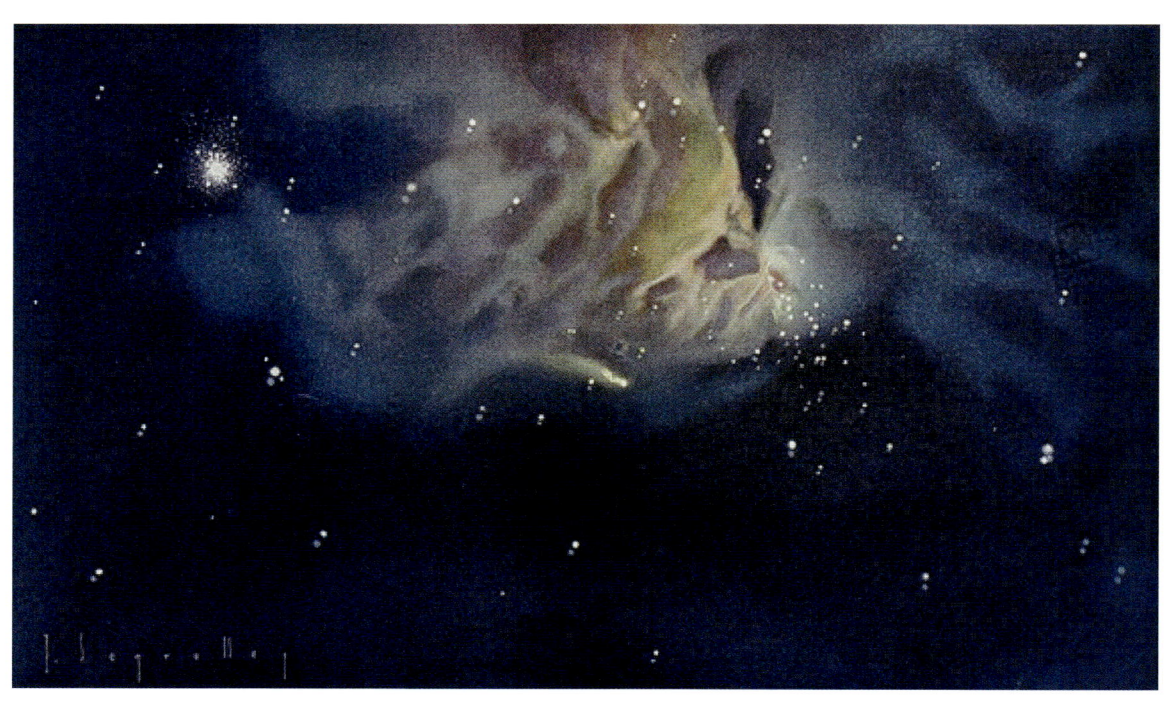

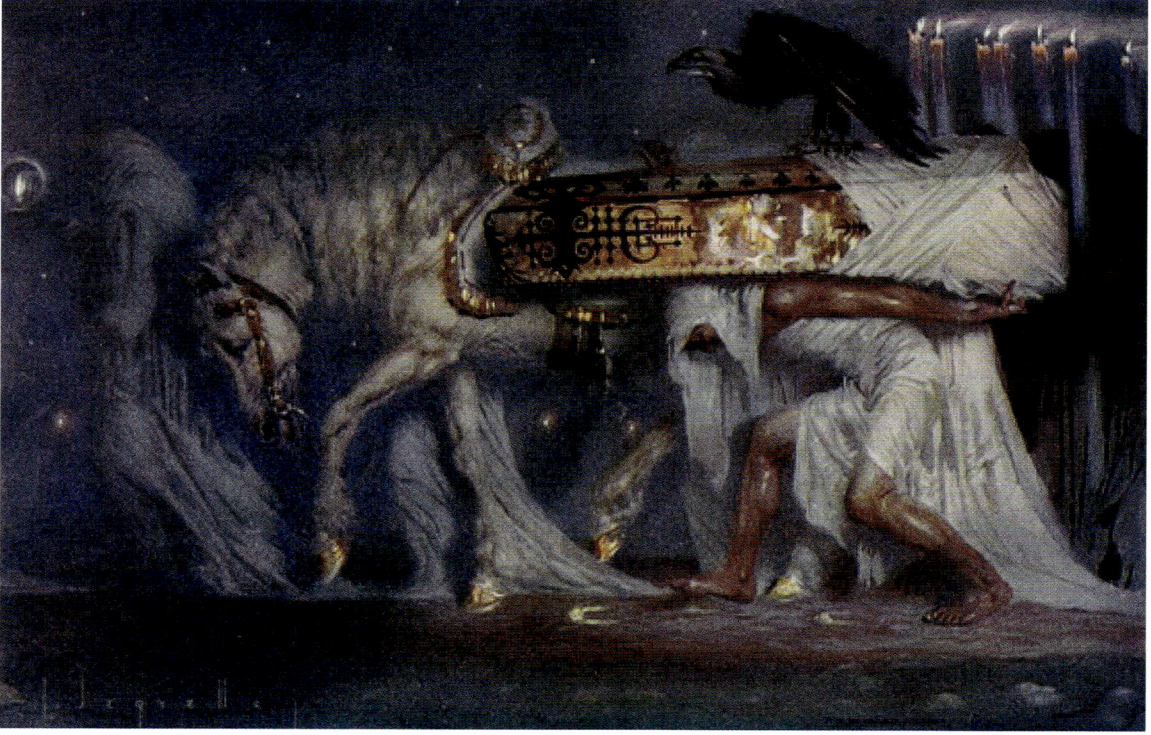

Figure 5.1 (both). José Segrelles (Spanish, 1885–1969), illustrations for Beethoven's music for *Illustrated London News*, 1927, *J. Segrelles Illustrador Universal*, 2010, ed. Institut d'Estudis de la Vall d' Albaida, p. 37, Casa Museu José Segrelles, Albaida, Valencia, Spain.

Segrelles utilized stark contrasts of light and dark as an expressive mechanism in his paintings.

Music would resurface throughout Segrelles's artistic career, specifically classical compositions by Wagner, Chopin, and Beethoven that were the consistent themes of his illustrations for *The Illustrated London News* in the 1930s (Fig. 5.1). His depictions of Beethoven's sonatas range from interpreting the literal music to representing its lyrical feel. For example, Segrelles translated Beethoven's *Sonata in F Minor (Op. 57)*, known as "Appassionata," as the birth of a celestial star in the vastness of a blue spatial field. The Korshak Collection features a musically inspired watercolor, *Chopin in the Charterhouse* (1933, Plate 45), depicting Polish composer Frédéric Chopin and his lover, French novelist George Sand. In the scene, Chopin is seated at the piano, his music wafting from the instrument in the form of ghostly muses.

Following the painful loss of his brother Vincente in 1902, Segrelles returned to Albaida. This would be the first of many cyclical returns there throughout the artist's life. His devout love and attachment to his family also characterized the artist's proclivity to return home and was a sustained source of inspiration for his artwork. Segrelles used his siblings as models for his paintings, and the architecture of his sleepy Spanish village resurfaces throughout his illustrations for *Don Quixote*. Detailed renderings of classical Spanish architecture such as archways, interiors, and ruins that appear as locations or backgrounds for his illustrations are not surprising, as they recall a love and longing for Albaida and its surrounding landscape.

In 1904, Segrelles continued his artistic studies in Barcelona, arriving there in a period of modernization, mechanization, and increasing European influence on the Spanish Peninsula. A chance encounter in a Barcelonian bookstore with the illustrations of Gustave Doré for the French publication of *Don Quixote* lead to the completion of his first large-scale oil painting on this theme. Although not exceeding Doré's contributions to the Cervantes story, Segrelles's illustrations of the Espasa-Calpe edition were colorful transfigurations of Doré's whimsical and movement-filled compositions.

In Barcelona, he was hired by the Photo Studio Napoleón under the tutelage of Santiago Feliú Fernández. The activity of the studio was adapted to technological advancements in photography including the emerging medium of silent film. Segrelles's role at the studio included coloring photographic stills and film reels with watercolor paint and serving as a sound effects actor during the screening of otherwise silent films. The borders between commissioned work/advertising film and autonomous art became more permeable and less defined in avant-garde cinema in this period. Film lighting techniques utilizing artificial light sources, such as diffusion, three-point lighting, and low-key effects creating stark contrasts between black and white, were already known to the young Luminist painter. Segrelles's highly effective use of light itself as an emotive and expressive influence can be traced to the backlit reels of a dark theater where techniques such as chiaroscuro, tonal modulations, and spatial recession were continuously practiced and refined. His unique work experience combined with early impressions from Sorolla's tutelage instilled a cinematographic quality in Segrelles's paintings unlike the monochromatic line work of some European illustrators from this period and the two-dimensional quality of their output. First, film impressed itself on Segrelles's artistic vision and, later, that vision influenced filmmakers. This is substantiated in the praise and admiration for Segrelles expressed by contemporary filmmakers and creators William Stout, John Howe, and Guillermo del Toro, all of whom made pilgrimages to the artist's studio in Albaida, with del Toro acknowledging Segrelles's direct impact on his vision of Pan in his film *Pan's Labyrinth*.[3]

Following his graduation from Higher School of Arts at Casa Lonja in 1910, Segrelles was hired by Spanish publishing agent Don Ramón Molinas as a cartoonist for the first children's newspapers, or "comics," in Spain. In this endeavor, Segrelles created the characters "Dick Navarro, the Terror of the Prairies" and "Montbars, the Pirate," making playful and colorful graphics well suited for the amusement of children. His proclivity for producing such whimsical illustrations was perhaps an extension of his role as older brother to his younger siblings. His work for Molinas gained him attention with other commercial publishers, and while maintaining employment at Studio Napoleón, Segrelles contributed illustrations for Granada y Compaña Publishing House for the stories "Conan Doyle" and "The Adventures of Sherlock Holmes."

Segrelles left Studio Napoleón to formally pursue commercial publishing opportunities and was promptly employed as an artist for Araluce Publishing House. He worked on a "Masterpieces Collection" for Araluce that included thirty-six small, abridged versions of classical literary titles such as *Cabeza de Vaca, The Knights of the Round Table, The Odyssey, Tom Thumb, History of Columbus, Tales of Mystery and Imagination, Julius Caesar, Uncle Tom's Cabin, Francisco de Goya, The Iliad, The Crusades*, and *Faust*, among others. Although his artwork for these popular stories did not cement his reputation as "The Illustrator" of any given their extremely limited circulation outside of Spain,

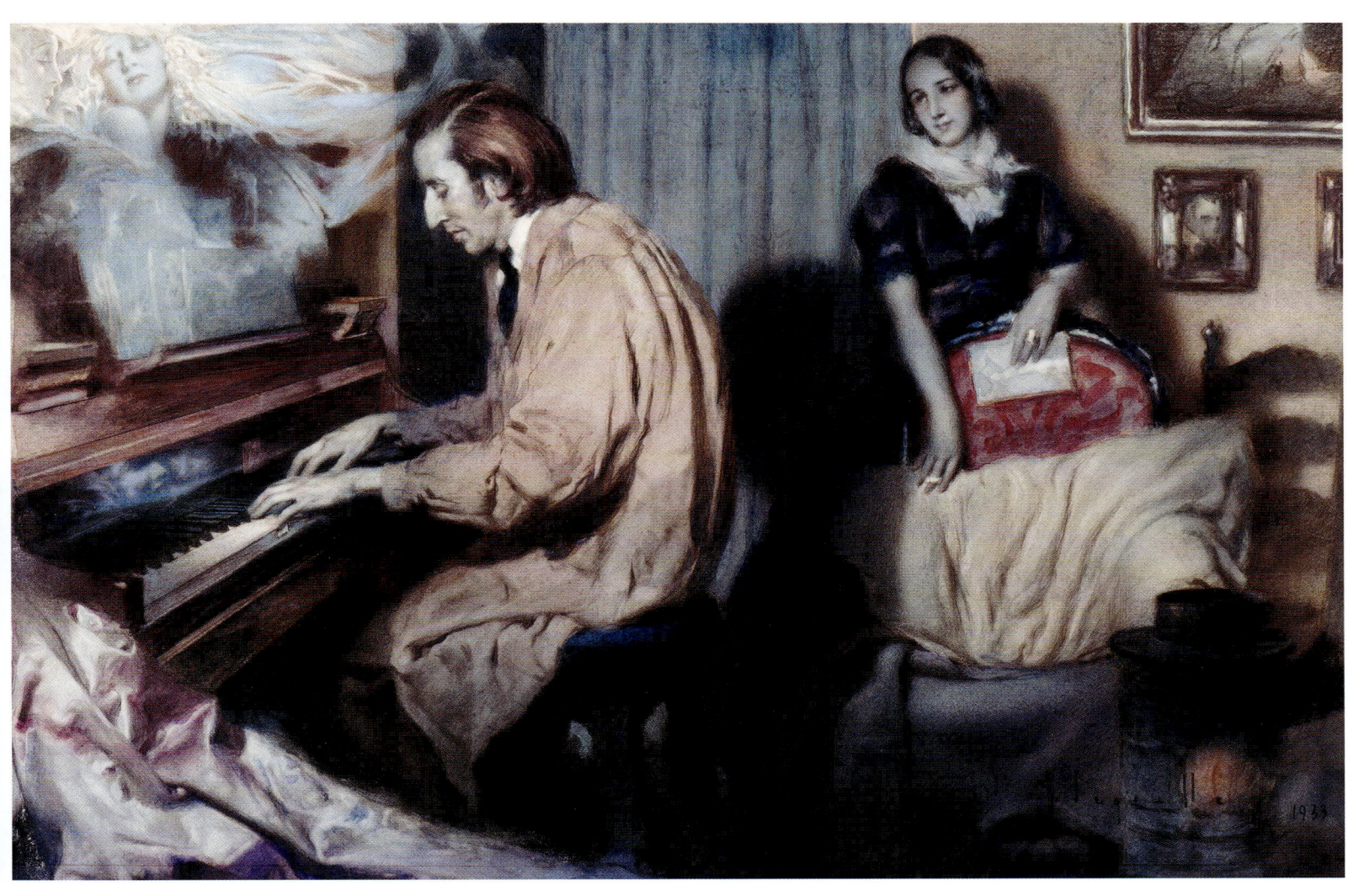

PLATE 45. José Segrelles (Spanish, 1885–1969), *Chopin in the Charterhouse*, 1933, watercolor, gouache, and pastel on paper, 11 × 17 inches, Casa Museu José Segrelles, Albaida, Valencia, Spain.

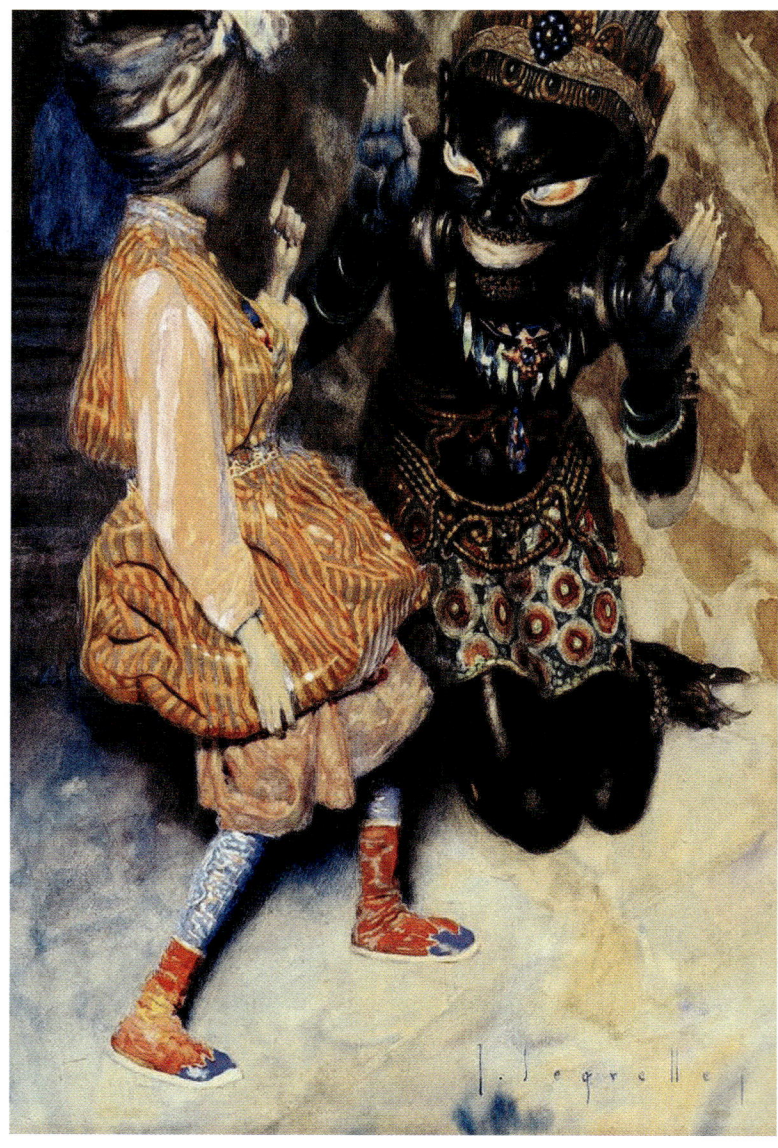

FIGURE 5.2. José Segrelles (Spanish, 1885–1969), "The Gold Bug" for *Tales of Mystery and Imagination*, *The Illustrated London News*, Christmas 1935, Casa Museu José Segrelles, Albaida, Valencia, Spain.

FIGURE 5.3. José Segrelles (Spanish, 1885–1969), ". . . a genius of terrifying appearance, who told him . . . ," illustration for *The Illustrated London News*, Christmas, 1930, Casa Museu José Segrelles, Albaida, Valencia, Spain.

his 1935 illustrations for Edgar Allan Poe's *Tales of Mystery and Imagination* are haunting and definitive images that would have gained him great favor had they been more widely distributed (Fig. 5.2).

Segrelles's career truly began to prosper in the 1920s, with various exhibitions of his work finding critical acclaim in the Spanish press. He was commissioned by advertising companies, submitted covers for Spanish magazines including *Joventut Catalana, Sports,* and *L'Esquella de la Torrata,* and produced posters for FC Barcelona, the Cycling Tour, the Real Aero Club, and the Catalan Motorcycle Club. He also submitted commissions for the Spanish government, the National Autodrome of Barcelona, and the Catalan Football Association Federation, while maintaining employment at the publishing houses Salvat and Seguí, and he received various private commissions, including one from the Vatican. This decade was arguably the most productive of Segrelles's career and one in which he produced increasingly mesmerizing fantasy works.

With the demand for his commercial work at an all-time high, and despite a relentless production schedule, Segrelles's personal artistic vision crystallized under pressure. His creative works from this period are characterized by elegantly rendered but bizarre, and often surreal, interpretations of his own nightmares and hallucinations. In 1922, Segrelles published his *Nightmare Series,* five watercolors inspired solely from such nightmares. He later produced elevated depictions of *The Seven Deadly Sins* (1925) and dream-like interpretations of the epic poem "La Atlántida" by Jacinto Verdaguer (1925; Fig. 5.3).

His well-received exhibitions throughout the 1920s caught the interest of author Blasco Ibáñez, with whom he went on to collaborate and maintain a lasting personal relationship. Segrelles was hired to complete nearly 120 oil, gouache, and watercolor submissions for Ibañez's novels *The Dead Mandan, The Intruder, The Cathedral,* and *Flor de Mayo.* As these commissions continued, Segrelles's fantasy work became more refined, more imaginative, and more recognizably "Segrelles." Thirty-six of these fantasy works were later exhibited in Madrid in 1923 at the Valencian Art Exhibition, where they were discovered by brothers Francisco and Ricardo Verdugo Landi, managers of La Prensa Gráfica. Through his relationship with the brothers, Segrelles would contribute to the European periodicals *New World, Graphic World, Las Elegancias,* and *The Sphere.* The distribution of these periodicals, particularly *The Sphere,* outside of Spain ultimately led to Segrelles's employment in England and the United States.

His illustrations first appeared outside of Spain in 1927 in *The Illustrated London News* Christmas issue, the most widely distributed issue of the popular periodical. Additional commissions ensued, including eleven interpretations of Beethoven's Fifth Symphony (1927), Dante's *Divine Comedy* (1928), *El Ingenioso Hidalgo Don Quixote de la Mancha* (1929), and *One Thousand and One Nights* (1930), among others. His illustrations for *The Illustrated London News*'s sister publication *The Sketch,* including various illustrations for H.G. Wells's *The War of the Worlds*, one of which can be seen in the Korshak Collection, brought Segrelles to the attention of American publishers. Unlike earlier interpretations of Wells's Martian invaders, depicted as if they were mobilized water towers, Segrelles's illustrations presented the tripod Martians as celestial beings, jellyfish-like creatures with large, curious eyes (Plate 46).

Segrelles's reluctant forays to New York took place between 1929 and 1932. His first submissions in the United States were limited to commercial work for *Redbook,* the New York cityscape *Metropolis* he created for the magazine in 1930 being a fine example of his evocative work that landed him additional contracts with *Cosmopolitan* and Packard Motors. These lucrative contracts drew Segrelles to return to New York annually in pursuit of commissions that would provide sustained financial stability, but for which his style was perhaps not best suited. His success led to contracts with *Good Housekeeping, Literary Digest, Fortune, The Spur,* and *American Magazine*. His illustrations in these years took on a luxurious blue palette that permeated his work through 1935 and distinguished him from American illustrators of the same period.

On April 15, 1931, Segrelles inaugurated, with notable success, his only exhibition in the United States, hosted by the Roerich Museum in New York City. The exhibition included a total of fifty-four watercolors depicting Don Quixote's escapades, *The Divine Comedy,* Beethoven's Ninth Symphony, and *One Thousand and One Nights*.[4] In the following Sunday's review in *The New York Times,* Segrelles's work was described as "a little resembling that of our own Maxfield Parrish but is more complex and generally subtler. Often the color is rich and clear, imaginatively adapted to the requirements of the design."[5] Other inadequate comparisons to illustrators of the period surfaced, including suggested relationships to the works of Arthur Rackham and Edmund Dulac.

Living in New York City, even on the temporary basis his visas allowed, was a struggle for the artist, who wrote longingly of his native Spain and his distaste for American cultural excesses.[6] Following his commercial success in the United States, Segrelles's reputation continued to grow, but his commercial

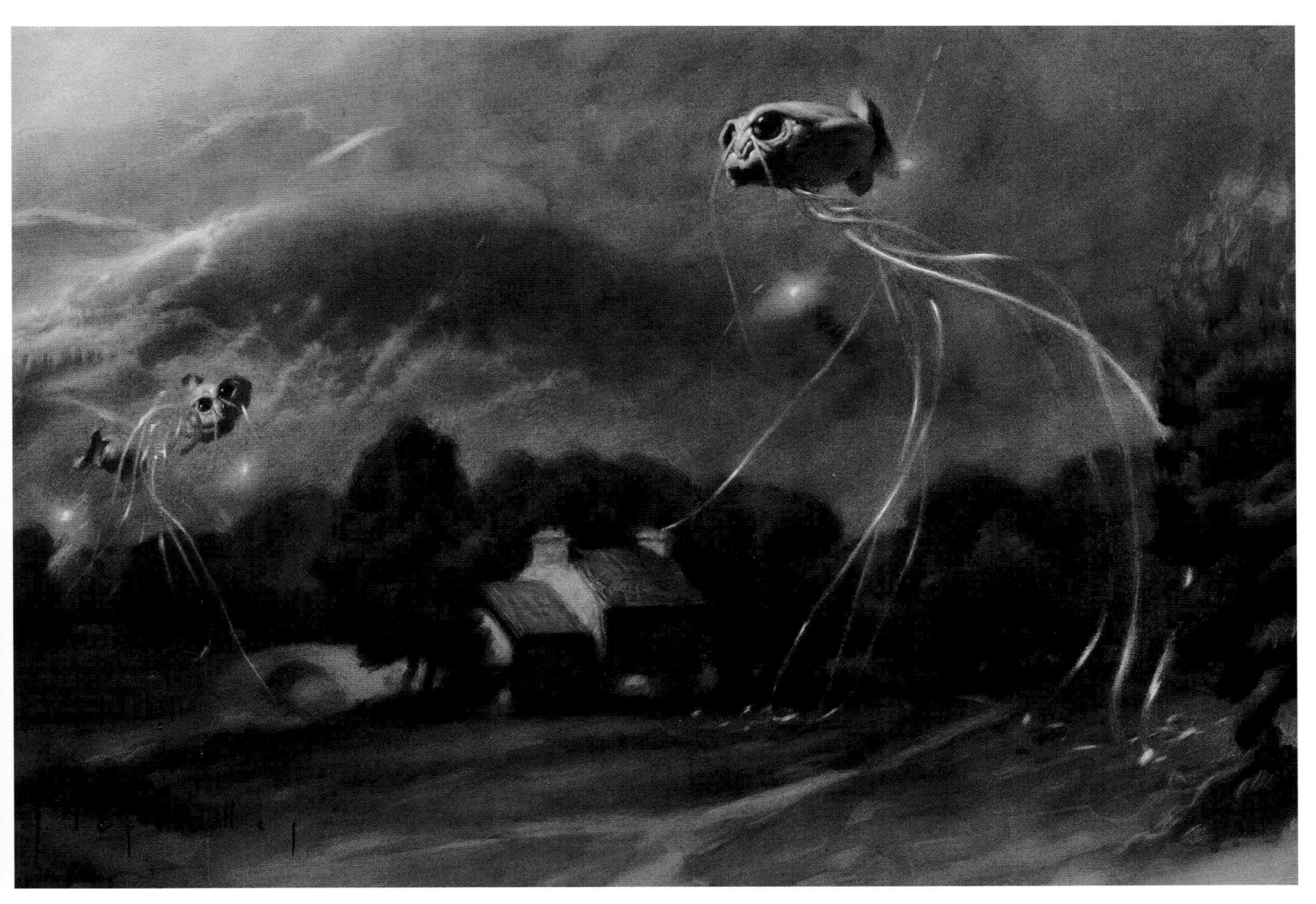

PLATE 46. José Segrelles (Spanish, 1885–
1965), *War of the Worlds*, c. 1930,
mixed media, 11 × 16 inches, Casa Museu
José Segrelles, Albaida, Valencia, Spain.

output cooled as he accepted teaching positions at the School of Valencia and the Royal Academy of San Carlos and began construction on the elaborate architectural vision that would become his home in Albaida. He labored over each minute detail of the house, which included an astronomical observatory, various libraries, elaborate archways and stairwells, an artist's studio, and themed interiors that now house a generous body of Segrelles's artwork.

This later period of the artist's formal career was characterized by his return to religious subjects for commissioned reproductions of religious artwork lost during the Spanish Civil War, and autonomous output on the themes of human and celestial bodies. Known as his Sidereal Period, Segrelles's fascination with astronomy led to an exciting body of work depicting lunar surfaces and the nebulous forms of outer space. Equally fascinating are the artist's interpretations of the interior of the human body (created circa 1958) in which the artist depicts arterial valves and ligaments as spatial landscapes.

Illustrator Roy Krenkel's discovery of Segrelles's work in the 1950s was probably the greatest factor in inspiring appreciation among modern American illustrators for Segrelles's artistic achievements in the fantasy genre. Krenkel, a gifted illustrator and passionate illustration historian, introduced Segrelles to artists Frank Frazetta and Al Williamson. Frazetta was impressed by Segrelles's illustrative works, commenting that Segrelles was the only artist that he was in awe of. Williamson shared a significant number of Segrelles's paintings with up-and-coming illustrators William Stout, Bernie Wrightson, and Michael Kaluta (Plate 37), among others. In this way, the Spanish artist's influence on contemporary illustration crept slowly into the modern creative consciousness but remained largely unexplored.

José Segrelles was a prolific artist of exceptional imagination and creative brilliance. Though widely acclaimed in his native Spain, his work unfortunately failed to gain wider international attention outside of very brief forays into European and American markets in the late 1920s and early '30s. Although his images were rediscovered and circulated via photographic stills among a small group of American artists in the latter half of the twentieth century, a general lack of awareness of Segrelles's captivating illustrative style severely limited the influence of his dynamic techniques on the broader American illustration genre. By presenting his work alongside artists more widely acknowledged for their artistic contributions to the field of fantasy illustration, the Korshak Collection posits Segrelles as a true master of the fantastic and encourages contemporary audiences to discover, explore, and reflect on the exceptional quality of his artistic visions.

1. Barry Klugerman, "Introducing José Segrelles," *Epic Magazine* (1985). I would like to thank Barry Klugerman for providing some research materials utilized for this article. His vast knowledge of the illustration genre and his appreciation for the artwork of Jose Segrelles cannot be overstated.

2. Vicente Gurrea Crespo, *Segrelles: José Gabriel Segrelles Albert (1885–1969) Biografía* (Valencia: Ediciones Marí Montañana, 1985). *Biografia* is the main reference for this essay, outlining the artist's education, exhibitions, travel, etc. This book was translated to English in collaboration with research assistant Sofia Oviedo in winter of 2023, but that translation was not published.

3. Joan Josep Soler Navarro, "The Influence of Segrelles on Current Art," *Synergies: Visual Art CV*, March 18, 2021, https://www.visualartcv.com/la-influencia-de-segrelles-en-el-arte-actual/; Soler Navarro and Juan Josep, "The Influence of Segrelles in Present-Day Art," in *Segrelles: The Labyrinth of Fantasy* (Spain: Gráficas Vernetta, 2015), 34–35.

4. *Exhibition of Paintings by José Segrelles, Under the Patronage of His Excellency, the Ambassador of Spain, Don Alejandro Padilla y Bell and Señora de Padilla* [exhibition pamphlet], International Art Center of Roerich Museum in cooperation with Roerich Colombian Cultural Association, New York, April 15–29, 1931.

5. Ruth Green Harris, "Seen in the Galleries: Some of the Current Exhibitions That Attract Attention as the Season Wanes," *The New York Times*, April 19, 1931, 136.

6. Gurrea Crespo, *Segrelles.*

Lisa Yaszek

MARGARET (JOHNSON) BRUNDAGE:
First Woman of Fantasy Art

Imagine it: one world where women defy the forces of cosmic horror that would terrorize them. Another where they are conduits of such horror, terrorizing men and other women alike. And yet another world where women are "sheroes" rescuing men in miserable straits. And still yet another world where they abandon humanity altogether to connect with weird gods and wild animals. All of this while impeccably coiffed, made-up, and dressed (or partially undressed) in glamorous Hollywood fashions.

Do these worlds sound familiar? They should—after all, they are the dreams that contemporary pop culture is made of, fueling everything from block-buster Hollywood horror films to award-winning fantastic feminist art. But more importantly, they are all worlds that were first visually dramatized by fantasy artist Margaret Brundage (1900–1976) in the 1930s and '40s. Brundage's groundbreaking artwork, produced largely over a thirteen-year period for the fantasy and horror pulp publication *Weird Tales*, catapulted that magazine to unprecedented levels of popularity—and notoriety. By filtering the techniques of commercial illustration and pinup art through the lens of radical race and gender politics, Brundage dramatized other people's stories while inserting her own perspectives on mythology, heroism, science, and futurism in ways still common to women's fantasy art today.

Born Margaret Hedda Johnson on December 9, 1900, in Chicago, Illinois, Brundage was raised by her mother and grandmother, both independent entrepreneurs and members of the female-led Christian Scientists, after her father passed away in 1908. Inspired by the women around her, Brundage pursued a career of her own from an early age. She was the editor of McKinley High School's newspaper and subsequently attended the Chicago Academy of Fine Arts, where she studied commercial art and fashion illustration. She sold drawings to local Chicago newspapers and worked at the Dill Pickle, a bohemian club frequented by artists, anarchists, and feminists including Studs Terkel, Emma Goldman, and Elizabeth Gurley Flynn. Here, she met and, in 1927, married house painter and radical activist Myron "Slim" Brundage, with whom she had one son, Kerlyn "Byrd" Brundage. Slim's drinking and womanizing made him a less-than-stable domestic partner, so Margaret's partially disabled mother moved in to help raise Byrd. The Brundages divorced amicably in 1939.

When the Great Depression reduced the demand for fashion illustration, Brundage pivoted to one of the few art markets that continued to flourish: that of the inexpensive, fiction-oriented pulp magazine. Chicago-based editor Farnsworth Wright was so impressed with Brundage's pastel illustrations that he immediately hired her to create six covers for *Oriental Stories* (later renamed *The Magic Carpet*) and then transferred her to the more popular *Weird Tales*. Between 1932 and 1945, Brundage produced sixty-six original covers for *Weird Tales* at the rate of ninety dollars per illustration (the equivalent of just over two thousand dollars today) and was the magazine's sole cover artist from June 1933 to August 1936. Like most of her male counterparts, she used her first initial and last name when signing paintings, but from the start, many readers suspected the artist was a woman—a fact Wright confirmed in October 1934 with the announcement that "M stands for Margaret."[1] Brundage earned the title "Queen of the Pulps" for her renderings of scantily clad women confronting or carrying out acts of near-cosmic horror.

Her pulp career wound down when *Weird Tales* moved to New York City— her fragile pastels were frequently smudged in transit from Chicago and the city's morality laws made it difficult to continue illustrating the themes that had catapulted the artist to fame. Once again, Brundage pivoted with the times, supporting her family with decorative painting and photo colorization. In the late 1940s and early '50s, she brought her passion for racial and sexual equality to the Chicago Black Arts movement, where she collaborated with artists such as Gwendolyn Brooks and served as president of the South Side Community Arts Center. Brundage continued to sell her paintings at art and craft fairs until her death from acute myocardial infarction on April 9, 1976.

Brundage may have been a pioneering female illustrator, but she was by no means alone. Rising literacy rates and new printing techniques made magazines the primary form of information and entertainment for Americans from the 1880s to the 1950s. Commercial artists were celebrities, and women were just as likely as men to become household names. Female illustrators including Rose O'Neill, Jesse Wilcox Smith, Anna Whelan Bates, and Clara Elsene Peck flourished in the first half of the twentieth century, producing romantic and domestic illustrations of women and children for women's magazines, children's books, and commercial household product advertisements alike.

Meanwhile, cartoonists Nell Brinkley and Ethel Plummer provided audiences with images of carefree, independent, and active modern women, whose frizzy hair and fashionable clothes paid homage to Mary Pickford and similar Hollywood icons.

Around the same time, Zoe Mozert, Joyce Ballantine, and Pearl Frush became leaders in the emerging field of pinup art. Like their male counterparts, Mozert, Ballantine, and Frush produced images of "wide-eyed, wholesome 'all-American girls'—who just happened to have voluptuous figures and tight, revealing clothes." However, they placed "less emphasis on breast size and legs," and clothed their subjects in swimsuits, nightgowns, and short-shorts outfits with low-heeled shoes rather than sexy black garters, stockings, and high heels.[2] Both male and female pinup artists often worked in pastels, which provided vibrant colors, could be manipulated to create both broad brushstrokes and fine lines, and involved minimal cleanup—all important qualities for illustrators on tight deadlines.

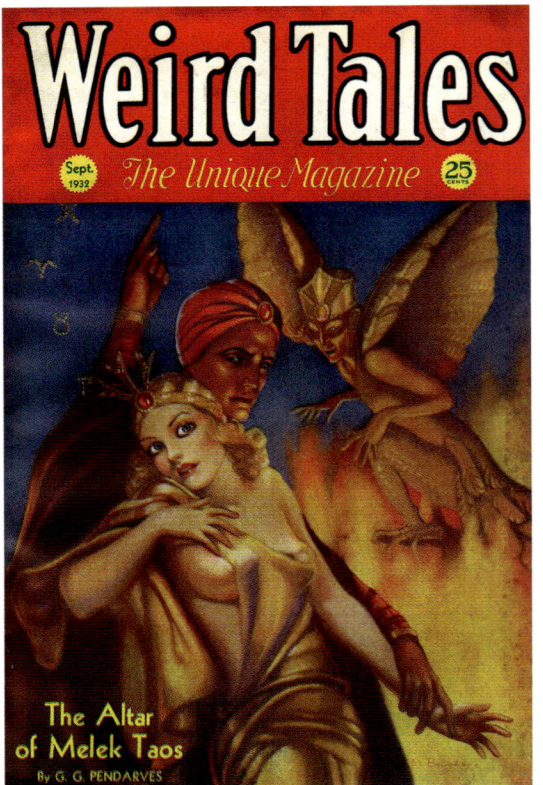

Other women found success in the cheaply produced speculative and spicy "pulp" magazines. Artists Nelly Littlehale Umbstaetter, Olivette Bourgeois, and Helen Higgins created most of the covers for the fantasy-oriented *The Black Cat* between 1901 and 1918. In the 1920s and '30s, commercial illustrators Doris Stanley and Lucille Holling brought their fashion and design sensibilities to horror and fantasy magazines such as *Ghost Stories* and *Oriental Stories*, while Irene Zimmermann produced pen-and-ink illustrations for spicy pulps *La Paree* and *Pep Stories*. Like their counterparts in the newspapers and slick magazines, women in the pulps typically created images of modern, active women, celebrating the female form through attention to textured clothing and hairstyles rather than traditional erotic signifiers.

This was certainly true of Brundage. Much like their Brinkley and Plummer counterparts, Brundage girls were always glamorous, fashionable, and active—whether that activity involved twisting away from the forces of evil, as in her September 1932 debut cover illustrating G.G. Pendarves's "The Altar of Melek Taos" (Fig. 6.1; Plate 4), or relishing their own cosmic power,

Figure 6.1. Margaret Brundage (American, 1900–1976), cover illustration for G.G. Pendarves's "The Altar of Melek Taos," *Weird Tales*, vol. 20, no. 3, Sept. 1932, Wikimedia Commons.

as in her January 1938 cover for Dorothy Quick's "The Witch's Mark" (Fig. 6.2; Plate 11) (these are the two pastels by Brundage found in the Korshak Collection). Brundage's use of pastels and fashionable if wispy clothing gave her female subjects, no matter how weird the circumstances were that they found themselves in, a sense of glamorous vivacity and freshness that echoed the work of Mozert and her peers. Finally, like pulp artist Zimmermann, Brundage refused to depict imperiled women in the classic passive, close-eyed, and prone manner common to much male-generated weird art. Instead, both created women who were wide-eyed and engaged with the world around them, even when they were lounging in baths or languishing on sacrificial altars.

Weird Tales editor Farnsworth Wright understood that brightly colored covers illustrating the sexiest scenes in each issue were key to capturing readers' interest in the middle of a crowded magazine stand. Brundage read carefully through each cover story and sketched out several versions of the scene she thought would be most dramatic; upon review, Wright "would always pick the one that showed a girl with the least amount of clothing."[3] While sexuality and sadism were present in the work of earlier *Weird Tales* artists including E.M. Stevenson, J. Allen St. John, and C.C. Senf, Brundage took Wright's preferences to a whole new level. In addition to bringing the conventions of modern fashion illustration and pinup art to her pulp magazine covers, she changed the way covers were composed. Earlier cover artists conveyed the other-worldliness of weird fiction by devoting attention to both the strange landscapes and the human forms within them, but Brundage channeled the emotional intensity of the genre by eliminating background details to better focus on the expressive faces and nearly naked bodies of her subjects.

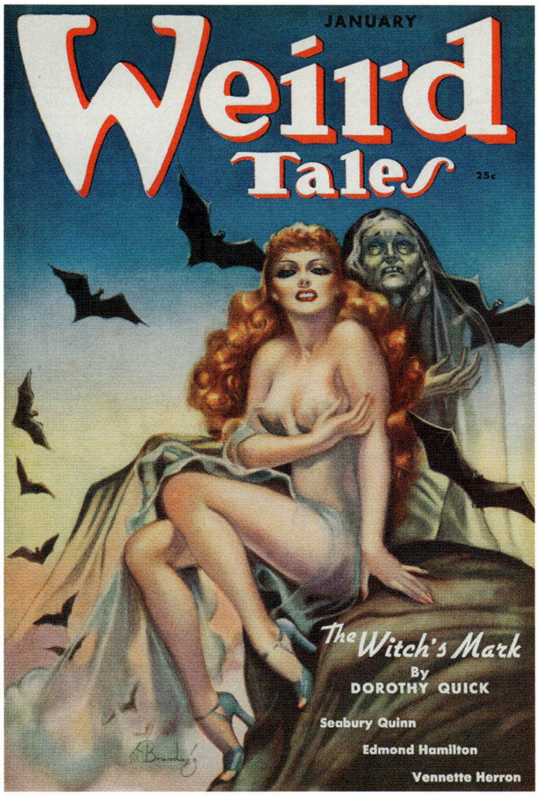

Brundage's art did indeed sell magazines—and it provoked lively debate within the pages of *Weird Tales*. During that period, 167 authors and fans wrote into "The Eyrie" letter column regarding her art. Over two-thirds (114) of their reviews were positive, twenty-nine were negative, and twenty-four were neutral. Nearly half (46.7 percent) of those who were critical admitted to enjoying Brundage's art, but thought it was not weird enough for the magazine. Others thought her images were too sexy for the stories they illustrated

FIGURE 6.2. Margaret Brundage (American, 1900–1976), cover illustration for Dorothy Quick's "The Witch's Mark," *Weird Tales*, vol. 31, no. 1, Jan. 1938, Wikimedia Commons.

(17.8 percent); disapproved of nudity in *Weird Tales* on principle (13.3 percent); had general complaints about Brundage's artistic ability (13.3 percent); or feared judgment by their peers for reading a magazine with suggestive art on the cover (8.9 percent). Wright's revelation that "M. Brundage" was a woman in the October 1934 issue did nothing to change readers' feelings about her work.[4]

While a few authors (led by H.P. Lovecraft and Clark Ashton-Smith, neither of whom ever received a Brundage cover treatment) dismissed the artist's "irrelevant nudes" as a calculated ploy on Wright's part "to attract two publics instead of one,"[5] most who lodged such criticism were fans. Author Jack Williamson championed Brundage's nudes as "masterpieces,"[6] and another author, Henry Kuttner, praised her cover illustrations as "beautifully done"[7] and, at their best, "embodying the spirit of the magazine excellently."[8] *Weird Tales*'s most popular female author, Elizabeth Counselman, concurred, noting that Wright was "very broadminded" about subjects that were "considered out-and-out taboos by other pulp magazines."[9]

The minority of fans who took issue with Brundage's work often appreciated its artistry but thought her nudes either "slightly out of proportion" or simply "out of place" in genre fiction.[10] Most, however, favored her work. Hazel Portelli called her September 1932 cover for "The Altar of Melek Taos" "beautiful and unusual," and Louis C. Smith concluded that, "I would have to write in rainbow colored ink to make my praise colorful enough" to truly honor the artist's accomplishments.[11] Dr. LeRoy C. Bashore thought Brundage's ability to make her heroines look "as if they were alive" was "magnificent," Elaine McIntire celebrated her nearly nude women as demonstrating "exquisite taste," and Mary Ashley called for even more, asking, "why not sandwich in a nude man on your covers once in a while?"[12]

Brundage's artwork was compelling in its time and remains so today because it complicates our culture's most dearly held beliefs about mythology, heroism, science, and futurism. Patriarchal folklore, mythology, and fantasy narratives have long revolved around "noble and brave knights [who] fought dragons and sorcerers, defended the poor and offended, [and] won the hearts of young beauties."[13] Since the late 1700s, however, women writers have created fantasy narratives of their own centered on avenging ancestresses, rebel princesses, and adventuring women. British author Ann Radcliffe pioneered this new mode of storytelling with her 1794 *The Mysteries of Udolpho,* written explicitly to counter the violent eroticism of male-authored gothic tales. This tradition continued through the 1800s with British fantasy poets Jean Ingelow, Julia Horatio Ewing, and Christina Rossetti, and by the opening decades of the twentieth century, feminist fantasy characters were central to works ranging from British modernist Virginia Woolf's *Orlando* (1928) to Swedish children's author Astrid Lindgren's *Pippi Longstocking* (1945). Even feminist-friendly men created new kinds of heroines for girls—most notably in American novelist Frank Baum's *Wizard of Oz* series (1900–19) and American psychologist William Moulton Marsden's comic book character Wonder Woman (1941).

Not surprisingly, many of the writers who contributed to *Weird Tales*, especially women including Dorothy Quick, Morgan Bassett, and C.L. Moore, made feminist fantasy characters central to their stories, and Brundage was highly skilled at creating cover art that visually dramatized the ideals embodied by such characters. Brundage's cover illustrations are conspicuously devoid of noble knights winning the hearts of young beauties. Instead, they present worlds where women take center stage, whether that involves young beauties trying to rescue themselves from sorcerers, as in "The Altar of Melek Taos"; beautiful young sorceresses consorting with dragons or other fantastic creatures, as in "The Witch's Mark"; or even, on occasion, young beauties becoming brave sheroes to defend men, as in Robert E. Howard's 1935 "The Hour of the Dragon" (Fig. 6.3).

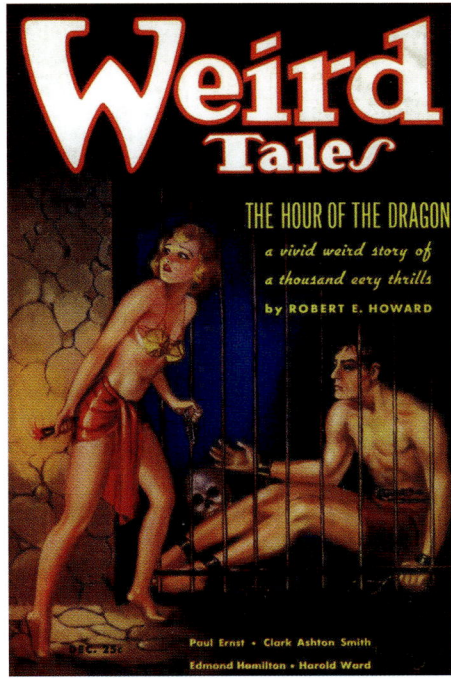

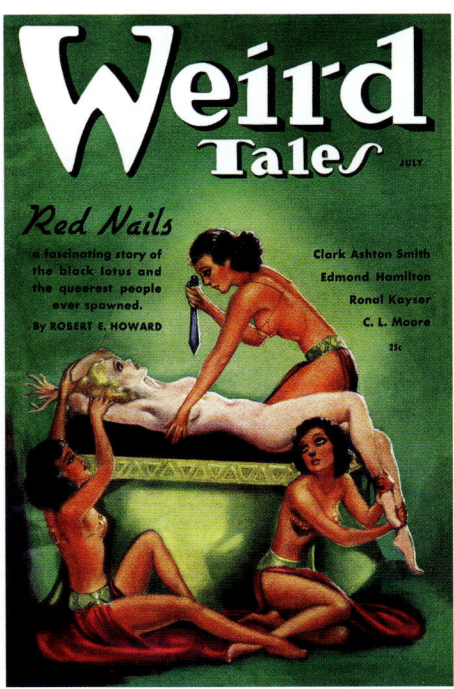

FIGURE 6.3. Margaret Brundage (American, 1900–1976), cover illustration for Robert E. Howard's "The Hour of the Dragon," *Weird Tales*, vol. 26, no. 6, Dec. 1935, Wikimedia Commons.

FIGURE 6.4. Margaret Brundage (American, 1900–1976), cover illustration tion for Robert E. Howard's "Red Nails," *Weird Tales*, vol. 28, no. 1, July 1936, Wikimedia Commons.

Sometimes Brundage's female-centered cover art walked a fine line between feminist statement and calculated play to the male gaze, as with the BDSM-inflected July 1936 cover for Howard's "Red Nails" (Fig. 6.4). Just as frequently, however, Brundage celebrated female desire in ways that subverted that gaze. This was particularly true of her illustrations for stories by women, such as the October 1934 cover for Moore's "The Black God's Kiss" (Fig. 6.5), and the cover for "The Witch's Mark." The former depicts Moore's heroine, the medieval warrior woman Jirel of Joiry, embracing a black statue, while the

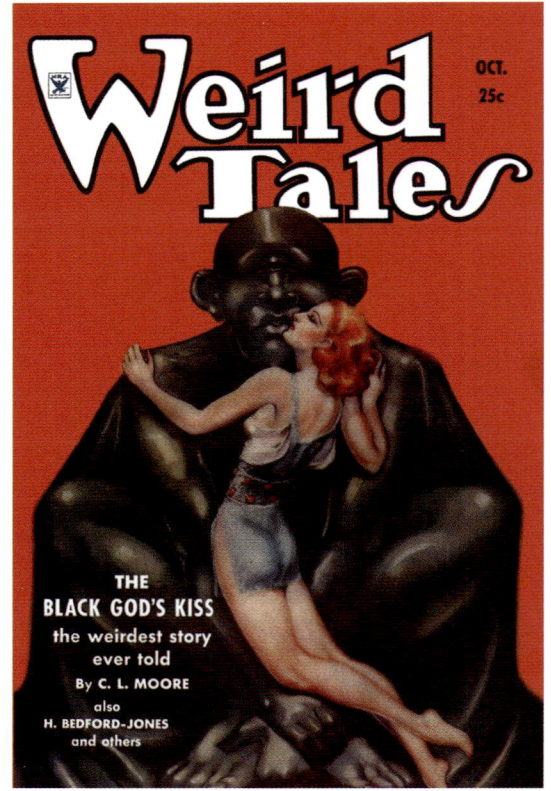

latter depicts Quick's antagonist, the witch-woman Cecily Maltby, exulting under an evening sky as bats swirl around her. In good pinup fashion, Brundage swaps Jirel's battle gear and Cecily's evening gown for wispy lingerie so readers can see even more of their pearly white flesh. At the same time, each image complicates conventional ideas about the gendered nature of agency and desire: the tension in Jirel's muscles contrasts sharply with the slack passivity of the idol's body while she seems to peer at readers through slitted eyes, and Cecily bares her teeth, snarling and staring directly back at those who would ogle her.

Indeed, Brundage's artwork often participated in the tradition of female gothic, ghost, and weird fiction initiated by Radcliffe in the late eighteenth century and continued in pages of *Weird Tales* by modern women writers. For instance, Brundage channeled Radcliffe's tendency to cast men who used technoscientific tricks to intimidate women as villains in her March 1937 cover for Quick's "Strange Orchids," with its image of a fearful but determined young woman standing defiantly between an offstage mad scientist—represented by a jagged shadow—and his victim (Fig. 6.6). Elsewhere, Brundage dramatized the ideals of modern weird fiction writers who celebrated women exchanging patriarchal civilization for the company of wild animals in pursuit of their "monstrous" desires for freedom. This is especially apparent in the January 1935 *Weird Tales* cover for Bassett Morgan's "Black Bagheela" (Fig. 6.7). Ostensibly the tale of a British white man searching for his lost brother, much of "Black Bagheela" revolves around an Asian mother and daughter who transform into leopards when they are endangered by men and use their abilities to

FIGURE 6.5. Margaret Brundage (American, 1900–1976), cover illustration for C.L. Moore's "The Black God's Kiss," *Weird Tales*, vol. 24, no. 4, Oct. 1934, Wikimedia Commons.

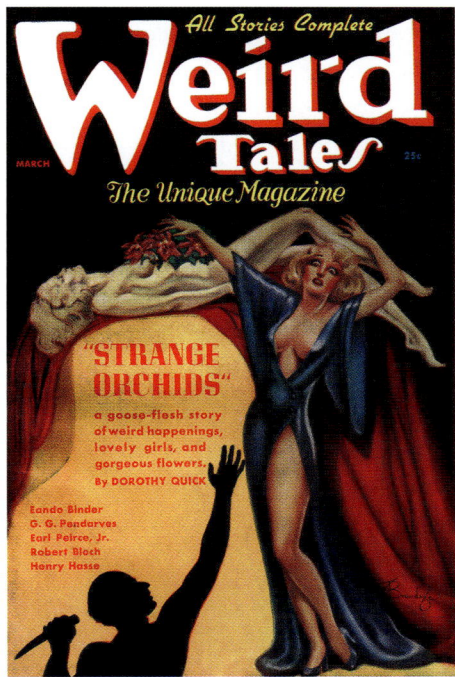

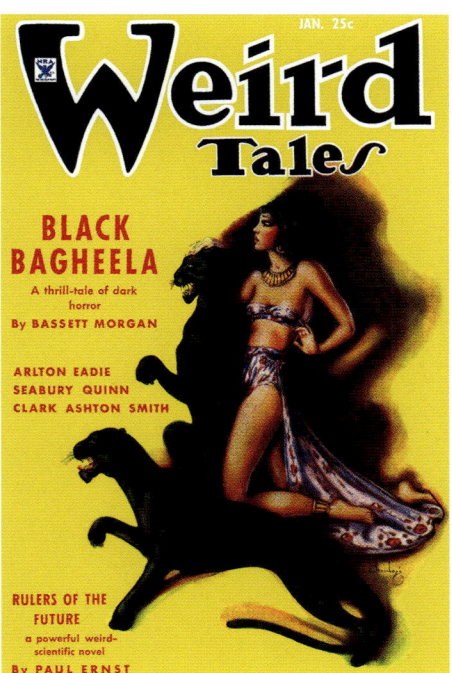

rescue the story's nominal hero from certain peril. Brundage's illustration dramatizes the action but adds her own political perspective by strategically ignoring Bassett's description of her heroines as mixed-race but possessing "the skin of a white woman."[14] Instead, Brundage endows her subject with dusky skin that stands in sharp contrast to the pale colors she used when depicting white people. As such, she gives readers a glimpse of a weird but potentially wonderful future that is feral, female—and in full color.

The aesthetic conventions first forged by Margaret Brundage have continued to serve as inspiration for women fantasy artists throughout the twentieth- and twenty-first centuries. In the 1940s and '50s, EC comics artists Lily Renée and Marie Severin followed Brundage by drawing women as fashionable and active subjects of both good and evil; Severin is particularly well known, like Brundage, for her strategic and highly effective use of color. Award-winning artists Julie Bell and Rowena Morrill made their debuts during the revival of feminism and fantasy art in the 1970s, crafting Brundage-esque covers for speculative magazines, paperback books, video games, trading cards, album covers, and movie posters featuring fashionably undressed women and men alike. Around the same time, Diane Dillon revived another unique aspect of Brundage's artwork, casting her heroines in a variety of races and ethnicities. Today, the quest for representational diversity continues

FIGURE 6.6. Margaret Brundage (American, 1900–1976), cover illustration for Dorothy Quick's "Strange Orchids," *Weird Tales*, vol. 29, no. 3, Mar. 1938, Wikimedia Commons.

FIGURE 6.7. Margaret Brundage (American, 1900–1976), cover illustration for Morgan Bassett's "Black Bagheela," *Weird Tales*, vol. 25, no. 1, Jan. 1935, Wikimedia Commons.

in the art of women like Mia Araujo, Rovina Cai, Winona Nelson, Tran Nguyen, Terese Nielsen, and Shelly Wan, all of whom draw on the myths of their respective cultures to depict women as strong protagonists connected to nature and the cosmos. Taken together, these artists point to the enduring legacy of Brundage's art.

1. Farnsworth Wright, "M Stands for Margaret," *Weird Tales*, October 1934, 526.

2. Lisa Hix, "Pinup Queens: Three Female Artists Who Shaped the American Dream Girl," *Collectors Weekly*, May 22, 2013, accessed Aug. 13, 2023.

3. Robert Weinberg, "Memories of Margaret," in *The Alluring Art of Margaret Brundage*, eds. Stephen D. Korshak and J. David Spurlock (Lakewood, NJ: Vanguard, 2013), 17.

4. Diya Patel, "Reviews on Margaret Brundage," June 28, 2023, unpublished report, the Center for Women, Science, and Technology, Georgia Tech.

5. H.P. Lovecraft, "Letter to Lee McBride White, 28 Oct. 1935," in *H. P. Lovecraft: Letters to J. Vernon Shea, Carl F. Strauch, and Lee McBride White*, eds. S.T. Joshi and David E. Schultz (New York: Hippocampus Press, 2016), 362.

6. Jack Williamson, "Letter to the Editor," *Weird Tales* 22, no. 6, Dec. 1933, 775.

7. Henry Kuttner, "Author's Comment," *Weird Tales* 28, no. 1, July 1936, 127.

8. Henry Kuttner, "Letter to the Editor," *Weird Tales* 22, no. 3, Sept. 1933, 391.

9. John Pelan, ed., *Conversations with the Weird Tales Circle* (Lakewood, CO: Centipede Press, 2009), 487.

10. Michael Liene, "Brickbats and Bouquets," *Weird Tales* 27, no. 3, March 1936, 378; Gertrude Gordon, "Letter to the Editor," *Weird Tales* 22, no. 5, Nov. 1933, 647.

11. Hazel Portelli, "Letter to the Editor," *Weird Tales* 20, no. 5, Nov. 1932, 716; Louis C. Smith, "Rainbow Colored Ink," *Weird Tales* 24, no. 6, Dec. 1934, 776.

12. Dr. LeRoy C. Bashore, "The February Cover," *Weird Tales* 25, no. 4, April 1935, 528; Elaine McIntire, "Keep Weird Tales Weird," *Weird Tales* 26, no. 2, Aug. 1935, 269; Mary Ashley, "Letter to the Editor," *Weird Tales* 23, no. 3, March 1934, 391.

13. "Fantasy," *Arthive*, accessed Aug. 13, 2023.

14. Morgan Bassett, "Black Bagheela," *Weird Tales* 25, no. 1, Jan. 1935, 61.

David M. Brinley

UNVEILING THE ENIGMATIC GENIUS
OF HANNES BOK

Elegantly stylized human figures, the symbolic and delicate pinch of a rose stem, and the juxtaposition of an effortlessly alien and musical landscape. In *A Rose for Ecclesiastes* (1963, Plate 47), Hannes Bok (1914–1964) was at his best—a visionary in a world invoking the sublime, filling his compositions with remarkable textures and uniquely bizarre aliens inhabiting strange and dreamlike worlds. Bok's iconic work is fine art in the world of weird fiction and illustration. Created at the very end of his career as an artist and nearly his life, *A Rose for Ecclesiastes* is a masterwork and one of the crown jewels in the Korshak Collection.

Considered one of the few stylists in the pulp magazine field and on par with Virgil Finlay (1914–1971) (Plate 48), Bok painted nearly 150 covers for various science fiction, fantasy, and detective fiction magazines, as well as contributed hundreds of black-and-white interior illustrations, throughout his career. Along with Finlay, Bok is now revered for creating the greatest science fiction art of the 1940s. Although a favorite of today's collectors in the genre, he received minimal recognition outside the field before and after his death.[1]

Bok was active as a book illustrator and painter in the late 1940s and early 1950s, when he found a renewed market for his art in book jacket illustration for science fiction and fantasy publishers, particularly Shasta Books in Chicago. His work for publisher Erle M. Korshak at Shasta is considered to be the finest of his career. Covers for *Slaves of Sleep* (1948), *Wheels of If* (1948), *Sidewise in Time* (1950), *Kinsmen of The Dragon* (1951) (Fig. 7.1), and the black-and-white *Who Goes There?* (1948) are some of the best jacket art in the fantasy field—ever. These five dazzling Shasta covers display not only the artist's impressive composition technique incorporating the spine of the jacket, but above all, his fantastic mastery of value, color, and intensity. The inspired wraparound jacket designs feature Bok's unerring feel for graceful line and mass. Bok had a natural inclination to stylize—his book jackets transcend illustration, as Shasta allowed Bok to experiment with form and concept. They represent an entirely novel approach for the time.

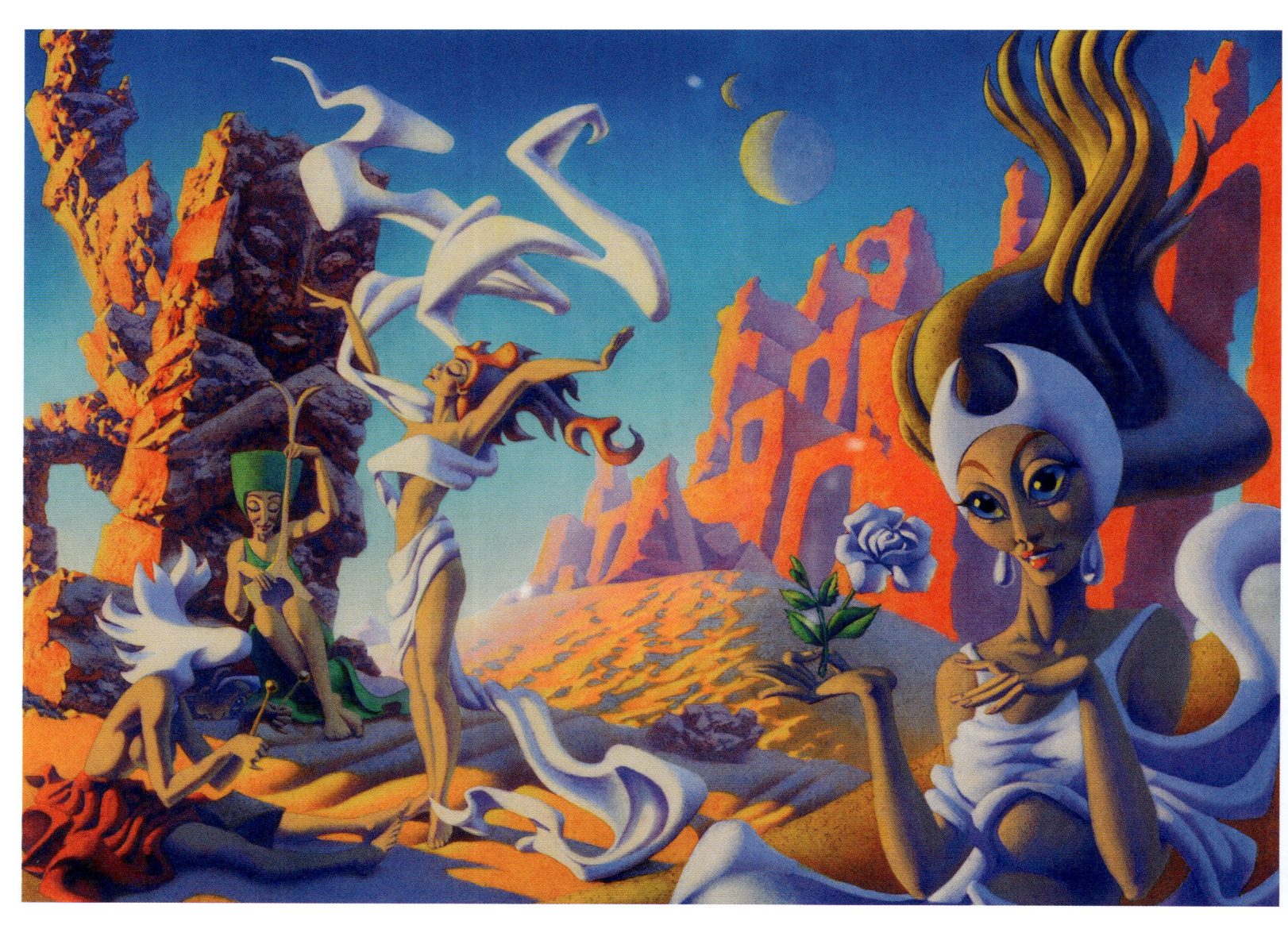

PLATE 47. Hannes Bok (American, 1914–1964), *A Rose for Ecclesiastes*, 1963, gouache on illustration board, 11 × 16 inches.

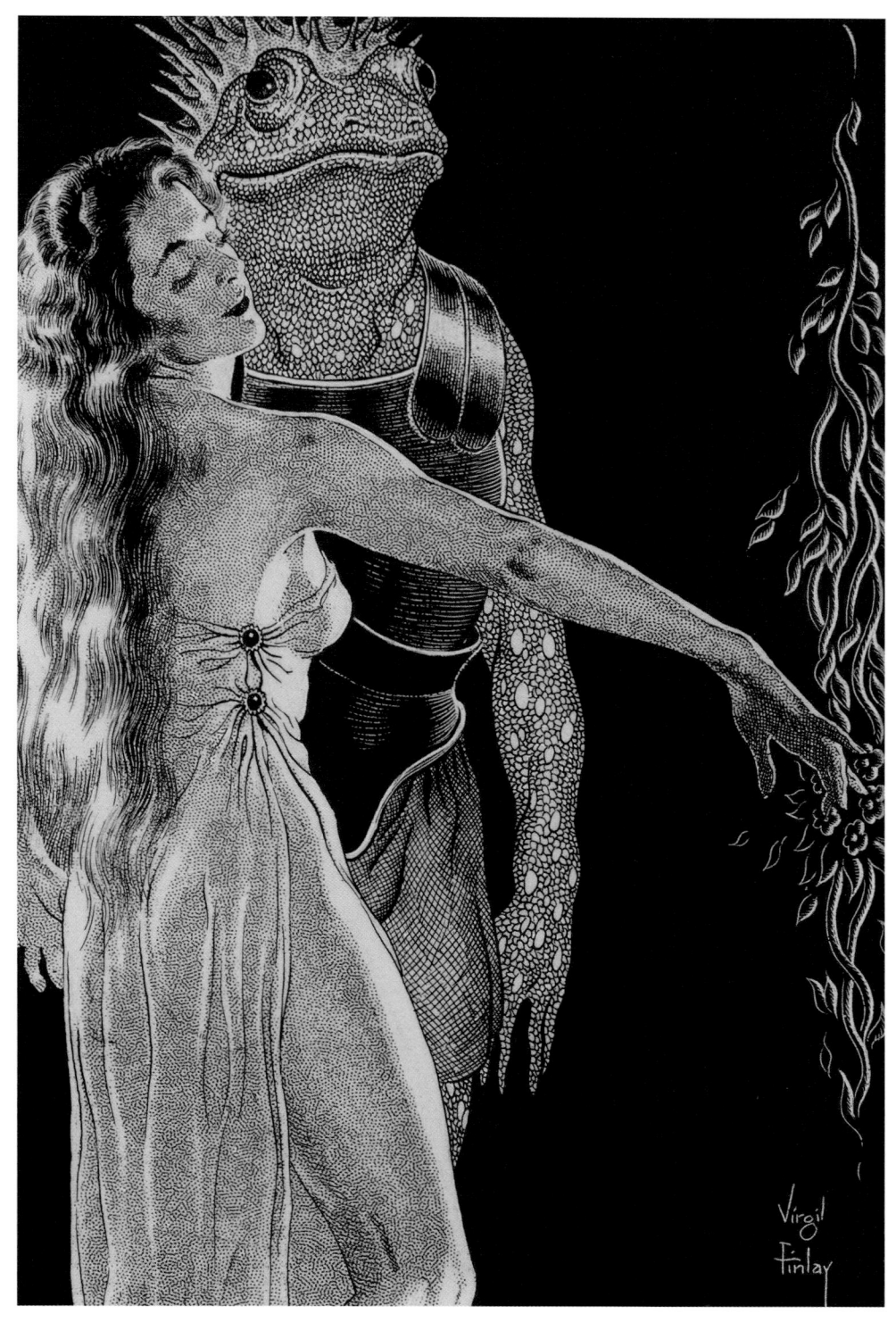

PLATE 48. Virgil Finlay (American, 1914–
1971), *Conquest of the Moon Pool*, 1948,
scratchboard, pen and ink, 8 × 5 inches.

Hannes Bok was born Wayne Francis Woodard in Kansas City, Missouri, on July 2, 1914, the youngest of four children. His parents divorced when he was five and his mother moved to Seattle, Washington, leaving her children in the custody of a strict, uncompromising father. When Wayne's father remarried, it was to a woman with views similar to his own, and together they discouraged the young man from becoming an artist. Wayne began using a pseudonym in 1932 at the age of eighteen; at first "Hans," and then "Hannes," in honor of the German composer and musician of the late Baroque period, Johann Sebastian Bach. Those in the know, however, believe that he changed his name mostly

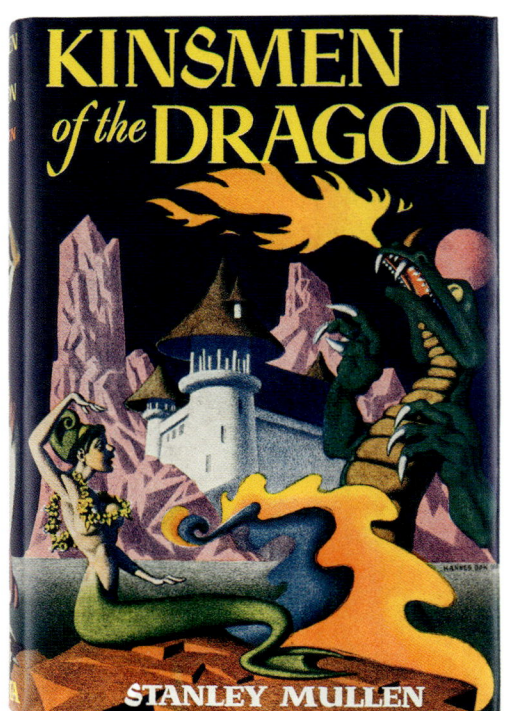

out of bitterness toward his father, which burned deep within him all his life. His name took its final form as Hannes Bok.[2]

A gifted and unusual talent starting out in a competitive field during the Great Depression years of the 1930s, Bok was a uniquely American artist and illustrator, as well as an amateur astrologer and writer of fantasy fiction and poetry. In 1937, a young author named Emil Petaja moved to Los Angeles, California, where he settled into the science fiction scene, befriending future star author Ray Bradbury, as well as other budding writers including Henry Kuttner, Henry Hasse, and Forrest J. Ackerman. By 1938, Bok also moved to Los Angeles, where he shared an apartment with Petaja. This allowed them to attend fan meetings together, haunt secondhand book shops, hang out at the movies, and help each other with their poems and burgeoning science fiction stories and artwork.

Bradbury became something of an avid promoter and un-official artist representative for Bok after he and Bok worked together on four covers of Bradbury's fanzine *Futuria Fantasia*. A teenage Bradbury, in July 1939, brought samples of Bok's art, including paintings, sketches, and ink drawings, from Los Angeles to New York to the inaugural World Science Fiction Convention.[3] Here, he passed along Bok's work to Farnsworth Wright, editor of *Weird Tales* magazine. Bok made his professional debut gracing the December 1939 issue with his cover art and interior illustrations. Considering this success, Bok pulled up stakes and moved to New York City that same month, where he would spend the remaining twenty-four years of his life.[4]

A Rose for Ecclesiastes originated as a science fiction short story written by American author Roger Zelazny in 1963 and nominated for the 1964 Hugo Award for Short Fiction.[5] Zelazny was a celebrated American poet and writer

FIGURE 7.1. Hannes Bok (American, 1914–1964), cover illustration for Stanley Mullen's *Kinsmen of the Dragon*, 1951, Shasta Publishers, Chicago, Korshak Collection.

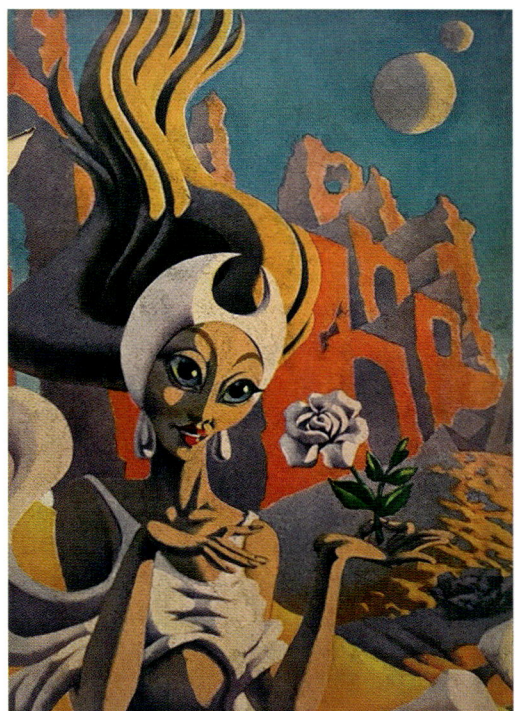
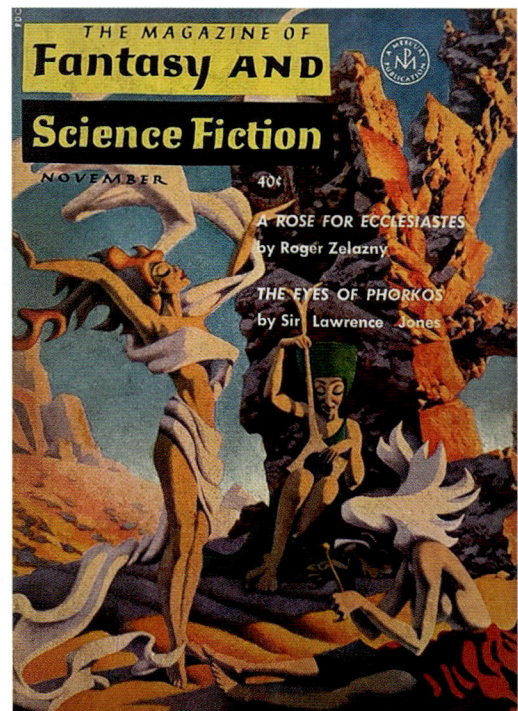

of fantasy and science fiction short stories and novels throughout his lifetime. *Rose* helped to blur the definition of science fiction into speculative fiction. It removed the scientific limitations of the genre and opened it to entirely new possibilities.

Zelazny's story is narrated by a gifted human linguist and poet named Gallinger, who is part of a mission studying Mars. He becomes the first human to learn the "high language" of the intelligent Martians, and to be allowed to read their sacred texts. He comes to believe that Martian culture is essentially fatalistic, following an event in the distant past that left the long-lived Martians sterile. The Martian high priestess regards Gallinger highly, and over the course of months, his theological and poetical discussion elevate him to a status something like a prophet. Ultimately, he is seduced by a Martian temple dancer and impregnates her, the first such pregnancy on the planet in hundreds of years. The Martians appear not to take this well, as it contradicts their religion's expectation of extinction. The High Priestess is gifted the rose from Gallinger, vowing to learn how to grow the flower. The story ends well for the Martians, though perhaps less so for Gallinger, who discovers his dancer was only fulfilling her religious duty by seducing him, not caring for him otherwise. He attempts suicide by taking forty-four sleeping pills, but when he wakes up, he is in the infirmary of his ship, and he sees Mars through a porthole, growing farther away as the ship leaves Mars to return to Earth.

Bok was commissioned to create the *A Rose for Ecclesiastes* wraparound cover for *Fantasy & Science Fiction* magazine's November 1963 issue (Fig. 7.2).[6]

FIGURE 7.2 (both). Hannes Bok (American, 1914–1964), wraparound cover illustration for *The Magazine of Fantasy and Science Fiction*, November 1963, Mercury Press, Inc., Concord, NH.

His artwork captures the essence of the narrative, transcending mere depiction by imbuing the work with his own spiritual intelligence.

Though not nearly enough documentation exists of Bok's entire process, there are enough tissue sketches, vellum drawings, and various tracings and rough compositions for other pieces in the Korshak Collection archives to surmise how Bok would have assembled and composed *A Rose for Ecclesiastes*. Such materials are a rather unique aspect of the Korshak Collection and have been particularly important for Bok studies (Fig. 7.3). Unfortunately, no tissue or specific compositional preliminary drawing for this painting exists.

However, having the opportunity to visually inspect the original surface of the piece provides a candid look into Bok's technical mastery as well as his imaginatively stylized figures. Judging by his sketchbook notes, he may have drawn the subject directly onto a primed board, then began to directly paint in layers over it, building to a rich and solid opacity. Quoting from a letter Bok wrote to acquaintance Mark Walsted, dated February 8, 1963: "Also working on wraparound cover for *MAG OF FANTASY AND SCIENCE FICTION* at last!— mainly becuz it's a wrap-around job with good reproduction (pays next to nothing). Only I sorta bit off a lot to chew; got carried away & designed it as if it were 11 × 16 feet instead of 11 × 16 inches. If it comes out as expected, it'll be a riot of reds & blue-greens, be as enamel-surfaced as a Dali original.

DAVID M. BRINLEY

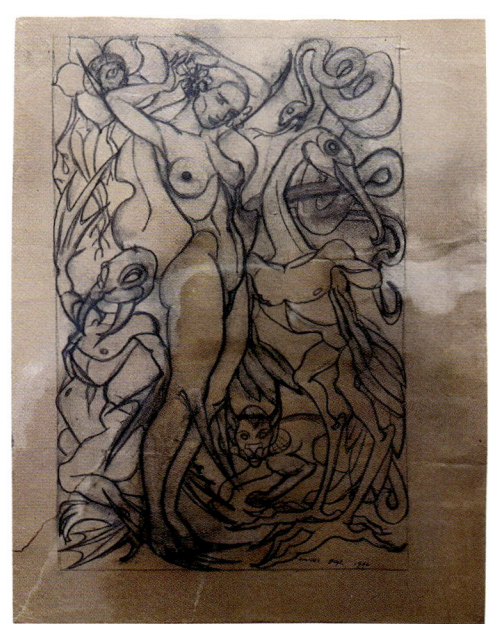 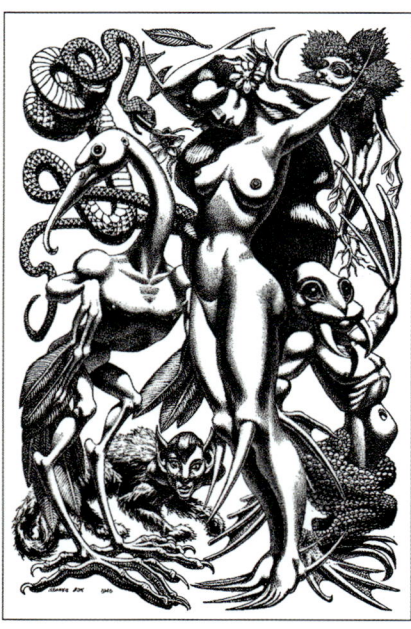 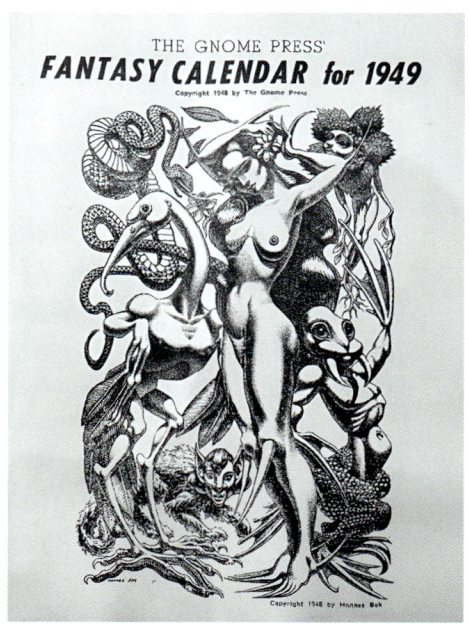

FIGURE 7.3 (all). Hannes Bok (American, 1914–1964), illustration and tissue study of "The Fox Woman and the Blue Pagoda," 1946, reprinted for cover of *Fantasy Calendar for 1949*, The Gnome Press, 1948, New York, NY, Korshak Collection.

I don't expect to paint other ones—easy way to go broke."[7] Ultimately, the original painting is more a "riot" of violets, oranges, and considered touches of green—impactfully rendered most notably as a beautiful triad of secondary colors in a world of cerulean and cobalt blues. The accent of primary red in the lower left figure helps sweep the viewer's eye around the entire composition. The audience of the wraparound cover artwork is looking through a portal to an environment where the atmosphere and the air quality have a spiritual weight unknown. Bok's figures almost always appear to be in motion, nearly flailing themselves around, a gestural ballet of fluid dancers upon a stage. Bok's figures are not realistic, but rather impish and softly angular.

The lighting of the figures utilizes core darks, cast shadows, and reflected light; all culminating with the beautiful warm Rembrandt-like lighting across the High Priestess's face.[8] Bok's prism for viewing fantasy themes is free-flowing, exaggerated in form and detail, and bizarrely sensual.

A distinct composition of foreground, middle ground, and background, *Rose* elevates every inch of the composition and subject matter. The mountainous orange and violet background rocks complement the sky while the triad used within the characters makes each distinct. The utilization of atmospheric perspective is critical in conveying the depth of the landscape, grounding the composition. Bok's very personal and idiosyncratic take on creating unique imagery that strives for variety rather than settling into static motifs and compositional shortcuts is unique and unforgettable.

The composition is also inexplicably reversed for publication. This most likely had more to do with the magazine cover designer's traditional needs for the typography and masthead placement, which all obscure much of the painting's power. The printing quality is desaturated and far more neutralized than Bok's original colorful vision, which distressed Bok to no end. After the cover's publication, in a letter to lifelong friend Petaja, dated November 28, 1963, Bok wrote: "Thankee for kind words re F&SF cover, but wait'll you get an eyeful of the original. I am cursed by stinko reproduction in my whole career—have had about only three good color reproduction jobs."[9] The poor reproduction quality inherent in mass market magazines of the time is unfortunate for posterity.

None of this, however, takes away from the aesthetics of the original art and its sophisticatedly considered original palette, which are all in tune with what Bok sought out philosophically in his work. Much like artist Aubrey Beardsley (1872–1898), Bok did not see fine art and illustration as mutually

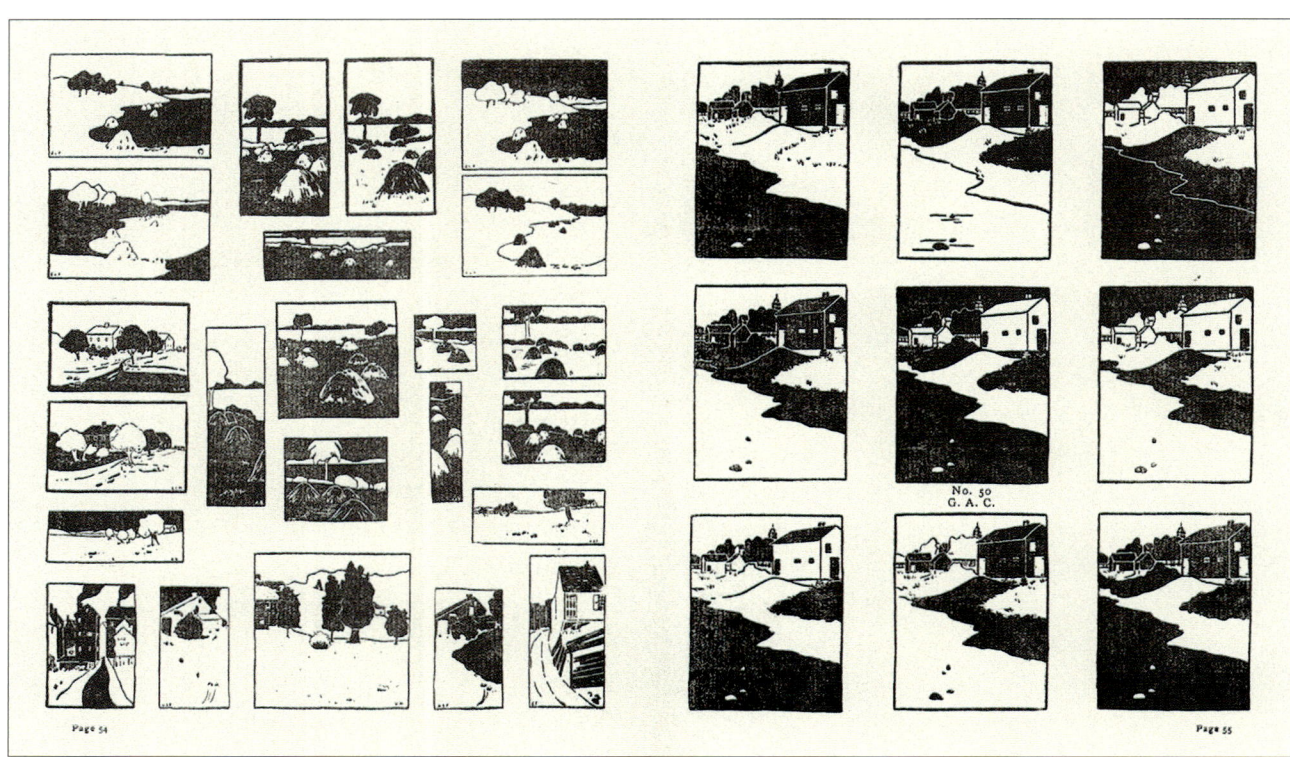

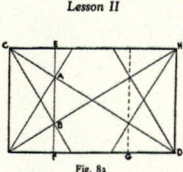

No. 50
G. A. C.

Page 54

Page 55

FIGURE 7.4 (above).
Arthur Wesley Dow,
Composition, 1905,
Baker and Taylor
Company, New York,
NY, 54–55.

FIGURE 7.5 (right, both).
Jay Hambridge, *The
Elements of Dynamic
Symmetry*, 1967, Dover
Publications, Inc.,
New York, 81 and 83.
This Dover edition, first
published in 1967, is an
unabridged and unaltered
republication of the
original 1926 work.

Lesson II   81

If the line HG, Fig. 78, represents unity or 1. and GE 1.618 then
CG equals .7236. The student is advised to construct this shape with
a metric scale and study closely the subdivided area. The reciprocal
of the square root of five is .4472. The line GE being the side of a
whirling square rectangle, is numerically expressed as 1.618. This
number multiplied by the reciprocal of the square root of five, that
is, .4472, gives us the numerical value of the line CG, or .7236. This
fraction .7236 divided into 1.618 equals 2.236, or the square root
of five. The area CE, therefore, is a root-five rectangle.

If, through the eyes AB of the whirling square rectangle CE, Fig.
79, the line FD is drawn parallel to the ends of the rectangle, it de-
termines the area CD. This area is that of a root-five rectangle and
is composed of the square GA and the two whirling square rectangles CA and HB. The student should remember that we are
dealing with similarity of shapes of areas and not sizes.

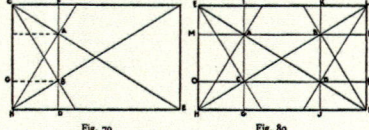

Fig. 79   Fig. 80

Arithmetical analysis:
If the line CH of Fig. 79, is unity or 1. and the line HE is 1.618,
and the area CD is a root-five rectangle, then the line HD is represented by .4472. HD or .4472 divided into CH or 1. equals 2.236
or the square root of five.

Obviously, from the above construction, we may draw lines
through the eyes A, B, C and D, as in Fig. 80, and divide the area of
the whirling square rectangle EF into four overlapping root-five
rectangles, MF, EP, EG and KF; AJ, ID, OA and BP are squares,
and EA, HA, HC, OI, BL, DF, KP and BF are whirling square rectangles.

Lesson II   83

Fig. 82

If the line EF is drawn through the eyes A, B of the whirling square
rectangle CD, Fig. 82, it defines the root-five rectangle CF. The line
CE equals .4472, and the line EH equals 1.618 minus .4472 or 1.1708.
This ratio divided into unity or 1. produces its reciprocal .854. The
area ED, represented by the ratio 1.1708 or its reciprocal .854, is
composed of the root-five rectangle GH plus the 1.382 area EG. If a
1.1708 were used for the purposes of design, one way of subdividing
that area would be as described.

Summing up this lesson the following ratios appear other than
those of the root-five and the whirling square rectangles:

Ratios	Reciprocals
1.382	.7236
2.618	.382
1.118	.8944
1.309	.764
1.1708	.854

The ratios 1.118 and 1.309 appear indirectly through their recipro-
cals, .8944 and .764. The ratio 1.118 may be found by dividing the
square root of five, 2.236, by 2. The 1.309 shape will be recognized
as a square plus two whirling square rectangles. .618 divided by 2
equals .309. The fraction .309 is the reciprocal of 3.236 or 1.618
multiplied by 2.

exclusive in the hands of artists with specific intent. Within one artist, there could exist an impulse toward popular culture as well as an impulse toward fine art. Beardsley's poster art and essay "The Art of the Hoarding" (1894) changed how the public thought about art and advertising. The two, according to the artist, were not mutually exclusive. His theater posters manifested his theory and helped revolutionize poster production in Europe and America.[10]

From a formal as well as conceptual perspective, academic art books by Arthur Wesley Dow (Fig. 7.4) and Jay Hambidge influenced Bok at a young age.[11] Hambidge's theory of dynamic symmetry was popular in the early twentieth century and was essentially concerned with the geometry of root rectangles and the golden ratio, a mathematical formula that artists utilize to create balance, harmony, and aesthetically pleasing compositions (Fig. 7.5).[12] The associated grid system helps create basic rhythm, movement, and unity via diagonals, spirals, and geometric themes; but ultimately, it is in the artist's mind and hands to utilize the system with intuition and creativity to create striking imagery (Plate 49).

These texts were foundational for Bok, a student of pictorial composition, as he incorporated the approach and dreamscapes of the immortal Maxfield Parrish (1880–1963) into his work. Reading Bok's notebooks in the Korshak Collection makes clear two of the ways in which Parrish directly influenced him: Parrish's use of dynamic symmetry and, most notably, his technique of meticulous glazing (Fig. 7.6).[13] Bok considered himself a student of the Parrish school of illustration, although he never studied with the artist; he only visited Parrish's farm on rare occasions in New Hampshire during the 1930s and corresponded with him.[14] In a 1928 letter to Bok, Parrish described what dynamic symmetry meant to him: "Of late years I have been doing all my work on a layout, so to speak, Of Dynamic Symmetry, a rediscovery on the part of Jay Hambridge of the old Greek method of making rectangles. Those familiar with this method consider that these dynamic rectangles are far more pleasing than just arbitrary rectangles, and not only that, but by their subdivisions they permit every feature of the picture to be part of the whole panel. If done with intelligence there is a certain balance to the design which is of great value."[15]

Parrish also used a "series-of-glazes" technique of oil painting like that employed by most of the great masters of the Italian and Flemish schools in which one color at a time is applied, then a thin coat of shellac, then another color, and so on. This was to remain Bok's favorite oil technique, although

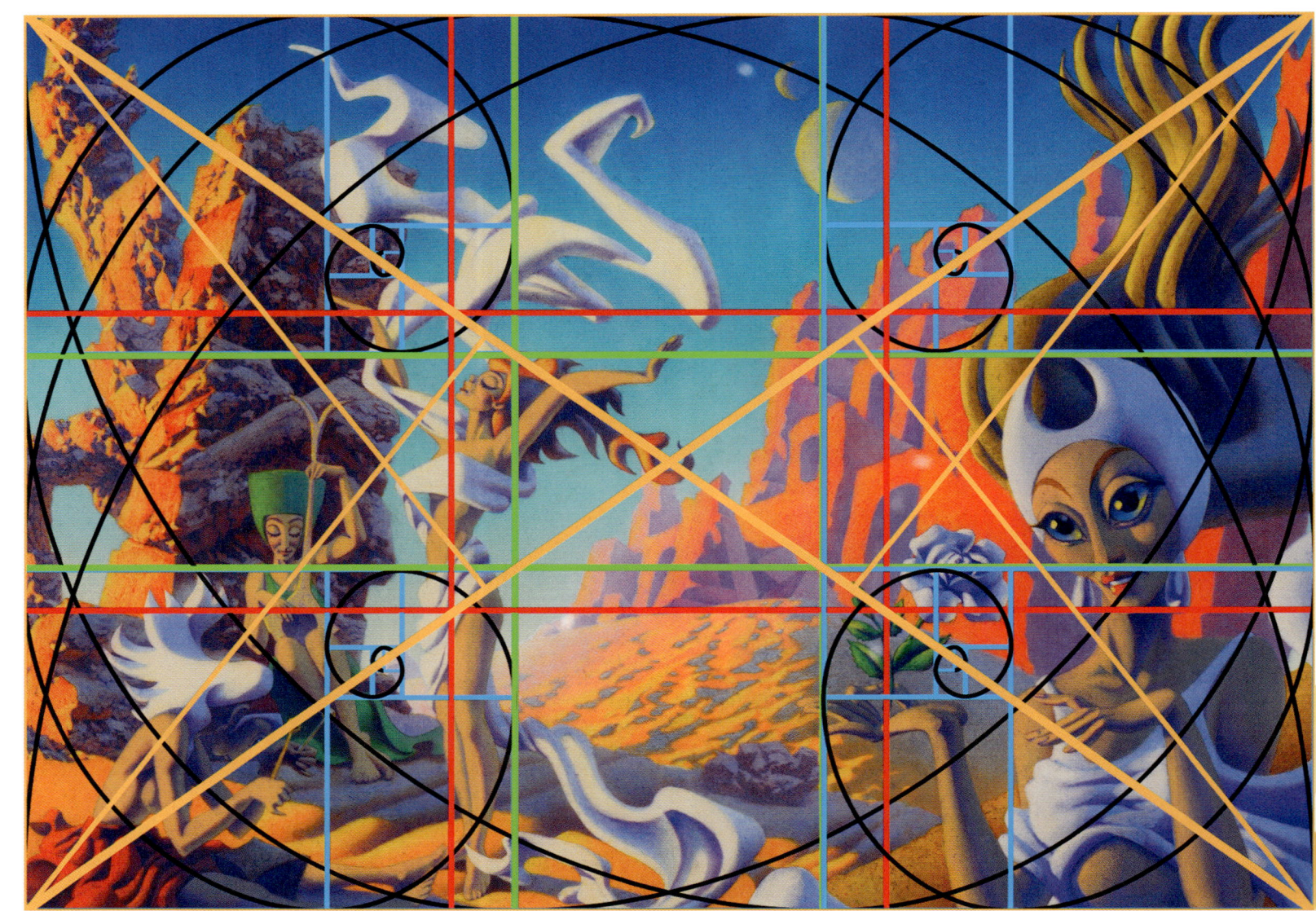

PLATE 49. Hannes Bok (American, 1914–1964), *A Rose for Ecclesiastes*, 1963, gouache on illustration board, 11 × 16 inches. "Dynamic Symmetry" diagram courtesy of the essay author, David M. Brinley, digital, 2024.

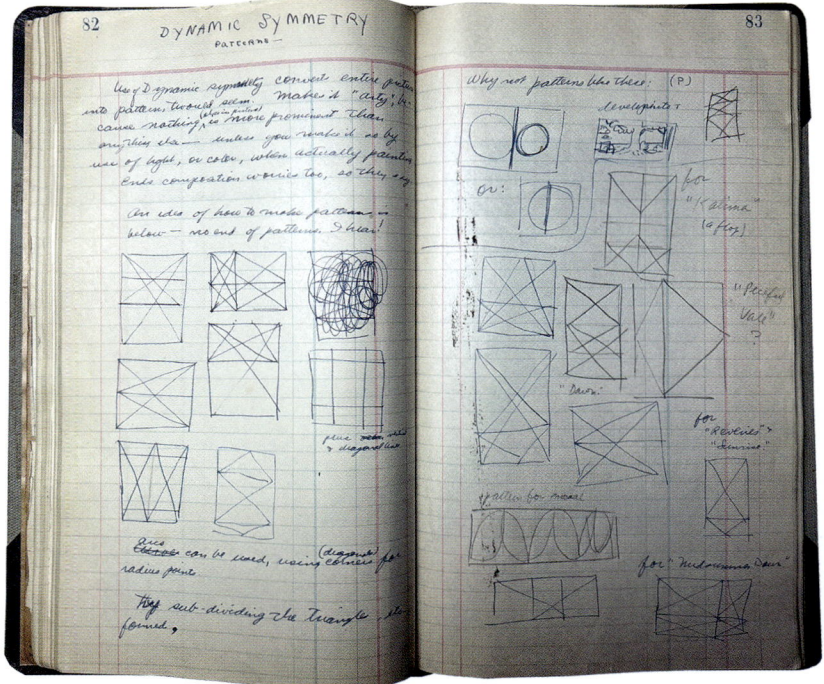

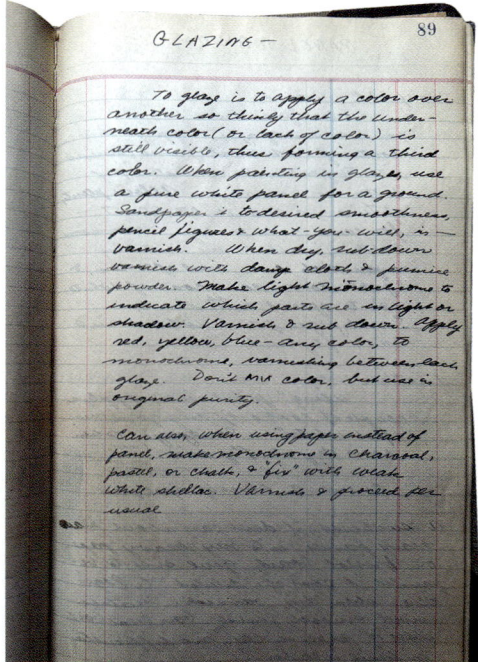

he worked in just about every art technique there is at one time or another. From studying the original surface of Bok's *A Rose for Ecclesiastes*, he appears to have incorporated this process of layering and glazing, as well as opaque mixing techniques, to complete the entire composition and satisfy specific needs for rendering complex elements with gouache at the eleven-by-sixteen-inch size.

Bok keenly understood Parrish's view on creating "pictures": "Why should not all such things, illustrations, decorations, miniatures, etc., be looked upon as pictures? … If they are good of their kind, they are good as pictures. The Museum [The Metropolitan Museum of Art] has on its walls many pictures which are purely illustrative and nothing else…. *Why not judge all these things by one standard? … It seems to me the original purpose of the work has precious little to do with the subject.*"[16] Parrish's and Bok's work holds back the assumed narrative of the image just enough that it demands the viewer create their own. This persistence comes from otherworldly qualities that provide the framework for our imaginations to take flight. When asked to tell the story behind *Daybreak* (1922), Parrish replied, "I know full well the public wants a story … but to my mind if a picture does not tell its own story, it's better to have the story without the picture…. The picture tells all

FIGURE 7.6 (both). Hannes Bok (American, 1914–1964), unpublished personal notes on Parrish's influence and his glazing techniques, c. 1940s, Korshak Collection.

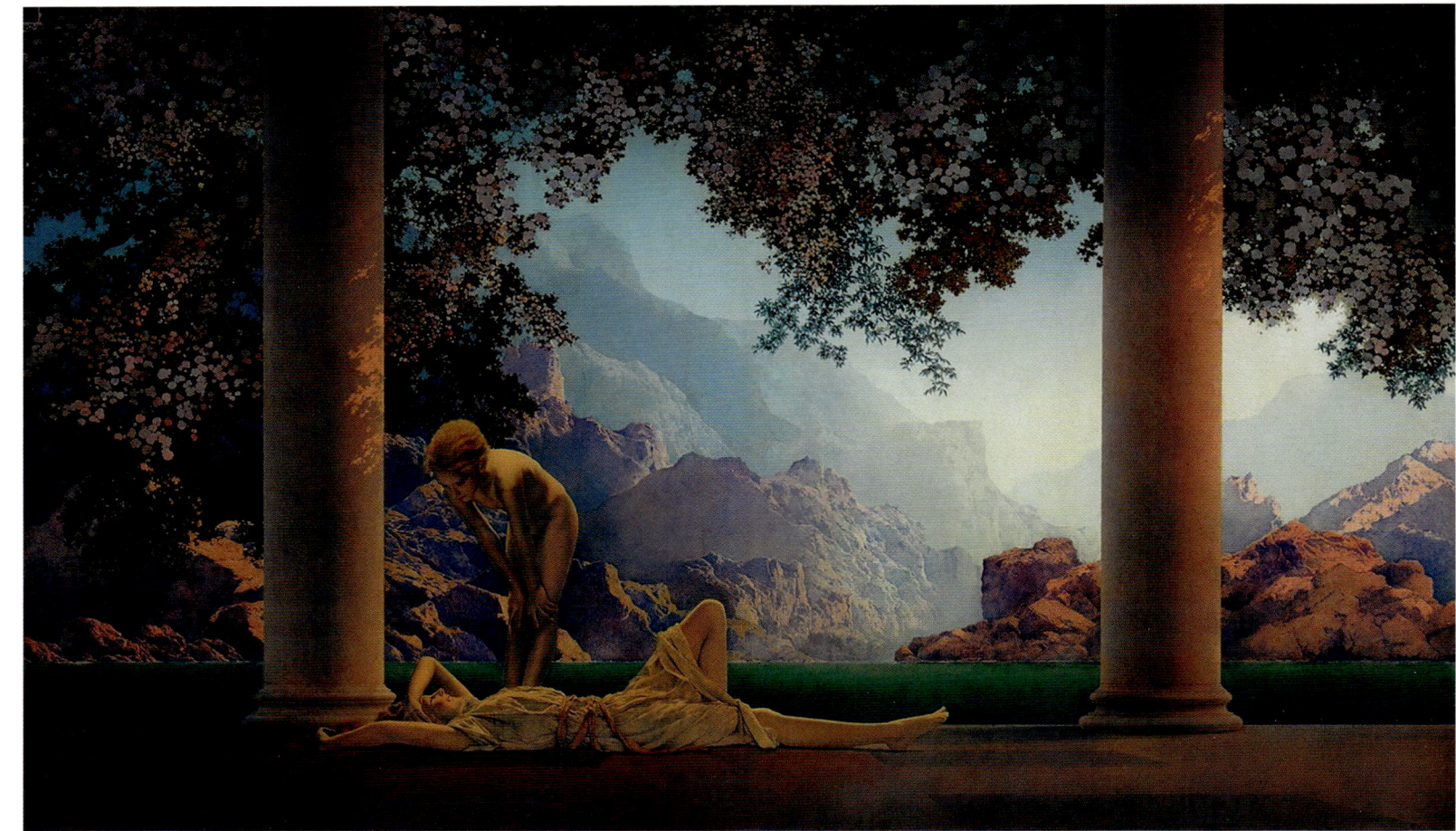

there is, there is nothing more" (Fig. 7.7).[17] Parrish had a feeling for subtle whimsy, purity of color, and value control (the use of light, halftone, and dark values), which people tend to overlook in his work. Bok has been accused of copying Parrish, but this is a superficial oversimplification. He was surely influenced both formally and conceptually by Parrish, much in the same way that great artists are influenced by other great artists and their dedicated vision to succeed. Parrish remained Bok's idol all his life.

Bok created considerable interior work in black and white throughout the 1940s for various pulp magazines including *Astonishing Stories*, *Famous Fantastic Mysteries*, *Future*, *Fantastic Novels*, *Planet Stories*, *Science Fiction Quarterly*, *Unknown*, and the aforementioned *Weird Tales*: "I aspired to become a magazine cover artist, so like Parrish—I studied current covers. A magnifying glass disclosed that the colors were made by the juxtaposition of microscopic dots of red,

FIGURE 7.7. Maxfield Parrish (American, 1870–1966), *Daybreak*, 1922, oil on board, 26½ × 45 inches, property of a private American collection, 2010.

yellow, and blue inks. Eureka! I spent weeks producing a cover, executing it by stippling colored inks. Without knowing it, I had rediscovered Seurat's pointilliste technique, although I learned the fact only much later"[18] (Fig. 7.8). His study of the printing process fueled his work on Michallet paper, which had a special texture that provided an inner light source as material was drawn on top of it. Bok utilized this paper to work in a pointillist fashion on coquille board. This unique board holds very tiny irregularly shaped pebbles that can be glazed over lightly with a lithographic crayon or hard graphite pencil to create value and shaded tones (Plate 1). Bok's definitive usage of reflected light makes these pointillist images feel alive and would carry over into his color and more meticulous glazed and opaque painted works (Fig. 7.9).

Bok's world of influence expanded through his admiration of Polish American painter, illustrator, and designer Władysław Benda. Publishers regarded Benda highly as an artist in the world of illustration art. His work illustrated magazine covers such as those of *Collier's, McCall's, Ladies' Home Journal, Good Housekeeping, Theatre Magazine*, and many others. Articles by and about Benda and his masks appeared regularly in many of the same magazines and publi-

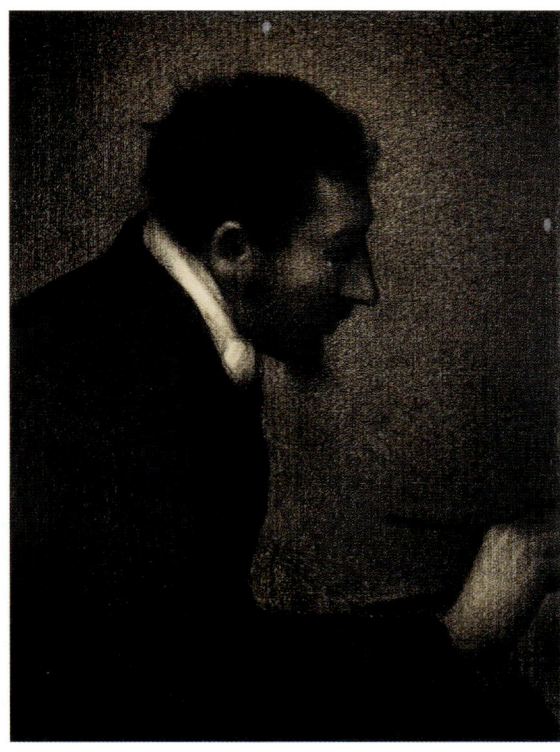

cations that carried his illustrations. Benda's book, *Masks* (1944), was a "how-to" study of his own stylized designs and unique construction techniques (Fig. 7.10), which were profoundly influential on Bok's aesthetic and own work of building beautiful and highly stylized masks (Fig. 7.11).[19] This solitary exploration would continue long after Bok left the publishers behind.

Bok was deeply intellectual but also highly emotional, with a distinct vision and intention behind all of his work. In many respects, he operated as an outsider artist in the world of cheap reproductions and even cheaper publishers. His pay was paltry, but still allowed for Bok to deliver work he believed in and work that best represented his superior process. Though he was perhaps resigned to working within this system, he was rather proud of the fact that his own philosophical approach to art-making didn't have an easily ascribed place in a commercialized world. Bok and artist Edmund Emshwiller (1925–1990) shared one of the inaugural 1953 Hugo Awards for science fiction achievement

FIGURE 7.8. Georges Seurat (French, 1859–1891), *Aman-Jean (Portrait of Edmond François Aman-Jean)*, 1882–83, Conté crayon on Michallet paper, Bequest of Stephen C. Clark, The Metropolitan Museum of Art, New York, 1960.

as the previous year's "Best Cover Artist" (both won in a tie). Even being presented this first Hugo by vote of science fiction fans did little to change Bok's attitude or fortunes. His cynicism toward the field was quite apparent by the mid-1950s. A complicated personality at odds with the establishment and a stickler for remaining true to his vision, Bok was completely at odds with editors, and these conflicts became more problematic. His inability to compromise limited his career as he started to withdraw from the field. Bok essentially left commercial art in 1954 to pursue his own creative indulgences.

Bok wrote articles on astrology for *Mystic Magazine* in the 1950s and eventually became more engrossed in his interest in the occult and mysticism as the 1960s dawned. In 1963, publisher Carl Weschcke of Llewellyn Worldwide embarked on an ambitious program to present the American public with two new magazines on mysticism. One entitled *Minute Scope* was printed on slick paper the size of *Time* magazine (8 × 10¾ inches) and included some of Bok's final printed illustrations.

Bok's own health was deteriorating rapidly at this time as he grew increasingly reclusive, dysfunctional, and malnourished. Wayne (Hannes Bok) Woodard sadly died alone in poverty of a heart attack at age forty-nine on April 11, 1964.

DAVID M. BRINLEY

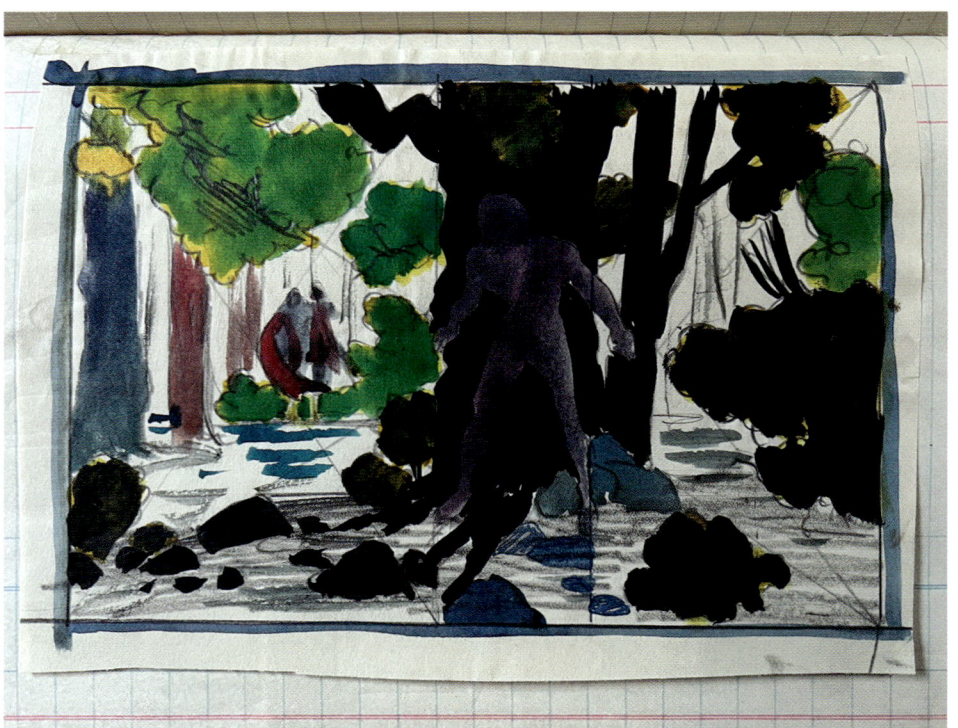

FIGURE 7.9. Hannes Bok
(American, 1914–1964), unpublished
ink and watercolor compositional
sketch, c. 1940s, Korshak Collection.

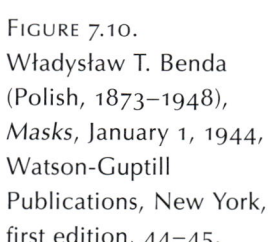

FIGURE 7.10. Władysław T. Benda (Polish, 1873–1948), *Masks*, January 1, 1944, Watson-Guptill Publications, New York, first edition, 44–45.

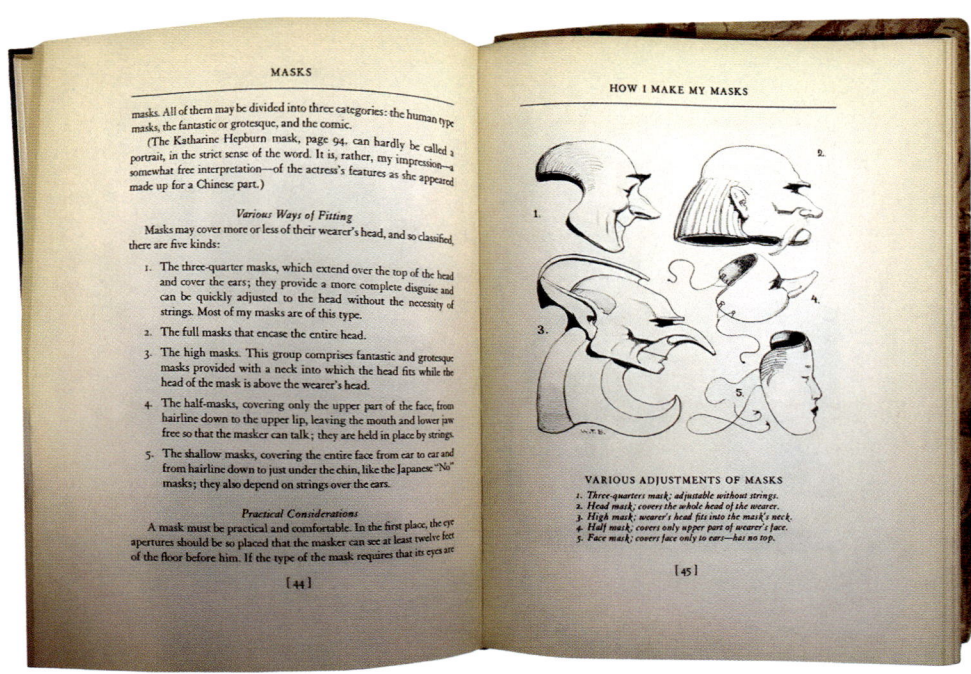

FIGURE 7.11 (both). Hannes Bok (American, 1914–1964), *Masks*, c. 1950s, Korshak Collection.

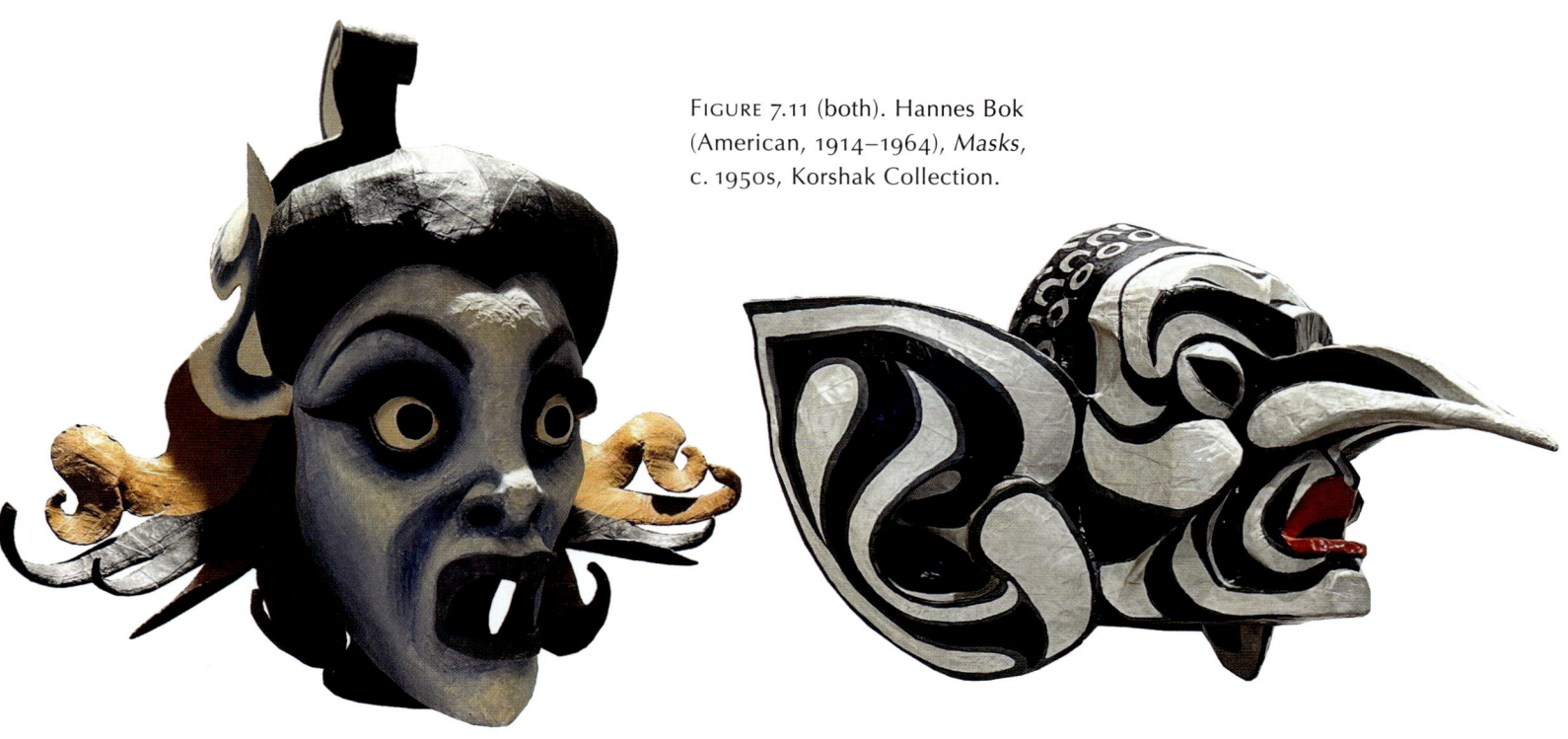

Despite some of the more esoteric published works at the end of Bok's life, ultimately, *A Rose for Ecclesiastes* would be Bok's masterpiece and last contribution to the field. An aching irony of life is that Bok worked over half of his to perfect a technique, did so, then unfortunately died one year later.

After Bok's death, Emil Petaja took responsibility for his estate and founded the Bokanalia Memorial Foundation in 1967 to keep Bok's memory alive and his work in the public eye through various collections and publications. The foundation was set up with the help and encouragement of Bok's friends, including Ray Bradbury and the Golden Gate Futurians of San Francisco.[20]

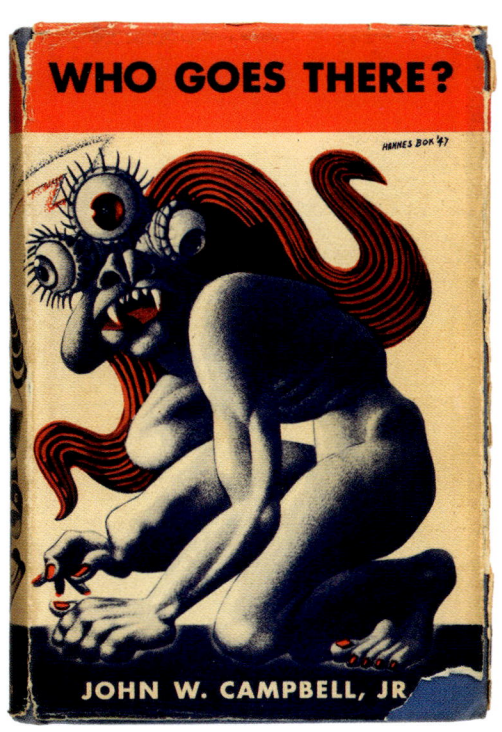

WHO GOES THERE?

JOHN W. CAMPBELL, JR.

Many of Bok's finest paintings were never published. He either sold them to private collectors or never let them go. In 1976, art collector Gene Nigra bought the bulk of Bok's estate from Clarence Peacock, a friend and neighbor of the artist who had inherited all of Bok's belongings when he died.[21]

Bok's formal influence is not as readily or directly apparent today as it should be, but his visionary approach to art-making certainly is. His work truly set the stage for more experimental science fiction, fantasy, as well as editorial illustration work in the ensuing decades, when artists developed a more personal voice and an approach to form and content that was more recognizably their own. Use of abstraction and surrealism carried on in science fiction artists such as Richard M. Powers (1921–1996) and in the fantasy art of artists not afraid to utilize juxtapositions of the beautiful with the grotesque, embracing texture and inspiring a sense of wonder when approaching subject matter more from the mind's eye and less from the clichés of the genre. Author John W. Campbell Jr.'s popular thriller *Who Goes There?*, first published in *Astounding Science Fiction* in 1938 as a novella, was adapted for the 1951 film *The Thing from Another World* and the John Carpenter–directed classic *The Thing* (1982).[22] Indeed, Bok's inimitable visualization for the cover jacket of the Shasta anthology *Who Goes There?* (1948) is fascinating and an undeniable influence on these filmic depictions of alien life forms (Fig. 7.12).

Bok's oeuvre leaves a complicated legacy in the world. He was not a household name, but the greatest visionary of his time in the fantasy genre. His creations have influenced artists working on the fringe of accepted fantasy tropes, as well as contemporary artists more broadly, to defy and push the boundaries

FIGURE 7.12. Hannes Bok (American, 1914–1964), cover illustration for John W. Campbell Jr., *Who Goes There?*, 1948, Shasta Publishers, Chicago, Korshak Collection.

of commercial and conceptual approaches to "illustration," and illustration of imaginative literature in particular. Eschewing banal depictions, Bok transcended the literal approach of visually narrating a snapshot in time. His symbolic and often metaphorical and allegorical work was deeper than that of contemporaries, more the metaphysical embodiment of a narrative, seen through his own personal interpretation and vision.

Hannes Bok maintains a relevant artistic legacy and is far from a pulp relic of the past. His experiences from the 1940s "pulp era," which held harsh treatment for creative souls such as Bok, ultimately led to his masterpiece. *A Rose for Ecclesiastes* is a tour-de-force in an alien world and in the history of great art—a culmination and triumph of all that Bok strived for in his remarkable and prestigious work.

1. Jane Frank, "Bok, Hannes Vajn," *Science Fiction and Fantasy Artists of the Twentieth Century—A Biographical Dictionary* (Jefferson, NC: McFarland & Company, Inc., Publishers, 2009): 116–18.

2. Stephen D. Korshak, "Introduction," in *A Hannes Bok Treasury*, ed. Stephen D. Korshak (Lancaster, PA: Underwood-Miller Publications, 1993), xi.

3. The first World Science Fiction Convention (Worldcon) was held on July 2–4, 1939, in the Caravan Hall in New York City.

4. The first magazine dedicated to fantasy, *Weird Tales*, appeared in 1923; it was followed in 1926 by *Amazing Stories*, the first science fiction magazine. Bok executed six color covers for *Weird Tales* between March 1940 and March 1942. *Weird Tales* also published five of Bok's stories and two of his poems between 1942 and 1951. More than fifty issues of the magazine featured Bok's pen-and-ink work until March 1954.

5. A "Hugo" is named after Hugo Gernsback, the founder of the pioneering science fiction magazine *Amazing Stories*. The Hugo Awards, first presented in 1953 and presented annually since 1955, are science fiction's most prestigious award. They are voted on by members of the World Science Fiction Convention (Worldcon), which is also responsible for administering them.

6. First published in 1949 by Mystery House, *The Magazine of Fantasy & Science Fiction* (*F&SF*), quickly became one of the leading magazines in the science fiction and fantasy fields, with a reputation for publishing literary material and including more diverse stories than its competitors. In 1958, *F&SF* won its first Hugo Award for Best Magazine, winning the award again in 1959 and 1960.

7. Emil Petaja, *And Flights of Angels: The Life and Legend of Hannes Bok* (San Francisco, CA: The Bokanalia Memorial Foundation, 1968), 53.

8. Rembrandt lighting is characterized by an illuminated triangle under the eye of the subject on the less illuminated side of the face. It is named for the Dutch painter Rembrandt (1606–1669), who utilized this type of lighting in many of his paintings.

9. Petaja, *Flights of Angels*, 53–54.

10. Aubrey Beardsley, "The Art of Hoarding (July 1984)," from *In Black and White: The Literary Remains of Aubrey Beardsley*, ed. Stephen Calloway (London: Cypher Press, 1998).

11. First published in 1899, Arthur Wesley Dow's *Composition* (New York: Baker and Taylor Company) has probably influenced more Americans than any other text to think of visual form and composition in relation to artistic modernity. While Dow is known as the mentor of Georgia O'Keeffe and Max Weber, his legacy as a proponent of modern art has suffered undeserved neglect by recent artists and art historians. *Composition*'s presentation of visual art as an analytic and constructive, rather than imitative, activity was the first tangible breath of abstraction to reach the American classroom.

12. Jay Hambidge's *Dynamic Symmetry* (New Haven, CT: Yale University Press, 1920)—originally published as a series of lessons in Hambidge's magazine *The Diagonal* (1919–20)—was popular in the 1920s and 1930s and influenced a generation of art, artists, and mathematics educators.

13. Korshak, "Introduction," xi.

14. In *And Flights of Angels*, Bok's biographer, Petaja, maintains that several visits occurred, although the exact dates are not known.

15. Coy Ludwig, *Maxfield Parrish* (New York: Watson-Gupthill, 1972), 128.

16. "Should Museums Form Collections of Illustrations?" *New York Herald*, December 1, 1907, as quoted in Sylvia Yount, *Maxfield Parrish 1870–1966* (New York: Harry N. Abrams, Inc.), 59.

17. Yount, *Maxfield Parrish*, 102.

18. Petaja, *Flights of Angels*, 108.

19. Władysław T. Benda, *Masks (Step by Step Series)* (New York: Watson-Guptill Publications, Inc., 1944).

20. A New York City circle of about twenty members and founded in 1938, the Futurian Society included distinguished science fiction professionals during the genre's formative years, including Isaac Asimov.

21. Gerry de la Ree, ed., *Beauty and the Beasts: The Art of Hannes Bok*, dust jacket text (Saddle River, NJ: Gerry de la Ree, 1978).

22. *Alternate Realities in Pulp and Popular Fiction, 1490–Early 2000s*, eds. Nicholas Egon Jainschigg, with R.W. Lovejoy, Jaleen Grove, and Whitney Sherman, *History of Illustration* (New York: Fairchild Books, 2019), 371.

David M. Brinley

INTERVIEW WITH MICHAEL R. WHELAN

Michael Whelan is a fine artist of imaginative realism and a renowned illustrator of science fiction and fantasy subjects whose work is featured in the Korshak Collection. He is a winner of fifteen Hugo Awards and a 2009 Science Fiction Hall of Fame inductee. This interview was conducted via email in February 2024. The entire transcript of the email exchange is included here, lightly edited for grammar and clarity.

BRINLEY: Erle Melvin Korshak was the publisher of the pioneering science fiction book company Shasta Publishers from 1948 to 1957. His son Steve Korshak has since curated a collection of illustration works that defined an entire generation's visualization of certain authors' work and literary characters. Three of your early pieces, *The Weird of the White Wolf* (1977), *The Master Mind of Mars* (1979; Plate 50), and *Swords of Mars* (1979), are included in the Korshak Collection. Could you please introduce your connection to the Korshaks and how these specific pieces were sought for inclusion?

WHELAN: Steve has a longstanding appreciation for fantasy art and I'm proud to have some of my works among his distinguished collection. In particular, the Korshaks and I share an avid interest in noteworthy fantasy/science fiction authors I've had the good fortune to illustrate. We soon got to know each other, having met at fantasy/science fiction conventions and art shows over the years, and developed a valued friendship.

What specific artists in the collection were an influence on you as a child, or inspired your love of the genre as you grew older and began pursuing art yourself?

Frank Frazetta (Plate 51) influenced virtually everyone of my generation of illustrators, and I was no exception. As soon as I saw his work, I was instantly attracted to it, and while a teenager, I sought it out in bookstores from L.A. to Denver. Though our painting styles were quite different, I can't deny that seeing his work has had an everlasting effect on me, especially in his convincing anatomy, color, and dynamic compositions. However, it must be acknowledged that there have been many artists whose work I found to be inspirational …

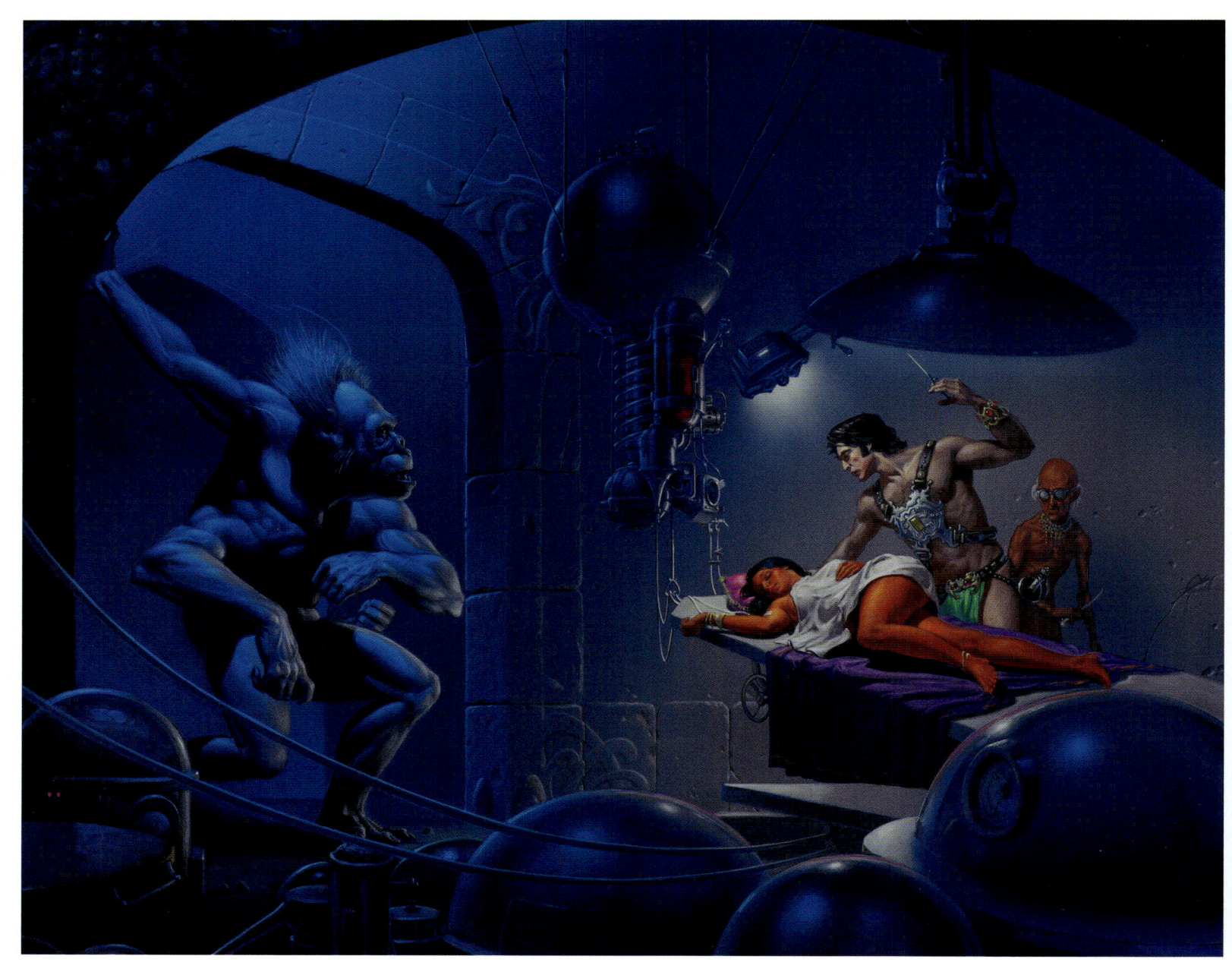

PLATE 50. Michael R. Whelan
(American, b. 1950), *The Master
Mind of Mars*, 1979, acrylic on
illustration board, 21 × 27 inches.

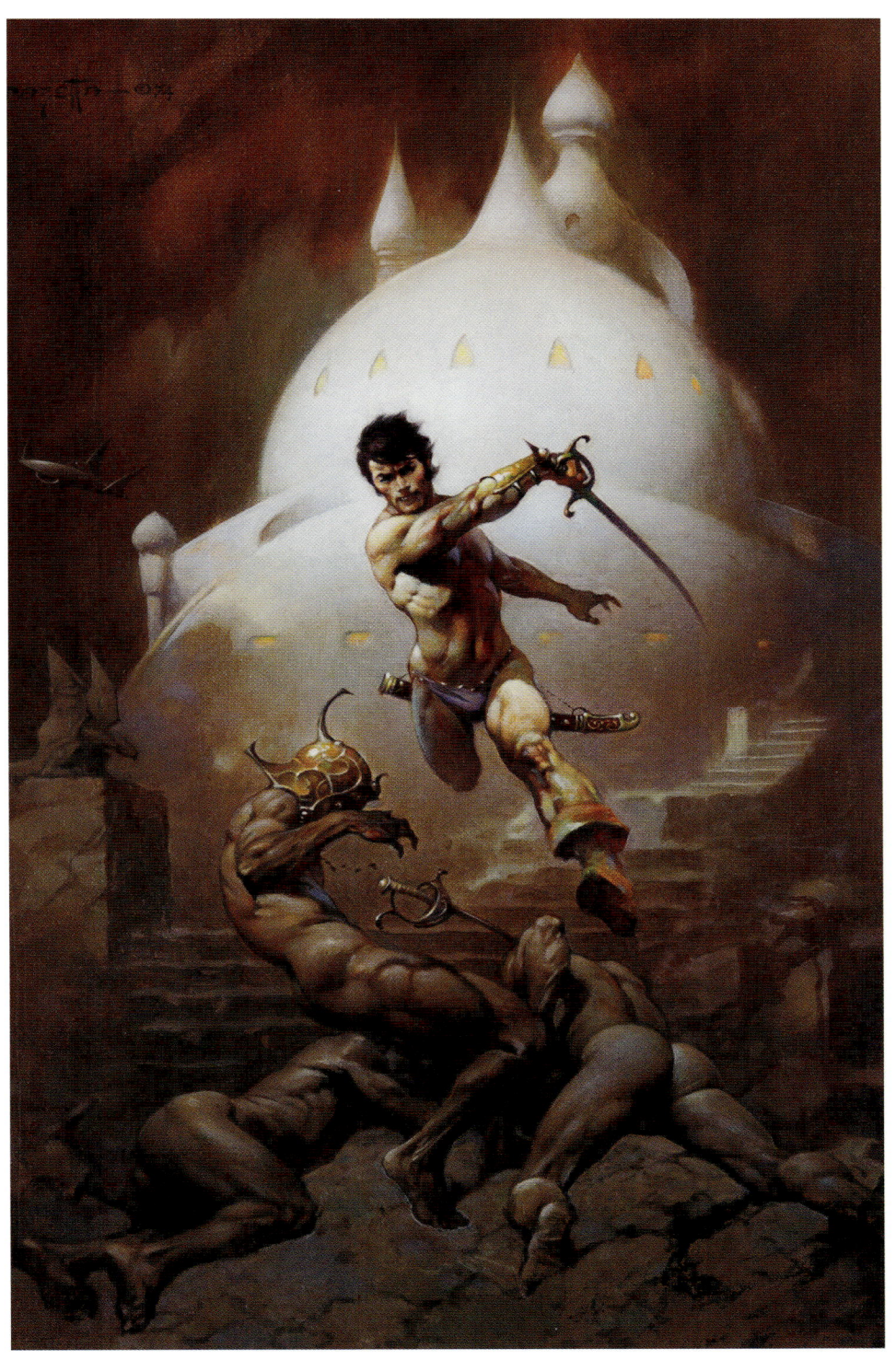

PLATE 51. Frank Frazetta (American, 1928–2010), *Swords of Mars*, oil on canvas board, 19 × 13 inches, jacket illustration for *Swords of Mars and Synthetic Men of Mars* by Edgar Rice Burroughs (Garden City, NY: Nelson Doubleday, Inc., 1975). Courtesy of Frazetta Girls, Inc.

so I feel that every admirable piece of artwork I encounter has some impact on me, conscious or unconscious.

Among the pieces in the Korshak Collection, there's the thrilling action and beautiful color of [J. Allen] St. John, Frazetta, and [Kelly] Freas (Plate 52). The way-out imagination of Frank R. Paul, the realism and precise rendering of [Arthur] Rackham and [Fortunino] Matania (Plate 53) … oh, I could go on and on. Both Hannes Bok and I were drawn to the work of Maxfield Parrish, though I never had the chance to meet or correspond with him.

Are there a few personal highlights in the collection that you simply respond to deeply for the quality and uniqueness of a particular artist, piece of art, or take on their visual interpretation of the literature?

Certainly. The Arthur Rackham paintings, for example: the way he so cleverly renders the fantastic creatures in a way that their surreal anatomies look as if they could actually exist; well, that's magic as well as art. I admire each of the artists in the collection for different qualities I see in their work; they all have something of the "sense of wonder" so enthralling in works of imagination. My mother had a wonderful collection of children's fantasy books from the early years of [the twentieth] century, so early on I grew up fascinated by the work of Rackham, [Edmund] Dulac, and their contemporaries. As I grew up and read books with cover art by Freas, [Ed] Emsh[willer], Frazetta, and others, that interest continued to expand. I sought out all the art of wonder I could find in local libraries and shows, and came to appreciate the astonishingly wide range of subjects, styles, and dramatic imagination that has been a hallmark of this ever-popular art genre.

Perhaps there are works outside of the collection that may have a particular importance in the field that captured your attention when you first saw them?

Definitely—too many to mention!—but I suppose I could single out a few particular examples. In my late teens, I was able to attend a showing of the art of Chesley Bonestell, a particular favorite of mine. I had seen reproductions of his art in magazines in the '50s, but I was astonished to witness firsthand the imagination, clarity, precision, and realism in his original paintings. It really opened my eyes wide to the possibilities in painting! In college, I saw a couple of exhibitions that—again—rocked my sensibilities and grasp of what was humanly possible. One was of the paintings of the West Coast visionary artist Bill Martin. The other show featured many works by M.C. Escher. I was never the same after seeing those two shows.

DAVID M. BRINLEY

PLATE 52 (opposite). Kelly Freas (American, 1922–2005), *Mars Minus Bisha* (*Planet Stories* cover), 1954, oil on canvasboard, 20 × 14 inches.

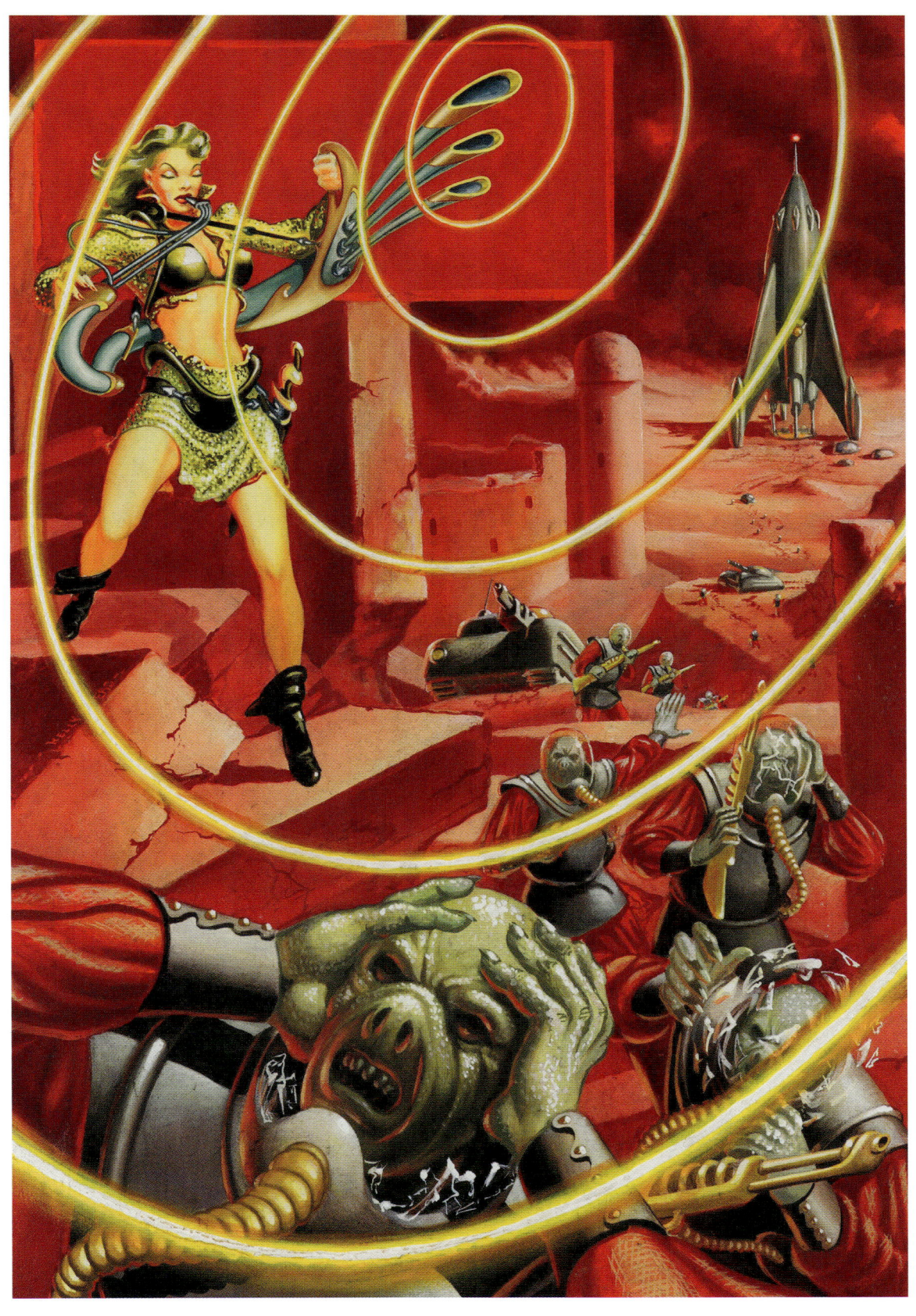

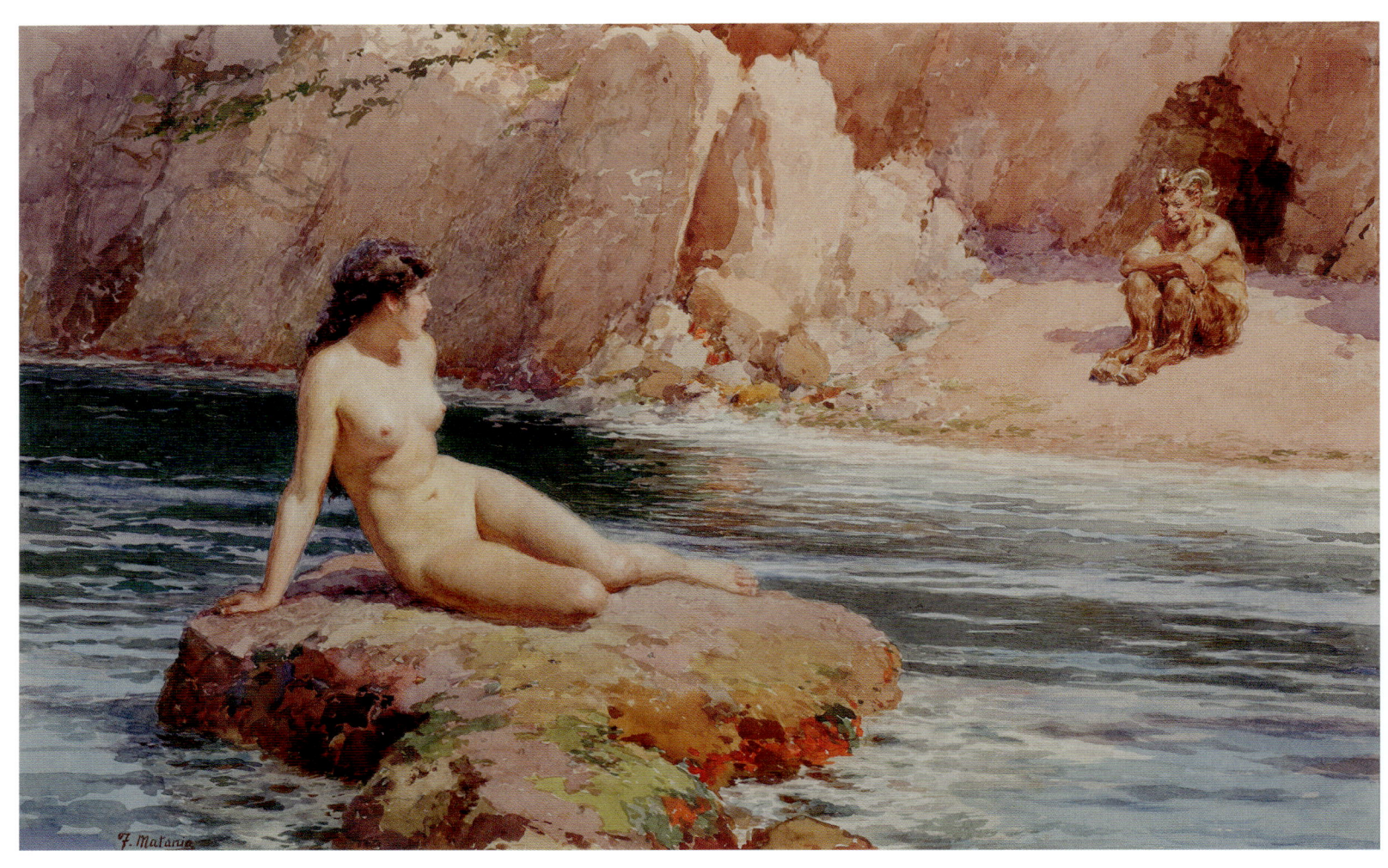

PLATE 53. Fortunino Matania (Italian, 1881–1963), *Checkmate*, c. 1950, watercolor, 10 × 16 inches.

How much did your pre-med education assist in your approach to anatomy and imaginative realism?

It had a profound effect on my knowledge base regarding the human form and its construction. At virtually the same time, I was taking life drawing and figure painting classes, so the two disciplines complemented each other neatly. I feel it helped me to paint figures without using models, which I couldn't afford early on in my career.

Was there a period of trial and error as well as experimentation with oil paint, acrylics, or other media in your earlier work?

Oh goodness, yes—and it is still going on, and will continue to do so as long as I live. "Life is for learning," sang Joni Mitchell, and I believe it to be true. I try to allow myself time to be experimental and have fun with whatever might produce an interesting or useful result, as long as it doesn't compromise the endurance of the final image in any significant way.

Was there a defining moment to utilize acrylic paint versus oil paint for you? I notice that *The Weird of the White Wolf* (1977) is listed in the Korshak Collection as "oil and acrylic on illustration board." Is this entirely correct for that specific piece?

In my younger years, I thought one should only use oils on primed canvas. When I learned that there were illustrators using (primed) illustration board as a surface, I was interested in giving that a try. I prefer canvas, but other surfaces can be effective in certain cases. Once I became too busy to wait for oil paints to dry in time to meet my deadlines, I had to switch to using acrylics. I enjoy both media very much; each has its advantages and disadvantages.

Do you reflect upon how your drawing, composition, and color palette influence your personal approach to a piece or do you collaboratively consider what the art director and project requires? Or both?

My first and foremost consideration after reading a text is "How can I best convey this novel into an image?" All other factors are secondary and selected to serve the needs of the first consideration, within the scope of my abilities and limitations. Any artwork painted on commission is a sort of balancing act, whether one is painting a pope, pop star, or paperback book cover. The one hiring the artist usually has some preconceived notions about what is expected, but even in the absence of any stated requirements, an artist is unfailingly affected by what he or she has done before, and where he or she would like to go.

Could you please discuss how collaborating with musicians and musical artists (and licensing particular works) may have influenced the content of and approach to your fantasy illustration work?

Creating artwork for musical projects has run the gamut from free expression on my part to dictated subjects and laundry lists of desired elements in an album's packaging. Often, the way I'd prefer that things go is that the painting was done, but someone connected with the music saw the piece, liked it, and licensed it for an album. However, in other instances, I've been asked to depict a certain rather specific topic or subject. In such instances, it's rarely as collaborative as I'd like it to be. For that reason, I rarely accept such assignments anymore.

Was developing your own personal content and fine artwork an important step that evolved from how you approached solutions for commercial pieces?

The key attraction of non-commissioned painting is in having no restrictions in size, image proportions, or subject matter. Not having to please anybody but myself is ideal, of course, and I've been extremely fortunate that the subjects of interest to me are enjoyed by others as well. Though it's hard to turn a deaf ear to the gallery owner who says, "I could have sold ten paintings of that image if you'd done more just like it."

DAVID M. BRINLEY

Illustration techniques have evolved and broadened over the past 160 years that the Korshak Collection spans, from European gift book illustrators' pen and ink, chromatic pulp covers, and 1960s and '70s heroic book covers, to the turn of the 2000s and entrance into the digital realm. Do you find that this trajectory goes hand-in-hand in some respects with the evolution of printing techniques and technology through the decades?

Artists have long been eager to employ new technology, and with advances in printing reproduction, history shows us a gradual evolution of techniques employed by each generation of illustrators. Nevertheless, appreciation for the styles and techniques of our predecessors remains constant, and their influence is easily seen among present-day artists, in spite of technical advances. Nevertheless, we are entering a new era now, where a particular long sought-after goal has been realized: the ideal of non-destructive editing power, now a reality via digital media. To be able to seamlessly correct one's work is almost irresistible.

One of the first artists I encountered as a student in the early 1990s who was working digitally in the field was David Mattingly. He described how he was moving from analog (acrylics and brushes) into the computer with digital tools.

How would you describe the evolution of digital painting and its contemporary impact in the field of fantasy? Does it offer speed? More flexibility with manipulating elements within a work?

Digital art has been a mixed blessing from my perspective. Without getting into the relative costs of tools employed, which platforms one chooses to work on, and the need to have electrical power in order to use it, there are several superficially attractive advantages to digital painting. For artists working on a deadline, or who are trying to satisfy a client requesting changes in an ongoing work, the advantages are obvious. But sometimes the learning curve can be daunting, especially if one hasn't grown up using digital tools as second nature. The initial danger with digital media for me was the temptation to "drill down," to edit the image down to the individual pixel level, which of course is the wrong idea altogether.

I'll end on this group of questions relevant to the future of the field. I'm curious how you feel. In speaking with author, editor, and historian Barry Klugerman, and Steve [Korshak], generative Artificial Intelligence (AI) inevitably came up. How do you feel about the emergence and training of AI and its unpredictable influence on the field? Are there pros and cons of AI as a tool, in your opinion? Do these tools influence the mind's eye to such a degree to stifle any future evolution of fantasy or, for that matter, any future original illustration?

Who can tell? History shows us that trends are transitory. In the early to mid-sixties, there was a slump in book cover illustrations due to editorial decisions to rely more on photography. It was claimed that "painted illustration would soon be dead." Well, then the popularity of fantasy/science fiction books soared and along came Frazetta and all that changed again! That's an outrageous simplification, I realize, but the point remains the same. I see AI as just a tool, and my instincts tell me that it won't replace artists any more than photography or digital media have done. Granted, it will narrow the niches some by adding content that wasn't there before, but in the end all it will do is reflect the current fashions in art and replicate some trends, but will mostly be a follower, not a leader. That's my gut feeling anyway. Time will tell. But generally if a thing can be done, humans will find a reason and a way to do it … and this genie is already out of the bottle.

MICHAEL R. WHELAN

Gary K. Wolfe

AFTERWORD: A Dialogue of Things Unseen

In early 1955, the author Algis Budrys was visiting the offices of *Fantastic Universe* magazine, where he spotted a cover painting by Kelly Freas, then one of science fiction's most prolific illustrators, of a man leaning over his desk whose head and arm had been replaced by gleaming metal, as though he were part robot. Intrigued by the image, Budrys wrote a short story called "Who?" that appeared in the April issue of the magazine (featuring that same Freas painting on its cover. He later expanded the story into a novel with the same title, published in 1958. The novel, one of the most direct expressions of Cold War anxiety from 1950s science fiction, was later reprinted in *American Science Fiction: Five Classic Novels of the 1950s,* published by the Library of America in 2012. It was even the basis of a now almost forgotten 1975 movie starring Elliott Gould. This is far from the only time a science fiction writer took inspiration from a pre-purchased cover painting, rather than a cover artist taking inspiration from a science fiction story.

In 1981, another distinguished author, William Gibson, published a short story titled "The Gernsback Continuum," now widely regarded as one of the defining texts of the literary and cultural movement known as cyberpunk. In it, an architectural photographer finds himself haunted by "semiotic phantoms, bits of deep cultural imagery that have split off and taken on a life of their own," depicting "a shadowy America-that-wasn't" based on the streamlined dreams of the 1930s.[1] In describing one of these visions, Gibson invokes "the covers of old *Amazing Stories* pulps, by an artist named Frank R. Paul…. Spire stood on spire in gleaming ziggurat steps that climbed to a central golden temple spire…. Roads of crystal soared between the spires, crossed and recrossed with smooth silver shapes like beads of running mercury."[2] The story has since been reprinted and translated more than sixty times.

In 2017, Ellen Klages published the novella *Passing Strange,* which would go on to win a World Fantasy Award. It describes a group of women, some involved with the LGBT community in 1940s San Francisco, one of whom is a successful pulp magazine illustrator named Haskell. One of Haskell's covers "showed a naked woman, her breasts barely concealed by a spill of blond hair, fleeing from a swarm of tiny-winged demons," while another showed a scantily clad woman, "this one threatened on one side by a lobsterish creature and on the other by a sinister-looking man in Chinese robes, his talon-like nails reaching for her throat."[3] The acknowledgments for the book include "Stephen D. Korshak and J. David Spurlock for their work on the art of Margaret Brundage,"[4] the prolific *Weird Tales* artist who partly provided the inspiration for the character Haskell, and whose work is insightfully discussed in this volume by Lisa Yaszek. (Incidentally, the delicacy of Brundage's pastels, described here by Michael Dirda as "so fragile that if you breathe heavily on them half the image will fly away as chalky dust," serves as a major plot point in Klages's story.)

As these three examples including artists whose work is featured in the Korshak Collection illustrate, the long relationship between fantastic literature and fantastic art has hardly been a one-way street. Just as the artists represented here have taken fiction as the launchpad for their own visions, so have science fiction and fantasy writers found inspiration in the visual arts, for which examples could be multiplied endlessly. British author Ian Watson's 1982 novel *The Garden of Delights* begins with a spaceship landing on a strange planet whose fantastic landscape seems identical to that of Hieronymus Bosch's sixteenth-century painting *The Garden of Earthly Delights*. Watson also edited an anthology, *Pictures at an Exhibition* (1981), featuring science fiction stories inspired by works of art by René Magritte, Albrecht Dürer, Salvador Dalí, Nicolas Poussin, Edvard Munch, Gustav Moreau, and even Frank Frazetta. And H.P. Lovecraft's "Pickman's Model"—the same story that inspired the chilling Hannes Bok illustration in the Korshak Collection—was itself partly inspired by earlier art. Lovecraft makes clear his debt by having his narrator mention Henry Fuseli, Gustave Doré, and other artists, and describing the work of his fictional artist Pickman in relation to other artists when he writes, "There was none of the exotic technique you see in Sidney Sime, none of the trans-Saturnian landscapes and lunar fungi that Clark Ashton Smith uses to freeze the blood."[5]

There is a long history of illustration being included in popular fiction in books and magazines, but it may be that science fiction and fantasy have had a more intimate, or more symbiotic, relationship with illustration than most genres, for one simple reason: both imaginative fiction and imaginative art try to show us things never before seen. Nineteenth-century book illustrations may have employed traditional tropes, depicting knights, castles, and even mythological creatures, but an *invented* manmade monster such as

Mary Shelley's *Frankenstein* was something few could clearly picture—at least until Theodore Von Holst's frontispiece for the 1831 edition. Nor had anyone seen a technologically designed spacecraft before Henri de Montaut's first illustrations for Jules Verne's *From the Earth to the Moon* (1865) appeared. Readers had few visual reference points for imagining the bizarre Martian war machines in H.G. Wells's *The War of the Worlds* (1898) until illustrations by Warwick Goble and Henrique Alvim Corrêa, and later José Segrelles, were circulated. Some of the most successful pulp magazine illustrators also worked for Western, romance, and crime magazines, but their familiar pictures of horses and caped, shadowy villains were not nearly as helpful for readers trying to visualize the texts as the spaceships and giant cities of Frank R. Paul or the monsters and surreal landscapes of Hannes Bok were. In other words, science fiction and fantasy gave writers and artists a license to invent, and readers a license to imagine, in ways that no other popular fiction attempted.

Publishers were well aware of this, and cover art became nearly as much a part of brand recognition as the authors featured between the covers—and not only in pulp magazines. Just as the work of Paul became emblematic of *Amazing Stories* in the 1920s or that of Brundage was synonymous with *Weird Tales* in the 1930s, so paperback publishers in the 1950s come to be associated with particular artists and styles. The relatively muted, realistic covers Stanley Meltzoff produced for Signet Books contrasted sharply with the more abstract, sometimes Yves Tanguy–inspired work of Richard Powers for Ballantine Books, the more sensational, pulpish covers of Ed Valigursky for Ace Books, or the deliberately retro images of Roy Krenkel for Ace's reprints of older classics by Edgar Rice Burroughs or Robert E. Howard. An astute reader of that era could quickly infer that the more painterly covers of Signet charac-terized classic science fiction by Isaac Asimov or Robert A. Heinlein, the more abstract Ballantine covers were used for writers like Arthur C. Clarke or Theodore Sturgeon, and the relatively garish Ace covers signified the old-school adventures inside. For many of us (including me), those distinctive cover styles represented our first awareness that different publishers did different things, and that publishers mattered.

The Korshak Collection thus represents not merely a historical survey of fantastic art and illustration, but an ongoing cultural dialogue that has since expanded to include everything from toys and movies to video games and industrial and commercial design. Given the often ephemeral nature of such work, it is something of a wonder that so many examples have been preserved,

GARY K. WOLFE

not only those of the genre from books and magazines, but also those of such important antecedents as Arthur Rackham, Edmund Dulac, and Harry Clarke. If there are occasional hints of the familiar in these fantastic images, it may well be because they have been a vivid part of our aesthetic landscape for well over a century, and continue to inspire us today.

1. William Gibson, "The Gernsback Continuum," *Mirrorshades: The Cyberpunk Anthology*, ed. Bruce Sterling (New York: Ace, 1988), 7, 5.

2. Gibson, "The Gernsback Continuum," 8.

3. Ellen Klages, *Passing Strange* (New York: Tor, 2017), 59.

4. Stephen D. Korshak and J. David Spurlock, *The Alluring Art of Margaret Brundage: Queen of Pulp Pin-Up Art* (Coral Gables, FL: Vanguard, 2013).

5. H.P. Lovecraft, "Pickman's Model," *Tales* (New York: Library of America, 2005), 203.

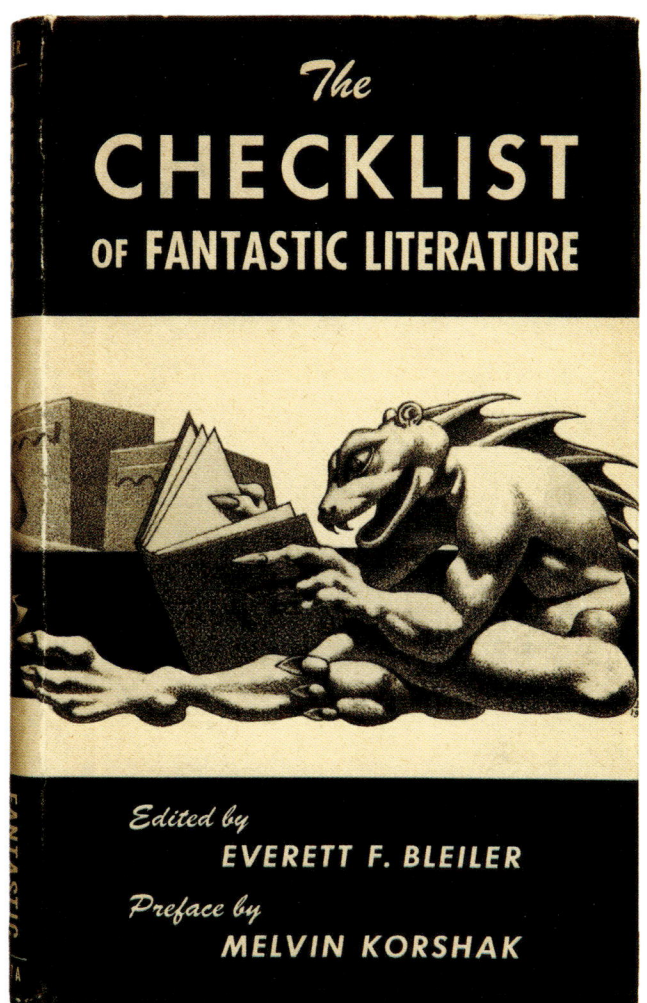

*The Checklist of
Fantastic Literature*
by Everett F. Bleiler
(Chicago: Shasta
Publishers, 1948).

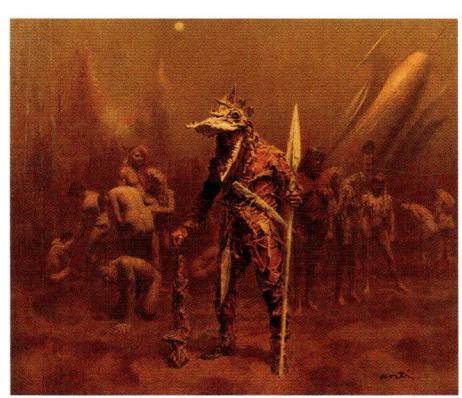

James Avati
(American, 1912–2005)
Deathworld 2, 1964
Oil on canvasboard
17 × 21 inches

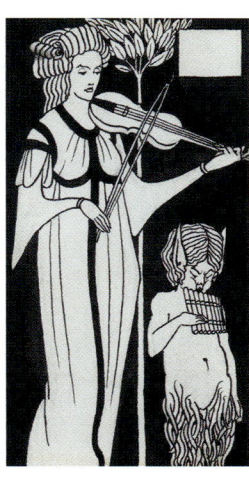

Aubrey Beardsley
(British, 1872–1898)
Le Morte d'Arthur, or *Woman Playing
the Violin and Satyr Playing the
Pipes for Le Morte d'Arthur,* 1894
Pen and ink on paper
5 × 3 inches

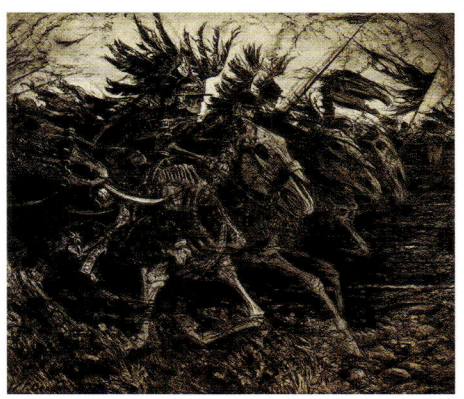

Władysław T. Benda
(Polish, 1873–1948)
The Army of the Dead, 1917
Charcoal on paper
29¼ × 34 inches

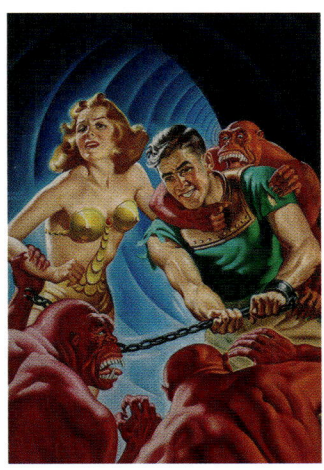

Earle K. Bergey
(American, 1901–1952)
Shadow over Mars, 1944
Oil on canvas
26 × 18 inches

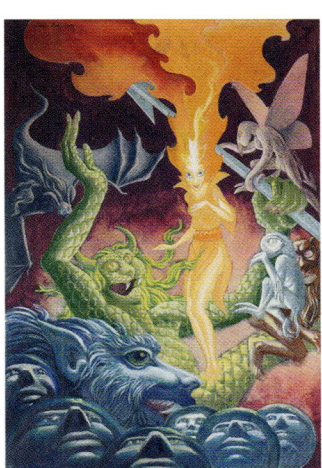

Hannes Bok
(American, 1914–1964)
Horror of the Glen, 1939
Gouache on illustration board
19¾ × 13½ inches

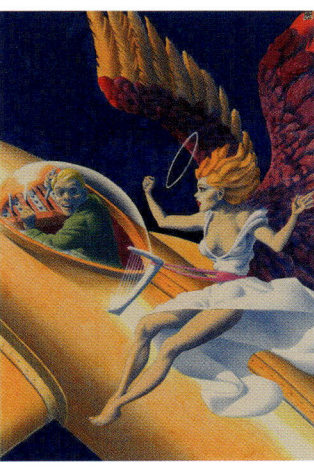

Hannes Bok
(American, 1914–1964)
Hell's Angel, 1951
Gouache on illustration board
16 × 11 inches

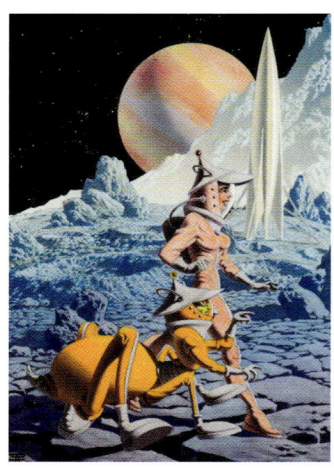

Hannes Bok
(American, 1914–1964)
Moonwalk (*Marvel Science Stories*
cover), 1951
Mixed media on illustration board
16 × 11 inches

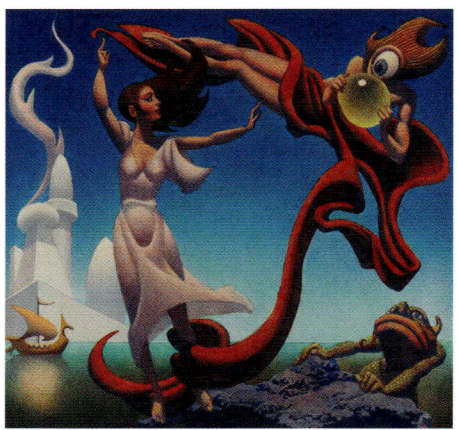

Hannes Bok
(American, 1914–1964)
Skull-Face and Others, 1946
Gouache on illustration board
6 × 8 inches

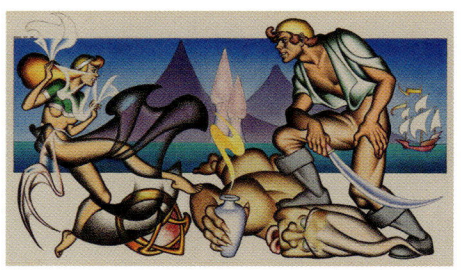

Hannes Bok
(American, 1914–1964)
Slaves of Sleep, 1948
Mixed media on illustration board
10 × 16 inches

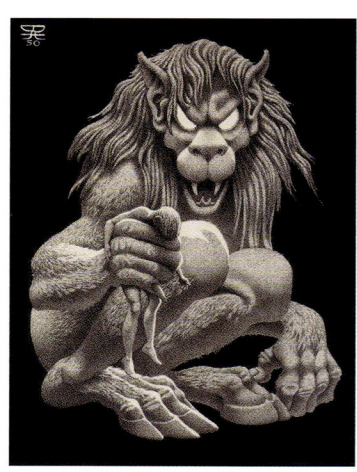

Hannes Bok
(American, 1914–1964)
Pickman's Model, 1950
Mixed media, pen and ink
on illustration board
8¾ × 6¾ inches

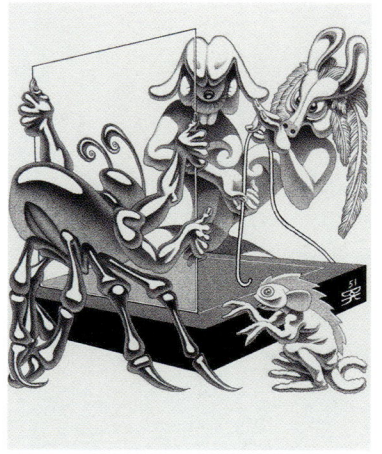

Hannes Bok
(American, 1914–1964)
Oblivion Quest, 1951
Pen and ink on paper
18½ × 15 inches

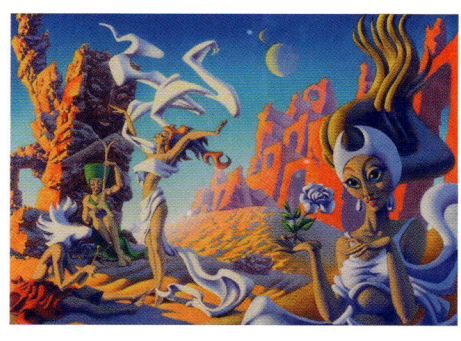

Hannes Bok
(American, 1914–1964)
A Rose for Ecclesiastes, 1963
Gouache on illustration board
11 × 16 inches

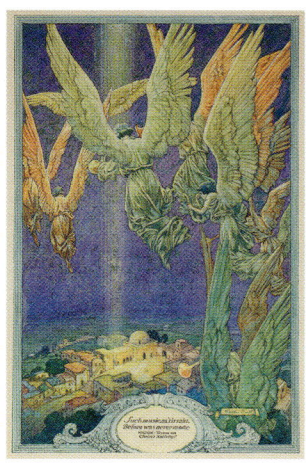

Franklin Booth
(American, 1874–1948)
Hymn on Christ's Nativity, 1929
Pen and ink with watercolor
18 × 12 inches

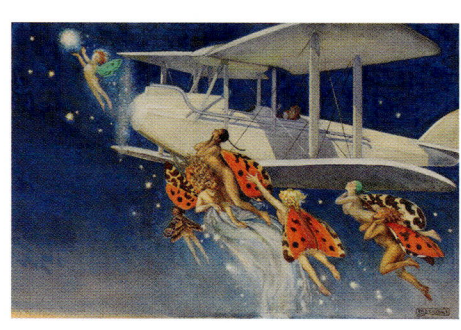

Eleanor Fortescue-Brickdale
(English, 1872–1945)
The Moth, 1917
Watercolor with gouache
on illustration board
11½ x 18½ inches

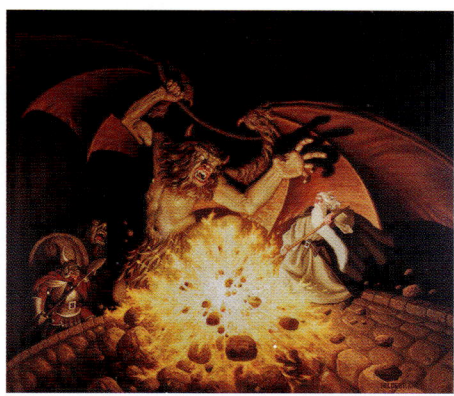

Brothers Hildebrandt
(American,
Greg Hildebrandt, 1939–2024,
and Tim Hildebrandt, 1939–2006)
The Balrog, 1977
Acrylic
35 × 42 inches

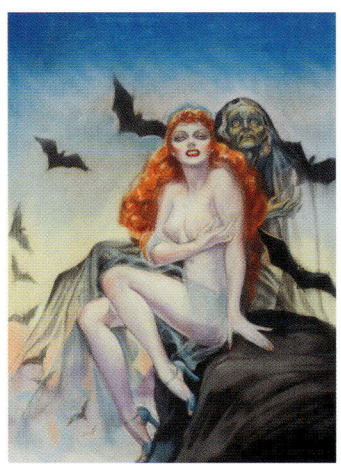

Margaret Brundage
(American, 1900–1976)
Witch's Mark, 1938
Pastel on paper
26 × 20 inches

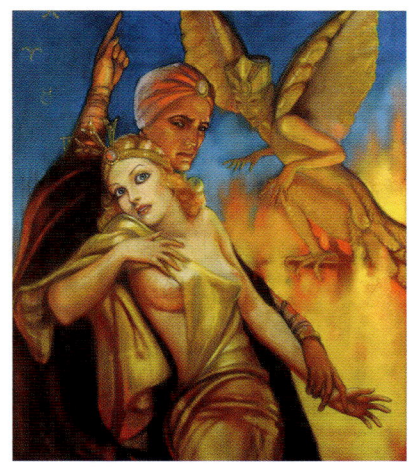

Margaret Brundage
(American, 1900–1976)
Altar of Melek Taos, 1932
Pastel on paper
23 × 16 inches

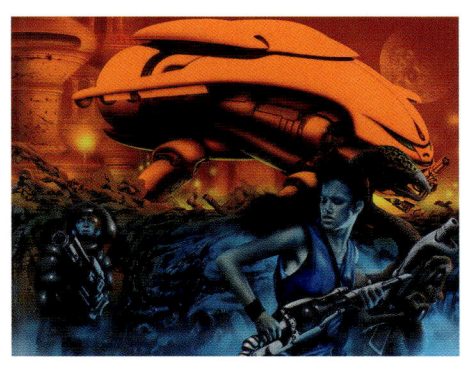

Jim Burns
(American, b. 1948)
Profiteer: Hostile Takeover #1
(*Odyssey*), 1995; Commissioned
by Daw Books, 1994
Acrylic on illustration board
21 × 28 inches
Courtesy of Jim Burns

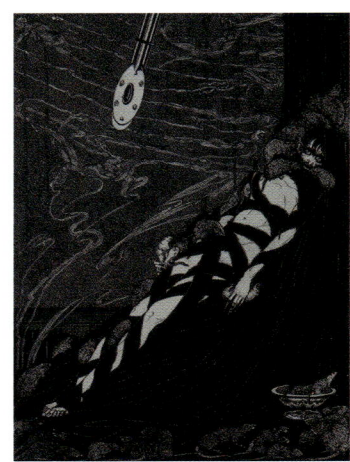

Harry Clarke
(Irish, 1889–1931)
The Pit and the Pendulum, 1919
Pen and ink
9 × 7 inches

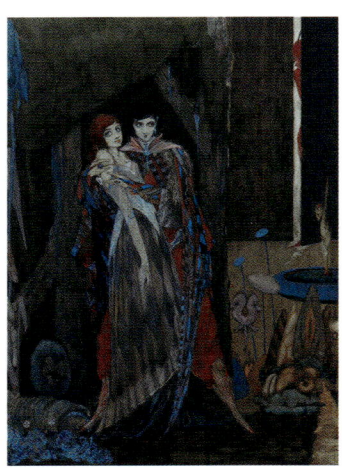

Harry Clarke
(Irish, 1889–1931)
Faust (frontispiece), 1925
Pen and ink, watercolor
12 × 9 inches

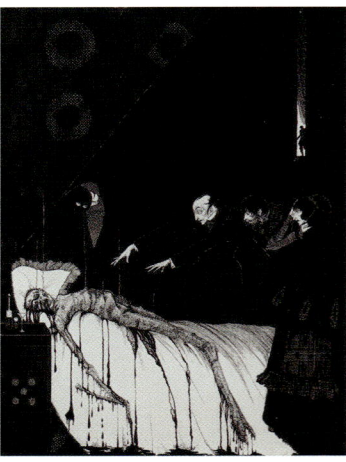

Harry Clarke
(Irish, 1889–1931)
*The Facts in the Case
of M. Valdemar*, 1919
Pen and ink
13 × 10 inches

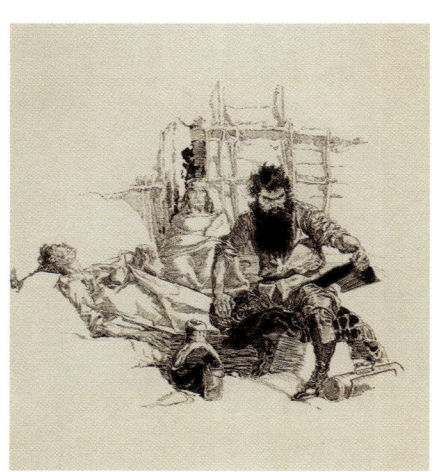

Joseph Clement Coll
(American, 1881–1921)
Professor Challenger
(*The Lost World*), 1912
Pen and ink
15½ × 14½ inches

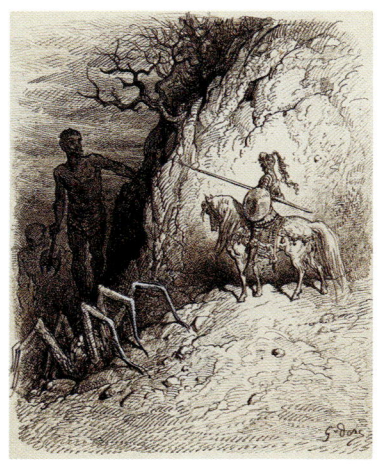

Gustave Doré
(French, 1832–1883)
Don Quixote, 1863
Pen and ink
10 × 8 inches

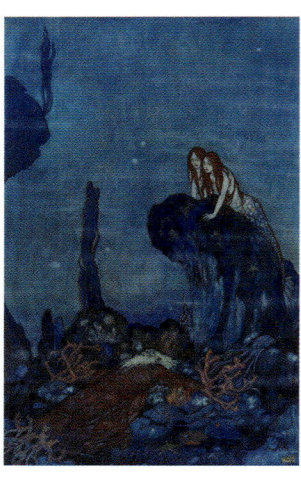

Edmund Dulac
(British, b. French, 1832–1883)
The Tempest
"*Full Fathom Five*," 1908
Watercolor, gouache, ink
17 × 11½ inches

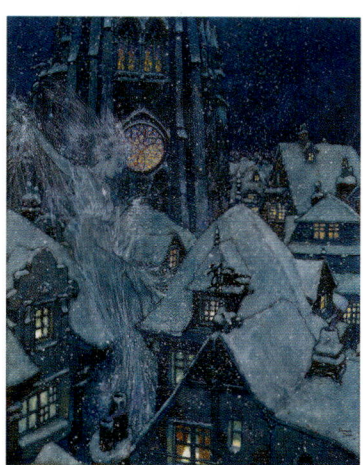

Edmund Dulac
(British, b. French, 1832–1883)
The Snow Queen, 1910
Watercolor, gouache,
pen and ink on paper
12³⁄₈ × 10 inches

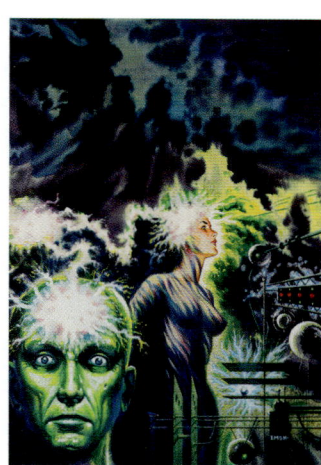

Edmund Emshwiller
(American, 1925–1990)
Science Fiction Stories
cover, 1955
Gouache on illustration board
17 × 12 inches; Courtesy
of the Ed Emshwiller Estate

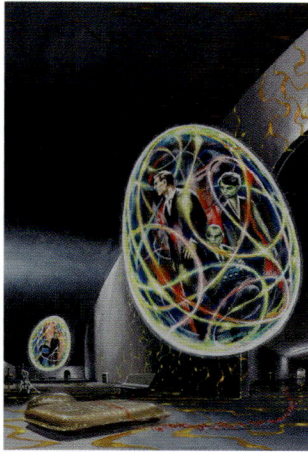

Edmund Emshwiller
(American, 1925–1990)
The Tree of Time, 1963
Gouache on illustration board
17 × 12 inches
Courtesy of the
Ed Emshwiller Estate

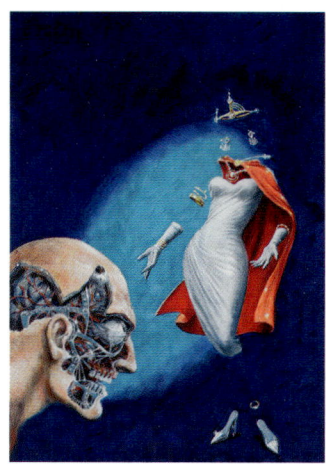

Edmund Emshwiller
(American, 1925–1990)
Towers of Toron, 1964
Gouache on illustration board
17 × 12 inches
Courtesy of the
Ed Emshwiller Estate

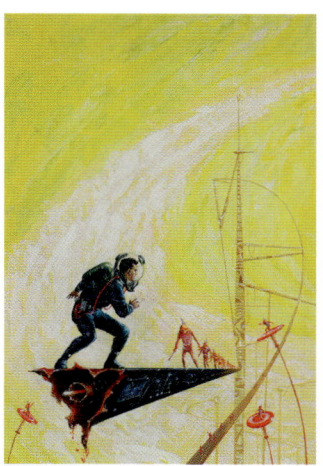

Edmund Emshwiller
(American, 1925–1990)
Spaceman, c. 1965
Gouache on illustration board
19 × 13 inches
Courtesy of the
Ed Emshwiller Estate

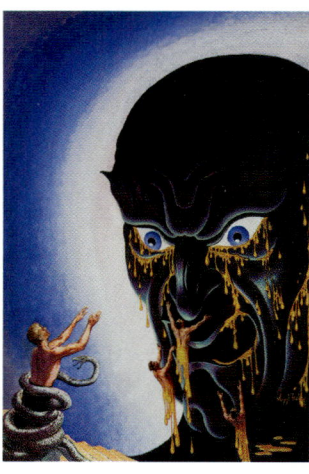

Virgil Finlay
(American, 1914–1971)
Face in the Abyss, 1940
Gouache on illustration board
18 × 13 inches

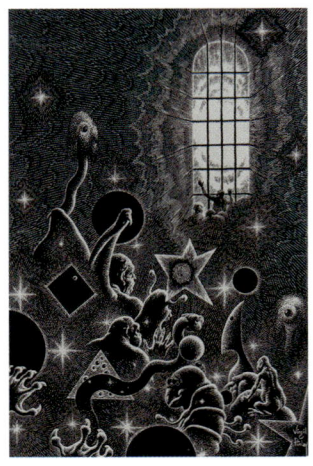

Virgil Finlay
(American, 1914–1971)
Three Against the Stars, 1950
Scratchboard, pen and ink
8 × 5 inches

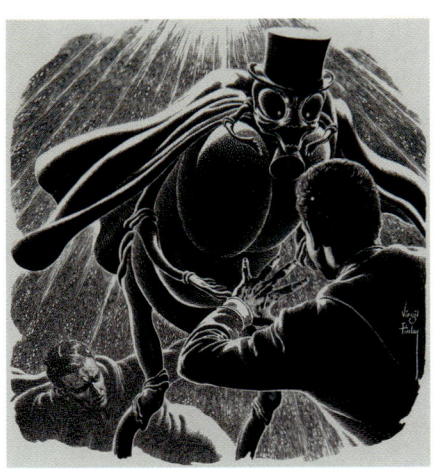

Virgil Finlay
(American, 1914–1971)
The Lovers, 1952
Scratchboard, pen and ink
6 × 6 inches

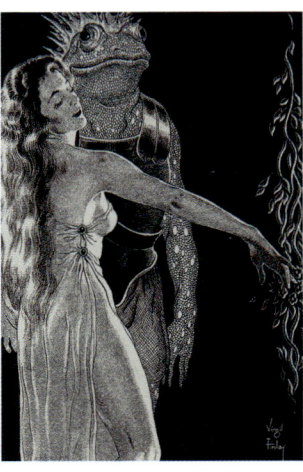

Virgil Finlay
(American, 1914–1971)
Conquest of the Moon Pool, 1948
Scratchboard, pen and ink
8 × 5 inches

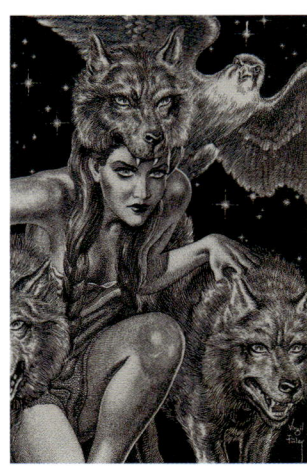

Virgil Finlay
(American, 1914–1971)
Dwellers in the Mirage (interior), 1949
Scratchboard, pen and ink
7 × 5 inches

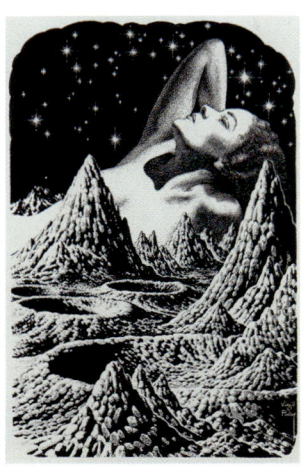

Virgil Finlay
(American, 1914–1971)
Woman in Lunar Landscape, c. 1955
Scratchboard, pen and ink
7 × 5 inches

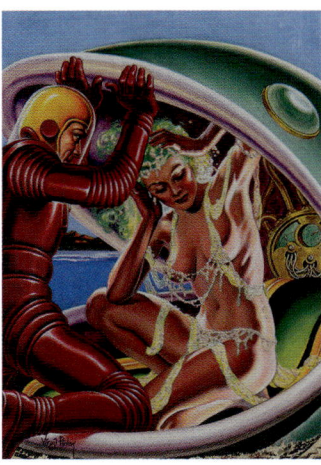

Virgil Finlay
(American, 1914–1971)
Other Worlds Science Stories
cover, 1956
Gouache on illustration board
10 × 8 inches

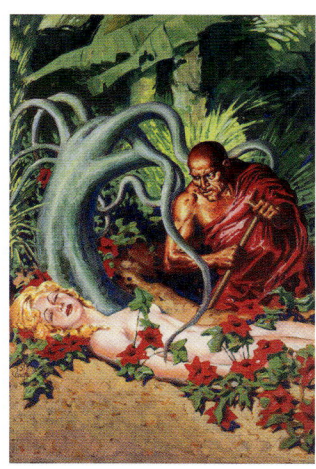

Virgil Finlay
(American, 1914–1971)
Garden of Adompha, 1937
Gouache on illustration board
19¼ × 13¼ inches

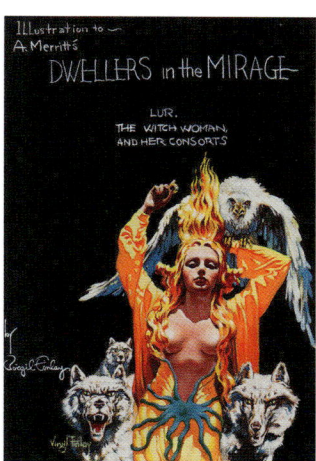

Virgil Finlay
(American, 1914–1971)
Lur the Witch Woman
(*Dwellers in the Mirage* cover), 1941
Gouache on illustration board
13 × 9 inches

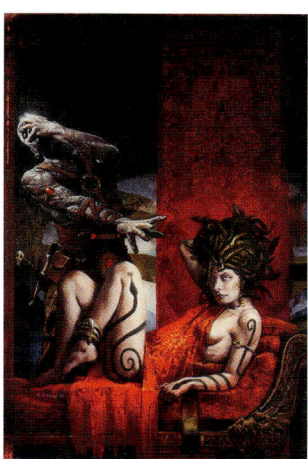

Scott Fischer
(American, b. 1971)
The Medusa, 2004
Oil on board
17½ × 12 inches

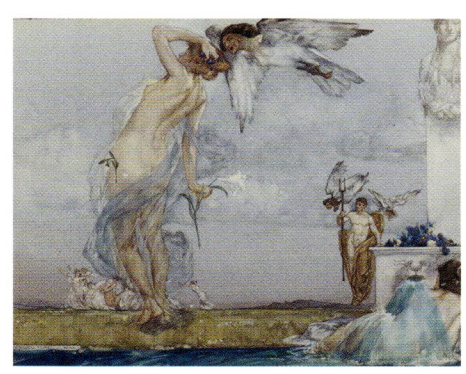

William Russell Flint
(Scottish, 1880–1969)
*For She Herself Had
Trod Sicilian Fields*, 1910
Watercolor, glazed
9¾ × 12¾ inches

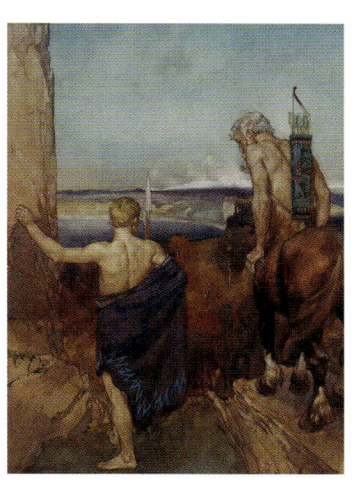

William Russell Flint
(Scottish, 1880–1969)
Cheiron the Centaur and Jason, 1911
Watercolor
11 × 8½ inches

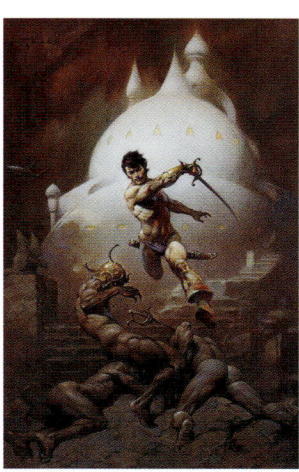

Frank Frazetta
(American, 1928–2010)
*Swords of Mars and
Synthetic Men of Mars*, 1966
Oil on canvasboard
19 × 13 inches
Courtesy of Frazetta Girls, Inc.

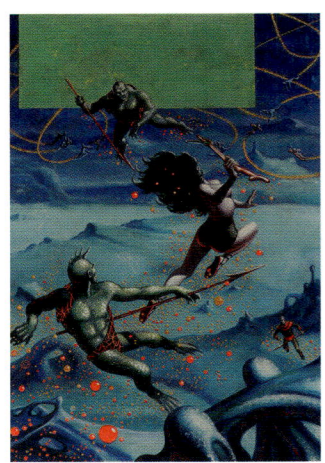

Kelly Freas
(American, 1922–2005)
Lost Tribes of Venus, 1954
Oil on canvasboard
19 × 13 inches

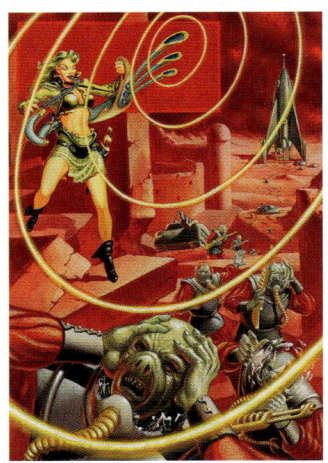

Kelly Freas
(American, 1922–2005)
Mars Minus Bisha
(*Planet Stories* cover), 1954
Oil on canvasboard
20 × 14 inches

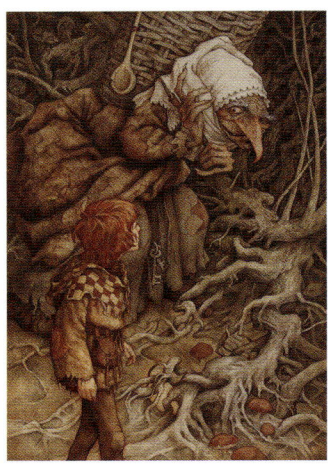

Brian Froud
(British, b. 1947)
Allison Gross, 1976
Watercolor, pen and ink
22 × 15½ inches

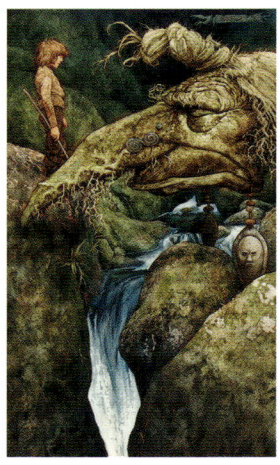

Brian Froud
(British, b. 1947)
Voice of the River, 1976
Watercolor, gouache
22¾ × 13½ inches

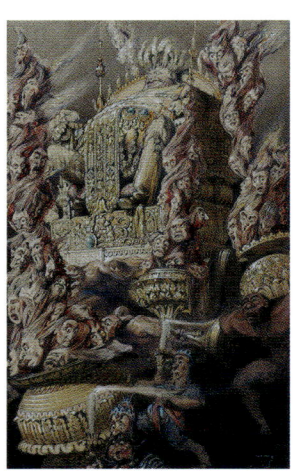

Álmos Jaschik
(Hungarian, 1885–1959)
Carnival of Souls, c. 1935
Watercolor with gouache, pencil
9 × 5¾ inches

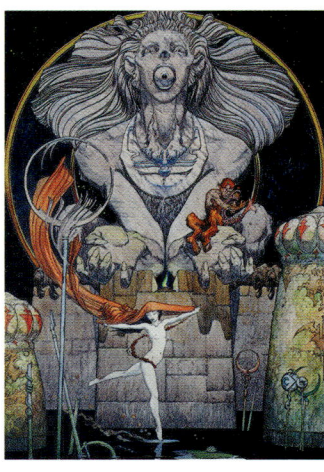

Michael Kaluta
(American, b. 1947)
Solo, c. 1976
Pen and ink, watercolor on paper
20½ × 15 inches

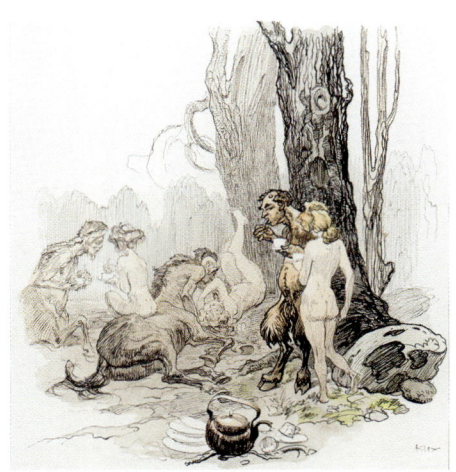

Heinrich Kley
(German, 1863–1945)
Picnic, c. 1930
Watercolor, pen and ink
9½ × 9½ inches

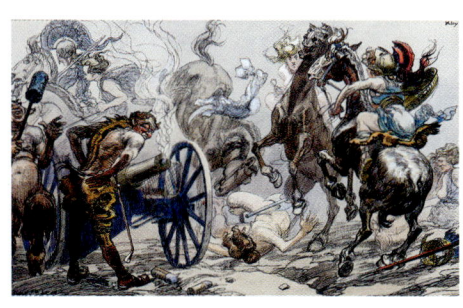

Heinrich Kley
(German, 1863–1945)
*Amazons During Shooting Practice in
Camp Lechfeld (Amazonen Bei Der
Schiessubung im Lager Lechfeld)*, 1910
Pen and ink, watercolor
9½ × 15½ inches

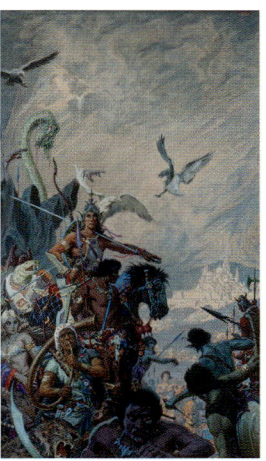

Roy Krenkel
(American, 1918–1983)
King Kull, 1967
Gouache on board
18½ × 11 inches

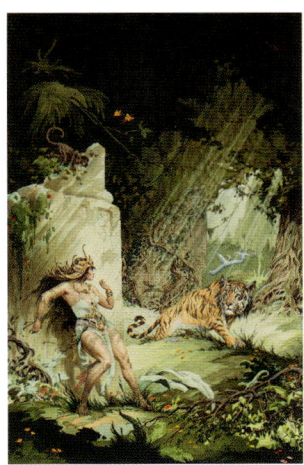

Roy Krenkel
(American, 1918–1983)
Land of Hidden Men, 1963
Watercolor with gouache
14 × 10 inches

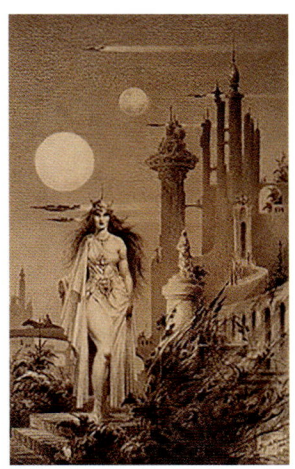

Roy Krenkel
(American, 1918–1983)
Erbania cover #13, 1963
Graphite on paper
18½ × 12 inches

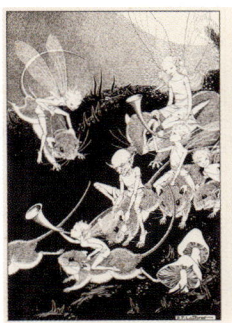

Dorothy Lathrop
(American, 1891–1980)
Fairy Riders, c. 1925
Pen and ink
10½ × 15¼ inches

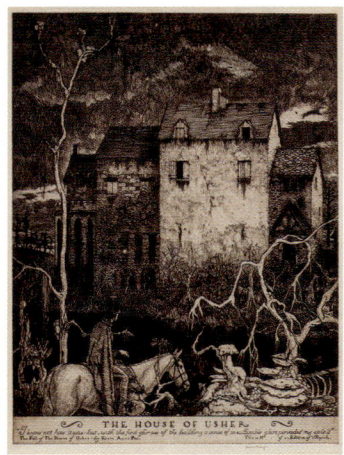

Robert Lawson
(American, 1892–1957)
The House of Usher, c. 1925
Etching
12 × 9 inches

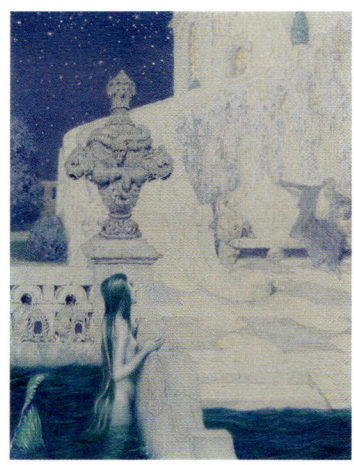

Heinrich Lefler
(Austrian, 1863–1919)
The Little Mermaid
(*Das Meefräulein*), 1911
Pen and ink, watercolor
9 × 7 inches

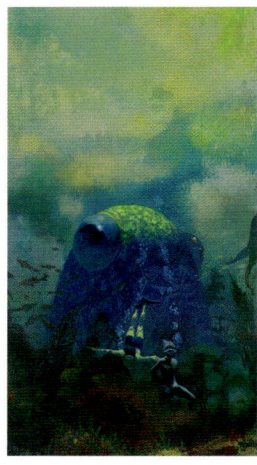

Paul Lehr
(American, 1930–1998)
Dolphin Island, 1971
Acrylic on board
17½ × 10½ inches
Courtesy of the Lehr Estate

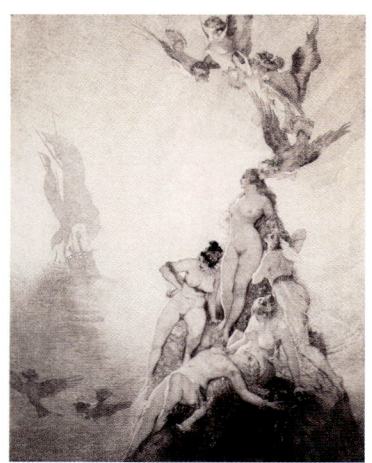

Norman Lindsay
(American, 1863–1919)
Unknown Seas, 1922
Etching with stippling
17 × 13 inches

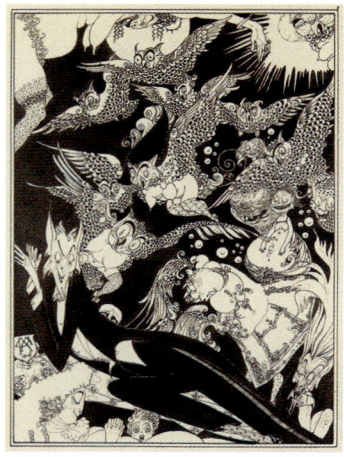

Paul Mak (Pavel Ivanov)
(Russian, 1885–c. 1967)
Scherzo, 1918
Pen and ink on paper
7½ × 5½ inches

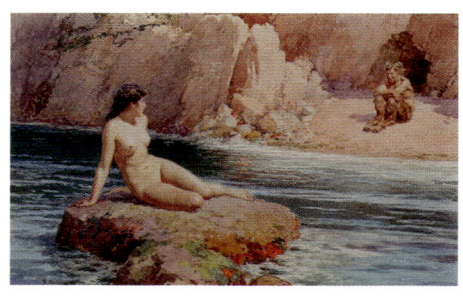

Fortunino Matania
(Italian, 1881–1963)
Checkmate, c. 1950
Watercolor
10 × 16 inches

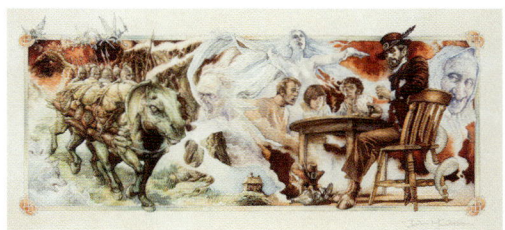

Iain McCaig
(American/British, b. 1957)
Irish Folk and Fairy Tales, c. 1984
Watercolor on paper
7½ × 17½ inches

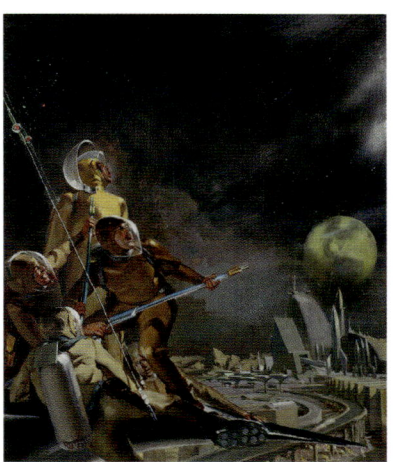

Stanley Meltzoff
(American, 1917–2006)
The Green Hills of Earth, 1952
Oil on canvas
20 × 18 inches

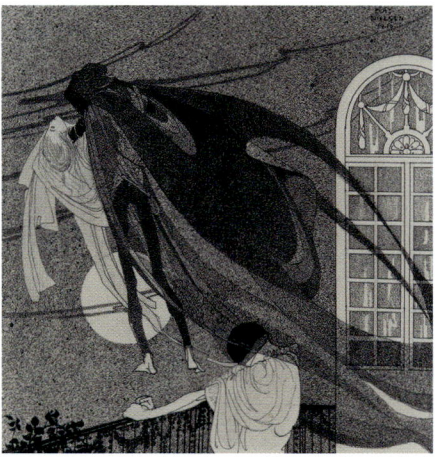

Kay Nielsen
(Danish, 1886–1957)
Book of Death I, 1910
Pen and ink
8 × 8 inches

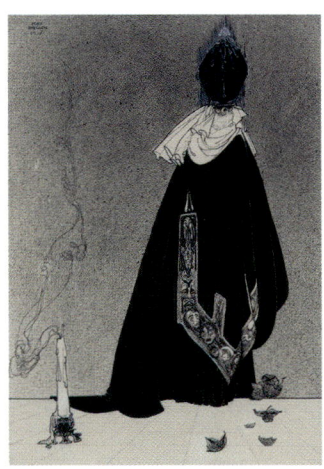

Kay Nielsen
(Danish, 1886–1957)
Book of Death II, 1910
Pen and ink
10½ × 7½ inches

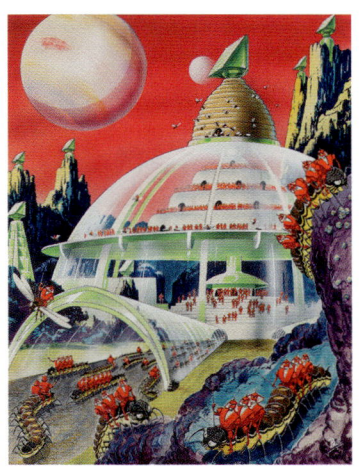

Frank R. Paul
(American, 1884–1963)
Glass City of Europa, 1942
Gouache on paper
22 × 16 inches

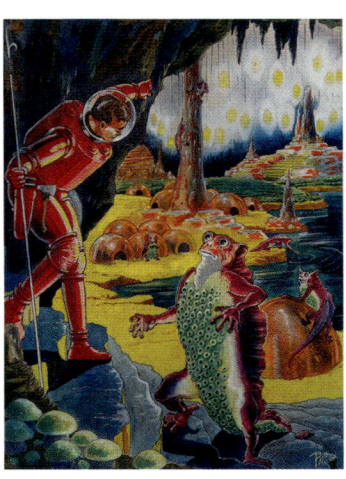

Frank R. Paul
(American, 1884–1963)
Life on Neptune, 1940
Gouache on illustration board
14 × 11 inches

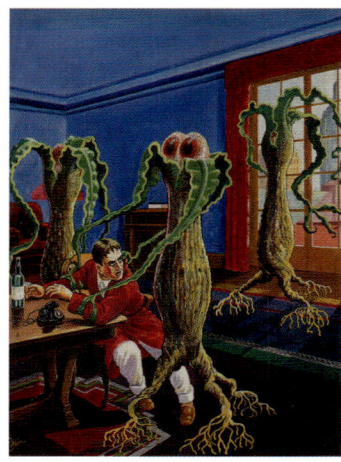

Frank R. Paul
(American, 1884–1963)
Seeds from Space, 1935
Oil on canvasboard
24 × 16 inches

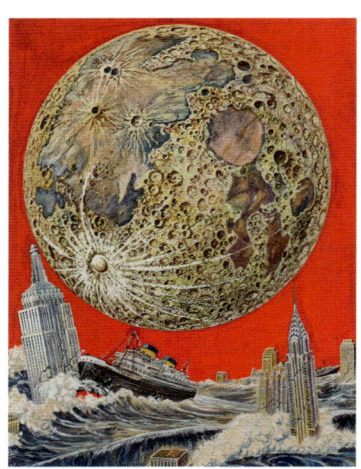

Frank R. Paul
(American, 1884–1963)
The Moon Doom
(*When Worlds Collide*), 1933
Gouache on illustration board
22 × 17 inches

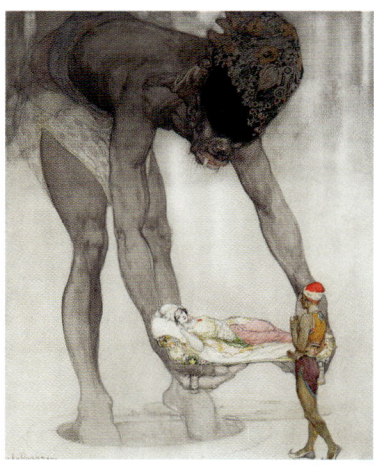

Willy Pogany
(Hungarian, 1882–1955)
The Sultan Misnar
(*Tales of the Persian Genii*), 1917
Watercolor
16 × 13 inches

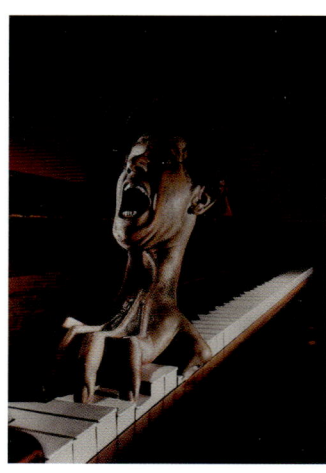

J.K. Potter
(American, b. 1956)
Alive and Screaming (Piano Man), 1985
Photography and digital illustration
14 × 10 inches

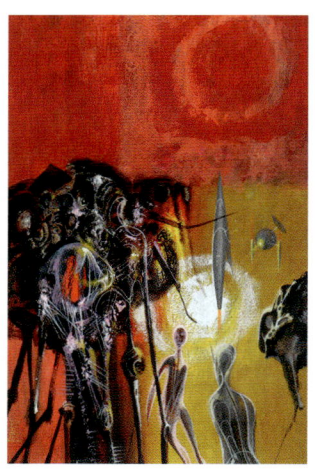

Richard Powers
(American, 1921–1996)
The Abominable Earthman, 1963
Acrylic on illustration board
17 × 11½ inches
© Richard Powers

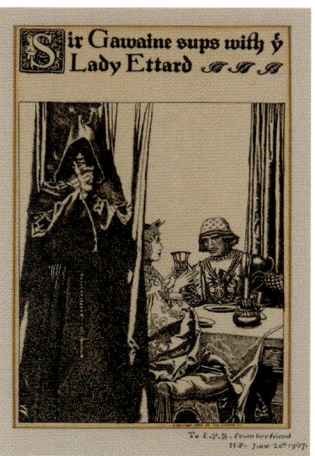

Howard Pyle
(American, 1853–1982)
Sir Gawaine Sups
with Ye Lady Ettard, 1903
Pen and ink
9¼ × 6½ inches

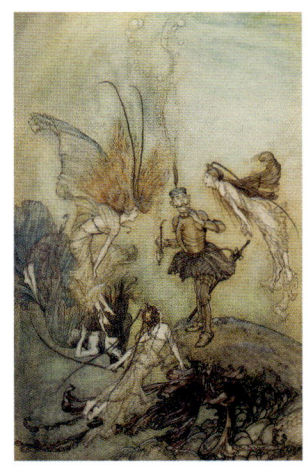

Arthur Rackham
(British, 1867–1939)
Sir Rupert the Fearless, 1907–8
Pen and ink, watercolor
10 × 8 inches

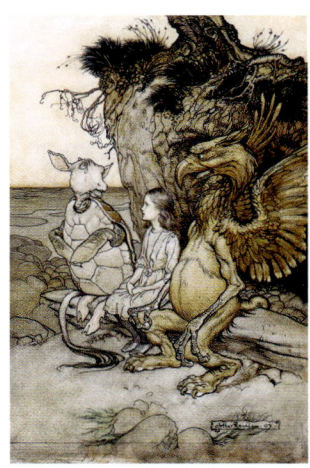

Arthur Rackham
(British, 1867–1939)
The Mock Turtle (*Alice's Adventure in Wonderland*), 1907
Pen and ink, watercolor
10½ × 7 inches

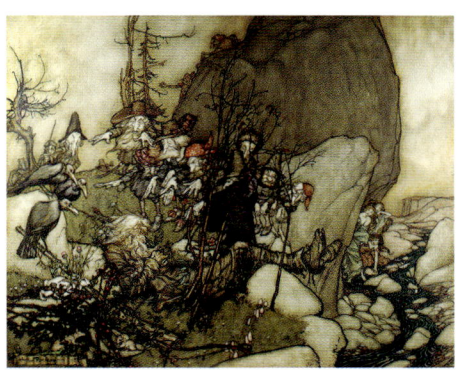

Arthur Rackham
(British, 1867–1939)
The Sleep of Rip Van Winkle, 1905
Pen and ink, watercolor
11¼ × 14 inches

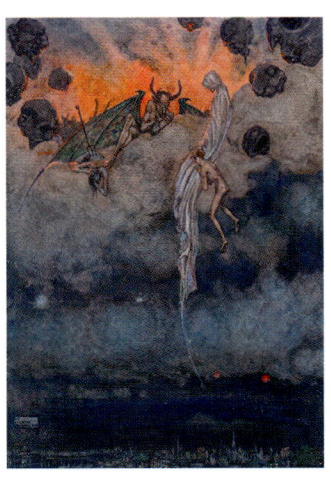

William H. Robinson
(British, 1872–1944)
Tomlinson (*The Collected Verse of Rudyard Kipling*), 1910
Watercolor
13½ × 9½ inches

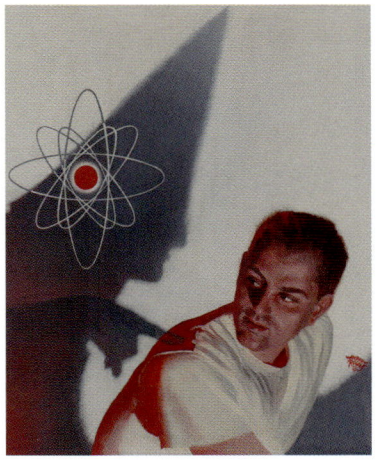

Hubert Rogers
(Canadian, 1898–1982)
Revolt in 2100, 1953
Oil on canvas
21 × 17 inches

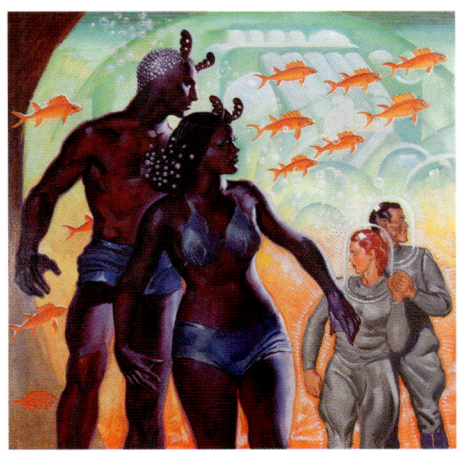

Hubert Rogers
(Canadian, 1898–1982)
Crisis in Utopia, 1938
Oil on board
21 × 21½ inches

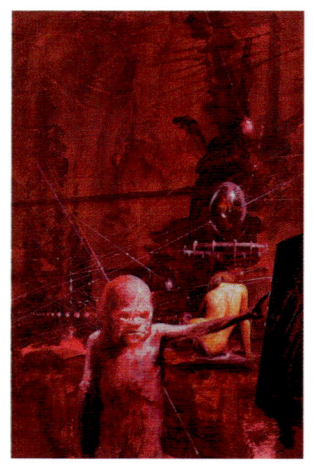

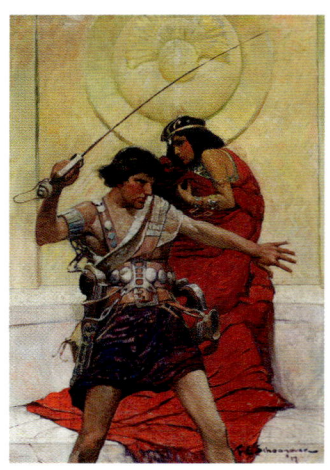

Alex Schomburg
(American, 1905–1998)
The Well of the Worlds, 1965
Gouache on illustration board
17 × 12 inches

John Schoenherr
(American, 1935–2010)
The Heaven Makers, 1968
Acrylic on illustration board
23 × 16 inches

Frank E. Schoonover
(American, 1877–1972)
A Princess of Mars, 1917
Oil on canvas
32 × 23 inches

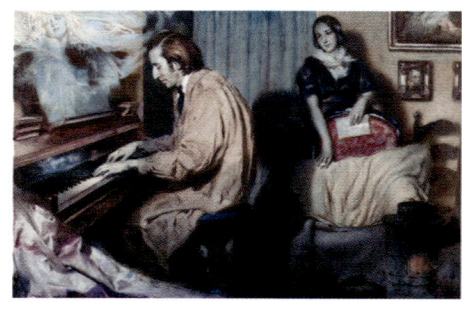

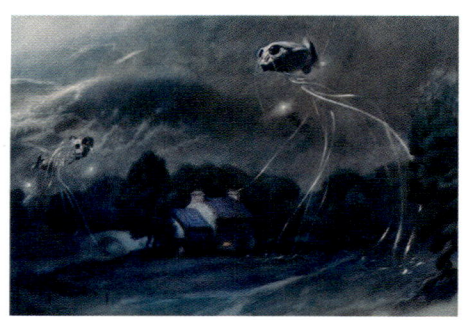

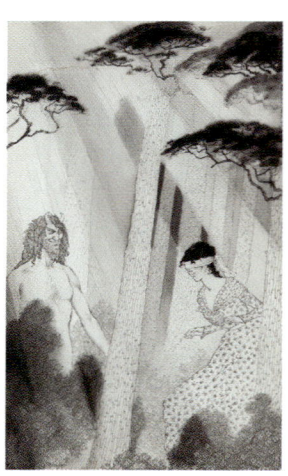

José Segrelles
(Spanish, 1885–1969)
Chopin in the Charterhouse, 1933
Watercolor, gouache, pastel
11 × 17 inches
Casa Museu José Segrelles,
Albaida, Valencia, Spain

José Segrelles
(Spanish, 1885–1969)
War of the Worlds, c. 1930
Mixed media
11 × 16 inches
Casa Museu José Segrelles,
Albaida, Valencia, Spain

Sidney H. Sime
(British, 1867–1941)
House of Souls (frontispiece), 1906
Pen and ink, watercolor
13½ × 9 inches

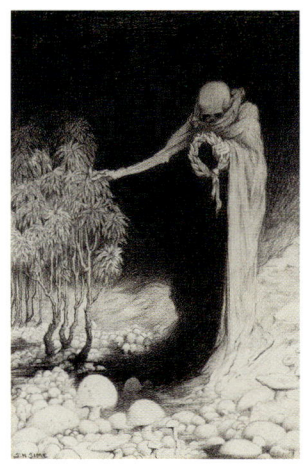

Sidney H. Sime
(British, 1867–1941)
Fame, c. 1905
Charcoal, pencil
16 × 10 inches

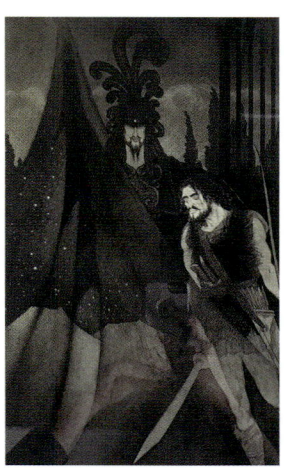

Sidney H. Sime
(British, 1867–1941)
The Dark Huntsman, 1899
Pen and Ink, watercolor (grisaille)
13½ × 8½ inches

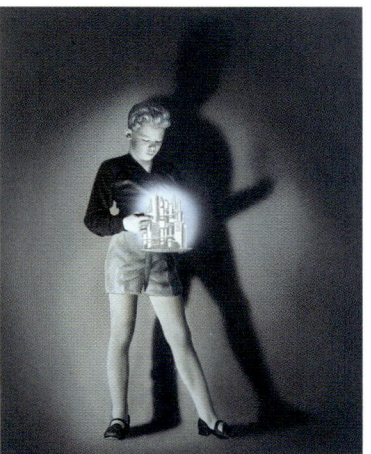

Malcolm Smith
(American, 1912–1966)
Cloak of Aesir, 1952
Photograph, mixed media
18 × 16 inches

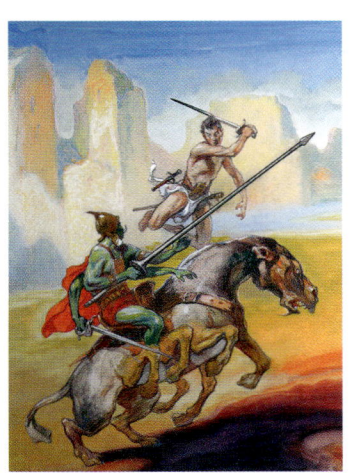

J. Allen St. John
(American, 1872–1957)
*John Carter and the
City of Mummies*, 1941
Gouache on paper
18 × 13 inches

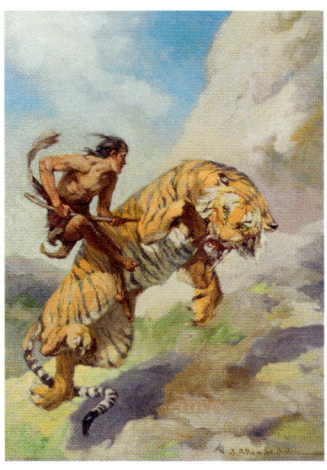

J. Allen St. John
(American, 1872–1957)
The Eternal Lover, 1925
Oil on canvasboard
25 × 18 inches

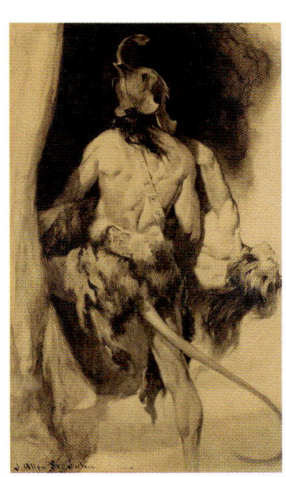

J. Allen St. John
(American, 1872–1957)
*The Abduction of Jane by Mo-sar
(Tarzan the Terrible)*, 1921
Watercolor on paper
25 × 16 inches

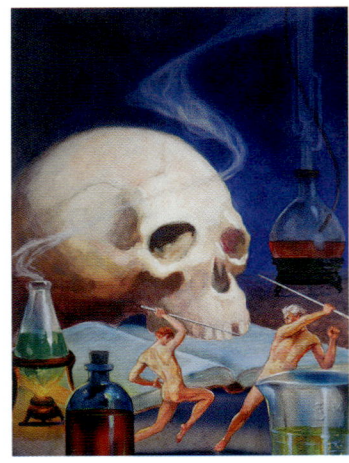

J. Allen St. John
(American, 1872–1957)
It's a Small World, 1944
Watercolor with gouache on paper
18 × 13 inches

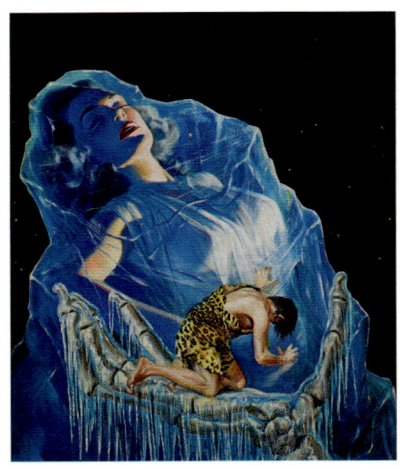

Lawrence Sterne Stevens
(American, 1884–1960)
Allan and the Ice Gods, 1947
Oil on board
16½ × 14 inches

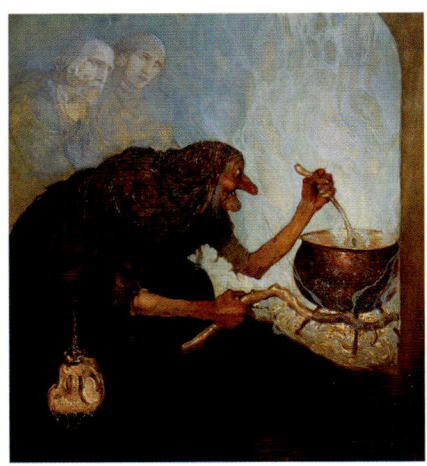

Gustaf Tenggren
(Swedish-American,
1896–1970)
Love In (Kärlekens Under), 1922
Watercolor, gouache
on illustration board
10½ × 9½ inches

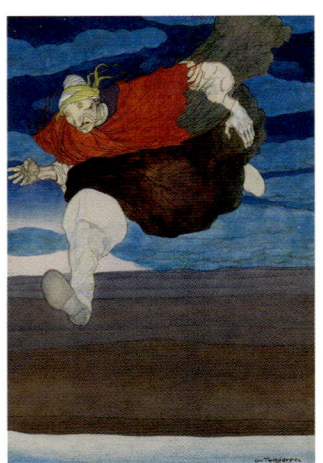

Gustaf Tenggren
(Swedish-American,
1896–1970)
The Witch (Grimms' fairy tale
"Sweetheart Roland"), 1923
Watercolor
13 × 9 inches

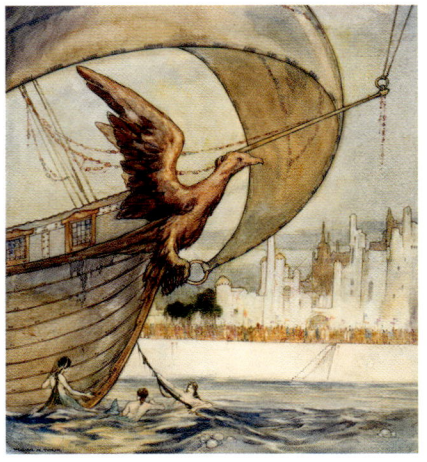

William Timlin
(British, 1892–1943)
The Landing (*The Ship That
Sailed to Mars*), 1923
Watercolor, pen and ink
11½ × 10½ inches

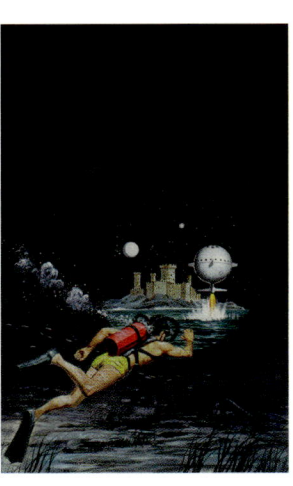

Edward Valigursky
(American, 1916–2009)
Key Out of Time, 1963
Gouache on illustration board
17 × 11 inches

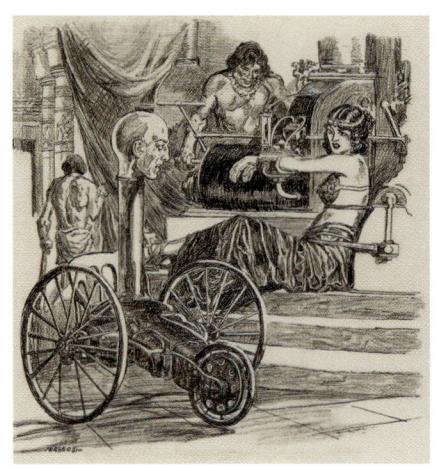

Hans "Wesso" Wessolowski
(American, 1894–1948)
The Heads of Apex, 1931
Pen and ink
10½ × 10 inches

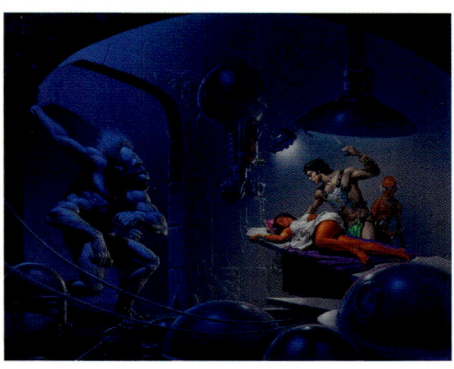

Michael Whelan
(American, b. 1950)
The Master Mind of Mars, 1979
Acrylic on illustration board
21 × 27 inches

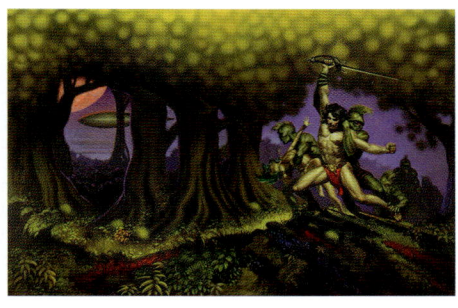

Michael Whelan
(American, b. 1950)
Swords of Mars, 1979
Acrylic on illustration board
18 × 28 inches

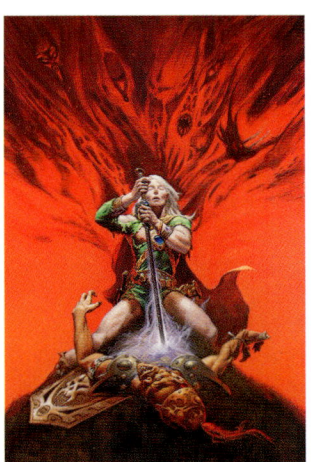

Michael Whelan
(American, b. 1950)
The White Wolf, 1977
Oil and acrylic on board
27 × 17 inches

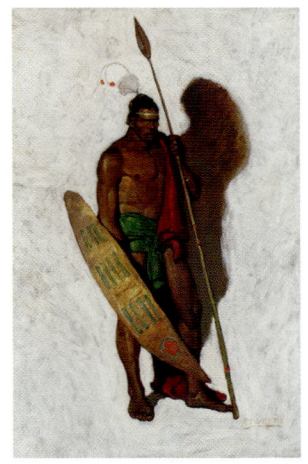

N.C. (Newell Convers) Wyeth
(American, 1882–1945)
Story of Allan Quartermain, 1914
Oil on canvas
40 × 30 inches

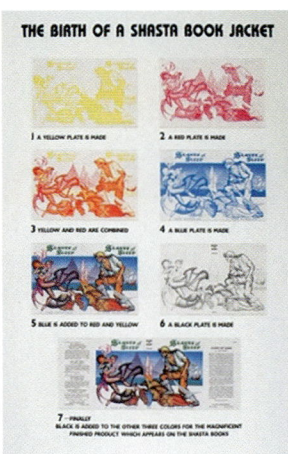

Shasta Publishers
The Birth of a Shasta Book Jacket
(featuring Hannes Bok's *Slaves of Sleep*)
Offset lithograph
c. 1950

CONTRIBUTORS

KEVIN J. ANDERSON has published more than 190 books, fifty-eight of which have been national or international bestsellers. He has written numerous novels in the *Star Wars, X-Files,* and *Dune* universes, as well as the *Clockwork Angels* steampunk trilogy. His original works include the *Saga of Seven Suns* series, the *Wake the Dragon* and *Terra Incognita* fantasy trilogies, humorous *Dan Shamble, Zombie P.I.* series, and *The Dragon Business* series. He has edited numerous anthologies, written comics and games, and composed the lyrics to three rock albums. Anderson is the director of the graduate program in Publishing at Western Colorado University, and he and his wife Rebecca Moesta are the publishers of WordFire Press.

DAVID M. BRINLEY is an award-winning artist and illustrator whose clients include *Time* magazine, *Rolling Stone, Newsweek, Sports Illustrated, GQ, The Washington Post,* and the *Los Angeles Times* and *New York Times* magazines. His personal, editorial, and portrait art is seen regularly in juried annuals including American Illustration, Communication Arts, The Society of Illustrators NYC, SILA Los Angeles, and 3x3 International Illustration. An artist member of the Society of Illustrators NYC since 2004, Brinley was selected by *Creative Quarterly* as one of the top 100 Creatives in 2015. His newest work was selected for 2023's *Lürzer's 200 Best.* David is a graduate with distinction from ArtCenter College of Design in Los Angeles, California, as well as Hartford Art School's prestigious MFA in Illustration program. He is a professor of Art and Design at the University of Delaware and is represented by Gerald & Cullen Rapp|Art Artist Representatives NYC.

GUILLERMO DEL TORO is a renowned filmmaker, writer, and artist, who has directed over a dozen films and created numerous television shows, including *The Strain* (2014–2017) and *Guillermo del Toro's Cabinet of Curiosities* (2022). His film *Pan's Labyrinth* (2006) won the Hugo Award for Best Dramatic Presentation, *Guillermo del Toro's Pinocchio* (2022) won the Academy Award for Best Animated Feature, and *The Shape of Water* (2017) won the Academy Award for Best Picture, with del Toro receiving the award for Best Director. He has written numerous books, including coauthoring the apocalyptic vampire trilogy including *The Strain* (2009), *The Fall* (2010), and *The Night Eternal* (2011), and from 2016 to 2018, he exhibited *Guillermo del Toro: At Home with Monsters,* featuring his collection of paintings, drawings, maquettes, artifacts, and concept film art, across the United States and Canada.

MICHAEL DIRDA is a Pulitzer Prize-winning journalist, a longtime book columnist for *The Washington Post,* and the author of the memoir *An Open Book* (2003), five collections of essays, and the critical appreciation *On Conan Doyle* (2012), which received an Edgar Award from the Mystery Writers of America. In another life, he earned a PhD from Cornell University in comparative literature, splitting his coursework between medieval studies and European Romanticism. He is currently completing a book about British popular fiction of the late nineteenth and early twentieth centuries tentatively titled *The Great Age of Storytelling.*

RACHAEL KANE is the Learning and Engagement Manager at Fuller Craft Museum in Brockton, Massachusetts, where she focuses on producing robust educational programing relating craft practices to a contemporary, local audience. Her work in equity-based museum education is informed by her time at Hamilton College and the Winterthur Program in American Material Culture at the University of Delaware. Her research explores conceptions of race, ethnicity, and gender presented through American illustration in the twentieth century, especially in children's media, toys, and games. She also specializes in Japanese print and textile media, with a particular interest in transnational material influences. Her work on paper dolls and performative domesticity was published through the Ephemera Society of America, and her work on embroidery was published in the magazine *PieceWork*.

STEPHEN D. KORSHAK is the owner, along with his wife Alma, of the Korshak Collection of Illustrations of Imaginative Literature. He received his B.A. from the University of Chicago in 1974 and his J.D. from the John Marshall Law School in 1980. He has authored the following books: *A Hannes Bok Treasury*, with a foreword by Ray Bradbury (1993); *A Hannes Bok Showcase*, with a foreword by Frederik Pohl (1994); *The Paintings of J. Allen St. John: Grand Master of Fantasy*, with a foreword by Jack Williamson (2008); *From the Pen of Paul: The Fantastic Images of Frank R. Paul*, with a preface by Sir Arthur C. Clarke (2009); and *The Alluring Art of Margaret Brundage: Queen of Pulp Pin-Up Art*, with J. David Spurlock (2013).

ASHLEY RYE-KOPEC is the Curator of Education and Outreach at the University of Delaware Museums, where she works to integrate the Museums' collections into the university's curriculum. She has taught courses in art history at several institutions and lectured widely on American, British, and Italian art and material culture. A specialist in nineteenth-century art, she holds an MA and PhD from the University of Delaware.

MARGARET D. STETZ is the Mae and Robert Carter Professor of Women's Studies and Professor of Humanities at the University of Delaware. Her books include a study of twentieth-century British women's comic fiction, an edited volume of essays on World War II military sexual slavery, and a catalogue of late Victorian portraits. She has also curated over a dozen exhibitions on art and print culture at museums and libraries in the United States and United Kingdom, including, with Mark Samuels Lasner, *Aubrey Beardsley, 150 Years Young* at the Grolier Club in New York City in 2022 and *Max Beerbohm: The Price of Celebrity* at the New York Public Library in 2023 to 2024.

LAUREN STUMP has served as Curator of the Korshak Collection since 2014. She is the owner of Hollingsworth Fine Arts, an Orlando-based firm specializing in collections management, and curatorial and valuation services. Additional curatorial projects include those with the Vinson Collection: *The Art and Story of Edgar Rice Burroughs*; and the Hollingsworth Collections: *American Victory Posters from WWI, Hungarian Trench Art from WWI and WWII*, and *Soviet Propaganda from the Cold War Era*, among others. Her background includes the study and practice of painting restoration techniques. She is an accredited member of the International Society of Appraisers and serves as chair of the society's membership committee. She received her Bachelor of Arts in History from the University of Central Florida.

MICHAEL WHELAN is one of the world's premier painters of imaginative realism. For more than forty years, he has created book and album covers for authors and musicians like Isaac Asimov, Stephen King, Ray Bradbury, Brandon Sanderson, the Jacksons, and Meat Loaf. His clients have included every major U.S. book publisher, the National Geographic Society, CBS Records, and the Franklin Mint. Whelan has won an unprecedented fifteen Hugo Awards, three World Fantasy Awards, and thirteen Chesleys from the Association of Science Fiction and Fantasy Artists. The readers of *Locus Magazine* (for science fiction insiders) have named him Best Professional Artist thirty-one times in their annual poll, and the Spectrum Annual of the Best in Contemporary Fantastic Art named him a Grand Master in 2004. Other noteworthy awards include a Gold Medal from the Society of Illustrators, a Vargas Award, a Grumbacher Gold Medal, and the Solstice Award from the Science Fiction Writers of America.

GARY K. WOLFE is emeritus Professor of Humanities in Roosevelt University's Evelyn T. Stone College of Professional Studies. A renowned science fiction editor, critic, and biographer, he has received the Pilgrim Award for Lifetime Achievement from the Science Fiction Research Association, the Distinguished Scholarship Award from the International Association for the Fantastic in the Arts, and a Special World Fantasy Award for criticism. He has received six Hugo nominations, two for his reviews collections and four for *The Coode Street Podcast*, which he has co-hosted with Jonathan Strahan for more than three hundred episodes. His books include *Harlan Ellison: The Edge of Forever* (2002), *Evaporating Genres: Essays on Fantastic Literature and Sightings* (2010), and he has edited multiple anthologies of science fiction novels for the Library of America.

LISA YASZEK is Regents' Professor of Science Fiction Studies at Georgia Tech, where she explores science fiction as a global language crossing centuries, continents, and cultures. Her books include *Galactic Suburbia: Recovering Women's Science Fiction* (2008); *Sisters of Tomorrow: The First Women of Science Fiction* (2016); and the series *The Future is Female! Classic Science Fiction Stories by Women* (2018–present). Yaszek's writings about science fiction have been featured in *The Washington Post, Food and Wine Magazine,* and *USA Today*, and she has been an expert commentator for CBS *Sunday Morning*, the BBC4, and AMC's *James Cameron's Story of Science Fiction*.

AMANDA T. ZEHNDER is the Chief Curator and Head of Museums at the University of Delaware Library, Museums and Press. She has curated dozens of exhibitions on a broad range of subjects over the course of her career, including the 2019 exhibition *Drawing Connections: Illustration and the Written Word,* cocurated with Curtis Small, which brought together selections from the Museums collections, University of Delaware Special Collections, and the Mark Samuels Lasner Collection at the University of Delaware. Zehnder's primary academic focus is late nineteenth- and early twentieth-century European and American art. Her publications include *Impressionism and Post-Impressionism: Collection Highlights* (2012), and "Forty Years of Artistic Exchange," in the exhibition catalogue *Degas/Cassatt* (2014) for the National Gallery of Art, Washington, DC. Zehnder holds a PhD in the History of Art from Bryn Mawr College.